UNVEILING THE SOCIOCULTURALLY CONSTRUCTED MULTIVOICED SELF

Themes of Self Construction and Self Integration in the Narratives of Second-Generation Korean American Young Adults

S. Steve Kang

University Press of America,® Inc.
Lanham · New York · Oxford

Copyright © 2002 by
University Press of America,® Inc.
4720 Boston Way
Lanham, Maryland 20706
UPA Acquisitions Department (301) 459-3366

PO Box 317
Oxford
OX2 9RU, UK

ISBN 0-7618-2450-2 (paperback : alk. ppr.)

TABLE OF CONTENTS

FIGURES

TABLES

PREFACE

This study seeks to understand the multiplicity of internalized voices, authorities, and values that are operative in the lives of second-generation Korean American young adults as they engage in the project of self. The research methodologies employed in this study were primarily ethnographic interviews, literature reviews, and participant observation. The study was guided by two research questions. First, what are the internalized voices, authorities, and values among the young adults, and how is this internalized multiplicity manifested in their lives and in their narrations of self? Second, given the prominent role of the church in the Korean American community, how does the church affect the self and function as one among the many internalized themes?

The findings of the study indicate five salient themes of internalized values (family, autonomy, relationship, community, and the combination of high ethnicity and high assimilation); two categories of authorities (the series of concentric spheres of "outside-in" authorities ranging from that of parents, the Korean American church, Korean American culture, and mainstream society, and "inside-out" authorities consisting the authority of peers, the revised authority of the parents, and the authority of spiritual leaders in their lives); and eleven salient voices (voices of mutual support and acceptance, absence and enmeshment, television as a voice in the absence, comparison, mediocrity and inadequacy, assimilation, womanhood, American dream, obligation and filial piety, companionship, and spiritual longings).

The findings of the study also indicate intricate relationship patterns among the internalized themes within the self, the intensity of reflexivity of the self, and the intentionality for further reflexivity and praxis of the self. Moreover, the findings of the study indicate that the Korean American church has had a constructive role in the lives of second-generation Korean American young adults and suggest that the church work toward becoming a community that embodies authenticity, grace, healing, and reflexivity, that practices intentional and integrative educational ministry, and that proactively engages the world.

ACKNOWLEDGEMENTS

I want to recognize several mentors in my life who have encouraged me to pursue the integration of faith, life, and learning. They are Mark Noll, the late Tim Phillips, and my colleagues at Christian Formation & Ministry Department at Wheaton College where I have been teaching for the past five years; Linda Cannell, Calvin Hanson, and Ted Ward from Trinity Evangelical Divinity School where I studied, worked, and taught for nearly a decade; the late Reverend Bob Harvey and Paul Heidebrecht from Immanuel Presbyterian Church where I and my family have been nurtured for the past ten years; and Peter Cha, whose friendship and support continue to amaze me.

My deep appreciation goes out to Jack Seymour, Robert Launay, Carol Lee, and Linda Vogel for their keen insights and perspectives toward this present work.

I am grateful to my and father and mother, Helen Yun Sik Kang, who has shaped me in more ways than she can imagine. This book is dedicated, with deep affection and gratitude, to Chris, my spouse of twelve years. Here I also thank my daughter, Ashley, and my son, Andrew, who have been the source of much joy and laughter in my life.

Soli Deo Gloria.

Chapter 1

Introduction

Over the years, I've come to learn that my identity is fluid, and that nothing can ever truly represent who I am. . . I am now, I think, aware of all my "issues" – the baggage I carry around. . . Now I refer to myself as either a MBP (multiple-box person) or a PWI (person with issues).[1]

Context for the Study

The United States of America has witnessed a steady influx of Korean immigrants since the passage of the Immigration Act of 1965. Most immigrated either as young couples without children or nuclear families seeking better standards of living and educational opportunities for their (future) children.[2] As many families settled in major cities of the U.S., immigrant parents had to adapt their Korean ways of life in order to pursue "the American dream." One major adaptation strategy for them was to establish churches, which functioned as a sociocultural center of Korean American community life and a safe-haven for its people.[3]

In the meantime, children of immigrant parents, second-generation Korean Americans, grew up in a sociocultural context characterized by complexity and confusion. While rapidly acculturating into

---

[1]Dredge Kang, "Multiple-Box Person," in *East to America*, ed. Elaine H. Kim and Eui-Young Yu (New York: The New Press, 1996), 82.

[2]Laura Uba, Asian Americans: Personality Patterns, Identity, and Mental Health (New York: The Guilford Press, 1994), 6-7.

[3]Sucheng Chan, *Asian Americans: An Interpretive History* (Boston: Twayne Publishers, 1991), 73-74; Won Moo Hurh and Kwang Chung Kim, "Religious Participation of Korean Immigrants in the United States," in *Journal for the Scientific Study of Religion* 29, 1 (1990), 19-34.

mainstream American society, they acquired American lifestyles and internalized America's value systems. However, while growing up culturally as Koreans, they struggled to fully assimilate into mainstream society due to various burdens placed upon them by the Korean American community.

At the same time, second-generation Korean Americans have experienced great pressure to maintain their Korean heritage and traditional Korean values on the home front.[4] They have also been expected to succeed in American society, often according to their parents' wishes. In the process, they were caught in a grueling tug-of-war between their Korean past and North American future. Trapped between conflicting cultural norms, they are often referred to as the lost generation.[5] Moreover, the Korean American church, functioning as an extension of the Korean immigrant family, has further reinforced these elevated expectations. Though many second-generation Korean Americans initially turned to one another for mutual support within the context of the church's education programs, many others left the church, disillusioned by its inability to provide resources for the pursuit of meaning in their daily lives.

The Problem and Purpose

Given their unique sociocultural context, second-generation Korean Americans have been constantly exposed to and have consequently internalized a multiplicity of voices, authorities, and values from both mainstream American society and the Korean American family and church. These internalized themes have become a concrete reality in their lives, playing a significant role in their construction of self.

Second-generation Korean Americans are currently going through their young adult years in the context of a multitude of life choices and various social responsibilities. They are engaged in a reflexive project, or what is also called a narration of the self.[6] In other words, these

---

[4]Jung Young Lee, *Marginality: The Key to Multicultural Theology* (Minneapolis: Fortress Press, 1995), 44.

[5]Ibid., 45.

[6]Anthony Giddens, *Modernity and Self-Identity: Self and Society in the Late Modern Age* (Stanford: Stanford University Press, 1991), 5, 35-69; Dan

young adults struggle to make meaning of life and to formulate appropriate concepts of the self in the midst of internalized voices, authorities, and values from the various sociocultural sources that surround them.

There is a dearth of literature on theoretical frameworks on which to guide a holistic understanding of the second-generation Korean American experience. This predicament can be traced to three broad methodological concerns.

First, Asian American studies, within which Korean American studies is a subset, has struggled as a developing discipline to form its own identity in academia. One of the ways the discipline gained access in academia was bringing together the experiences of Japanese, Chinese, and Korean Americans as pan-Asian American phenomena. While pan-Asian American literature has provided some common threads within these very distinct American ethnic groups, it has not fully served the populations it intended to describe. Moreover, due to the brevity of Korean immigrant history, literature on the Korean American experience is minimal and has largely focused on the first-generation's experience.

Second, other works on the Korean American experience have been comparative studies either with other ethnic groups or with the majority American population. Although these studies may have contributed to the advancement of literature on ethnic studies, they have provided little insight into the unique experience of Korean Americans, especially the second-generation experience.

Third, the unit of analysis in existing literature on the Korean American experience has often been a single aspect of the first-generation's experience. A particular aspect is imposed onto an existing framework in a given discipline in order to analyze a singular experience. Moreover, most studies have utilized a quantitative approach to fit people's experience into a convenient form of analysis, therefore missing the qualitative reality of the individuals the studies seek to represent. Some aspects that have been studied include ethnic identity development among Korean American children, adaptation strategies of Korean American immigrant families, and intervention strategies for immigrant families in which risk behaviors and addictions are involved.

McAdams, *Power, Intimacy, and the Life Story* (New York: Guilford, 1988) and *The Stories We Live By* (New York: W. Morrow, 1993).

This research, in contrast, is exploratory in nature, providing an opportunity for second-generation Korean Americans to describe their experience in a holistic and comprehensive manner. This framework needs to be multi-disciplinary and multi-faceted in nature, in order to embrace fully unique experiences and to allow the major themes of experiences to emerge through narration.

Toward that end, this research has a three-fold objective. First, from the narratives of second-generation Korean Americans, the study seeks to describe the internalized voices, authorities, and values found within various sociocultural sources. The study then explores the ways in which these young adults construct their views of themselves and function in daily life in the midst of the multiplicity of internalized themes. Finally, the study examines the role of the Korean American church on the construction of the self and daily functioning of these young adults.

Definition of Terms

1.   Second-generation Korean American young adults – Americans of Korean ethnic descent who were either born in the US or who came to the States before the age of 5, and whose primary language is English. At the time of the present study, the subjects for the study ranged from 23 to 29 years of age.[7]
2.   Acculturation - adoption of cultural patterns of host society in terms of cultural attitudes, values, and behaviors that result from contact between two distinct cultures.
3.   Assimilation - integration into host society which involves various aspects such as acculturation, structural assimilation, amalgamation, identification assimilation, attitude receptional assimilation, behavior receptional assimilation, and civic assimilation.[8]

---

[7]For more detail, refer to Chapter 6.

[8]Structural assimilation refers to large-scale entrance into cliques, clubs, and institutions of host society, on the primary group level; amalgamation involves large-scale intermarriage; identification assimilation indicates the development of a sense of personhood based exclusively on the host society; attitude receptional assimilation refers to the absence of prejudice; behavior receptional assimilation refers to the absence of discrimination; and civic assimilation indicates the absence of value and power conflict. For further discussion, see

4. Ethnic identity - the part of an individual's self-conception related to "knowledge of one's membership in a social group together with the value and emotional significance attached to that membership."[9] This sense of belonging, of shared values, and of self-identification is central to defining ethnic identity. While research on acculturation tends to focus upon intercultural contact at the group level, ethnic identity research focuses on individuals and "how they relate to their own group as a subgroup of the larger society.[10]

5. Mainstream American society – a social order that holds to cultural norms that have been unilaterally constructed and strictly maintained by European Americans throughout North American history.[11]

6. Voice – a speaking personality, the speaking consciousness. A voice always has a will or desire behind it, its own timbre and overtones. Voices always exist in a social milieu in that they are "rented" from previously internalized voices.[12]

7. Authority - an aspect of social organization and interaction in a relative world, with many differentiations (i.e., power, expertise, etc.). Sometimes, authority can be construed as possession of the "right" answers in the "absolute," or the mediation of the same.[13]

8. Values – the basis upon which desires are founded to justify what *we* do and to endow it with legitimacy. Values, therefore, are inherent in commitment to "ways of life" in that they are "communal" and "consequential" in terms of our relations to a cultural community.[14]

9. The self – All of our knowledge, feelings, and ideas as unique persons. It is the very essence of that which we are. The self can be

---

Milton Gordon, *Assimilation in American Life* (New York: Oxford University Press, 1964), 71-81.

[9]H. Tajfel, *Human Groups and Social Categories: Studies in Social Psychology* (London: Cambridge University Press, 1981), 255.

[10]Jean S. Phinney. "Ethnic Identity in Adolescents and Adults: Review of Research" *Psychological Bulletin*, 108:3 (1990), 500-501.

[11]See Robert Stam and Ella Shohat, "Contested Histories: Eurocentrism, Multiculturalism, and the Media," in *Multiculturalism: A Critical Reader,* ed. David Theo Goldberg (Cambridge: Basil Blackwell, 1994), 296-324.

[12]Mikhail Bakhtin, *The Dialogic Imagination* (Austin: University of Texas Press, 1981), 327-366.

[13]William Perry, *Forms of Intellectual and Ethical Development in the College Years* (New York: Holt, Rinehart and Winston, Inc., 1970).

[14]See Jerome Bruner, *Acts of Meaning* (Cambridge: Harvard University Press, 1991), 28-30.

construed in two ways: (1) knower/subject/process and (2) known/object/structure. The self is not a stable object, a pure and enduring core, but the sum and swarm of participations in social life.[15]
10. Reflexivity - the systematic exploration of the assumed or presupposed categories of thought which delimit the boundary of thinking, predetermine the thought, and guide the practical carrying out of social or psychological inquiry. The reflexive self, then, is the quality of the self that reflexively engages in an ongoing process of ordering one's personal-narratives.[16]
11. The construction of self – the emergent process of the self through dialogical interactions with various sources and people in a sociocultural context. Thus, the process is characterized by *joint action* between self and society, where issues of power are involved.

Significance of the Study

This study contributes to a holistic understanding of second-generation Korean American young adults. First, the study discloses the multiplicity of internalized voices, authorities, and values that operate in the lives of these young adults. Thus, instead of fragmenting various aspects of their experience, the study demonstrates the dialogical, confluential inner-workings of the major facets of their lives.

Second, the study discusses ways in which these young people attempt to tell their life stories and make meaning from their life experiences in the presence of myriad internalized themes.

Third, this study suggests strategies for young adults to become more critically aware of the influence and interplay of the multiplicity of internalized themes in their everyday lives. This reflexive process will allow them to disentangle the many complex threads that have come to shape the lives of Korean American young adults, resulting in a more authentic construction and understanding of the self.

---

[15]William James, *The Principles of Psychology* (New York: Dover Publications, 1981); George H. Mead, *Mind, Self, and Society* (Chicago: University of Chicago Press, 1934); Bruner, *Acts of Meaning*, 107.

[16]Pierre Bourdieu and Loic Wacquant, *An Invitation to Reflexive Sociology* (Chicago: The University of Chicago Press, 1992), 40; Giddens, *Modernity and Self-Identity*, 35-69.

Finally, the study discusses how the life of the church can assist these young adults, as they engage in the construction and narration of the self, thus claiming and living out their lives as more whole people.

Assumptions and Limitations

This study assumes there exists a multiplicity of internalized themes, i.e., voices, authorities, and values, that are operative in the lives of second-generation Korean American young adults. Moreover, the study assumes that the young adults have been engaged in or, at least, are capable of self-reflexion about these themes. Also, it is assumed that this study's findings have implications for the theory and practice of Christian education in the Korean American church.

There are several limitations of this study, especially in relation to its purpose, sample, methodology, and analysis. This study utilizes primarily the self-reporting of participants, which has its inherent bias. While follow-up interviews were conducted to triangulate data from individual interviews, the study does not claim to have deciphered all the intricacies and functioning of the multiplicity of internalized themes among these young adults.

While a variety of experiences and backgrounds are represented, the study sample is by no means a representative sample of second-generation Korean American young adults in the United States. Thus, the intent of this study is not to infer to a larger population of young adults based on the rather limited findings revealed in the interview analysis. Instead, the study purports to gain insight into how some Korean American young adults engage in self-construction and narration. The research findings are intended to provide a theoretical perspective that can be drawn upon in the formulation of future Christian education theory and practice in the Korean American church.

Chapter 2

The Socioculturally Constructed
Multivoiced Self

Exploration of the meaning of the phrase, "socioculturally constructed
multivoiced self," is a preliminary step to understanding the narration
of self of second-generation Korean American young adults.
Examination of the sociocultural construction of self leads to scrutiny
of this concept in light of the disciplines of anthropology and
psychology. Various theories of the multivoiced self lay the
groundwork for understanding the project of self amidst the multiplicity
of voices, authorities, and values, which exist simultaneously in the
lives of second- generation Korean Americans.

The Sociocultural Construction of Self

The theory of sociocultural construction of self is primarily
concerned with how a human being comes to describe, explain, and
envision his or her life and the world. It maintains that the self and
world can only be construed as sociocultural artifacts — products of
historically situated interchanges among people. Thus, the construal
process of the self and world is the ongoing result of the active,
cooperative and creative endeavors of human beings in relationship to
and in the world.

Social Constructionism as a Critique of the Modern Epistemology

At its roots, social constructionism is a reactionary movement in that
it critiques the positivist-empiricist conception of knowledge and thus
casts serious doubt on the notion that scientific theory reflects reality in

a direct, decontextualized, and abstract manner.[1] It argues for prior existence of possession of categories (*a priori* principle) before a person can claim to have derived theoretical categories from observation (*a posteriori*). It also argues for the necessity of a definition in describing or defining theoretical categories that reflect the reality. However, social constructionism does not swing back to the other extreme by resorting to the notion that the world is a reflection of reality in any indirect or decontexualized manner.

Critiquing from the social construction perspective, Kenneth Gergen asserts that exogenic knowledge (the nature of knowledge as the copy of the contours of the world, resulting in, for instance, behaviorism) and endogenic knowledge (knowledge as the product of internal processes of human beings, leading to cognitivistic perspectives of knowledge) have functioned as two major foundations in the history of social theory.[2] His major contention is that these perspectives or the combination of the two have not adequately served either general inquiry of the human life and the world or psychological and anthropological inquiries of human beings.

All construal processes are, instead of being static and unambiguous, fluid and precarious in their nature. Moreover, social constructionism calls for inquiry into the historical and cultural bases of various forms of world construction. It contends that any inquiry into the construal process in itself, whether by the investigator or the investigated or even by the collaboration between the two, is socially constructed, thus raising the question as to what or who constitutes *truth*.

Soundings of Sociocultural Constructionism in the Discipline of Anthropology

A prominent figure of the sociocultural constructionism in the discipline of anthropology has been Clifford Geertz. Geertz contends that human action and thought can only be understood in a culturally relative way. He distances himself from the notions of universal epistemology and science of human motivation as a framework. For

---

[1] Kenneth Gergen, *An Invitation to Social Construction* (Thousand Oaks: Sage, 1999), 1-32.
[2] Kenneth Gergen, *Realities and Relationships* (Cambridge: Harvard University Press, 1994), 30-63.

instance, in "Person, Time and Conduct in Bali," he analyzes conventional naming practices, village ritual and everyday etiquette among its people, theorizing that the ordinary interactions in life intermingle to construct a particular concept of self in Balinese culture.[3]

He conceptualizes culture, then, not as a set of chosen value orientations, but as multiple "games" played out according to commonly accepted rules.[4] Yet, Geertz does not claim to have the holistic picture of the basic configurations of the culture. Instead, he professes that his job is to search out significant symbols and underlying regularities of human experience.[5] Unfortunately, what is consistently missing throughout his work is his own presence as an ethnographer/anthropologist. Geertz does not discuss the constitutive role he plays in his interaction with the observed. Conversely, another anthropologist, James Clifford, writes a reflexive ethnography on anthropology, and specifically locates himself directly in his critique of his constitutive role as an ethnographer.[6]

Geertz has been concerned with the cultural configurations that shape particular agents. His approach is a shift from traditional anthropology in his wariness of putting inordinate emphasis on human agency in the multiple symbol systems of culture. Instead, Geertz has been more concerned with the constitutive or even constraining force of cultures working through individuals in largely unconscious form.

In a similar vein, Pierre Bourdieu has downplayed the role of human agency in constructing a coherent society and self through social solidarity and collective thinking by human beings.[7] His social constructionistic orientation is similar to that of Geertz and Clifford in that Bourdieu has consistently opposed essential (both objectivism and

---

[3]Clifford Geertz, "Person, Time, and Conduct in Bali" in *The Interpretation of Cultures* (New York: Basic Books, 1973), 360-411.

[4]Clifford Geertz, "Deep Play: Notes on the Balinese Cockfight" in *The Interpretation of Cultures* (New York: Basic Books, 1973), 412-453; Idem, *Islam Observed* (Chicago: University of Chicago Press, 1971).

[5]Clifford Geertz, "Thick Description: Toward an Interpretive Theory of Culture" in *The Interpretation of Cultures* (New York: Basic Books, 1973), 3-30.

[6]James Clifford, The Predicament of Culture: Twentieth-Century Ethnography, Literature, and Art (Cambridge: Harvard University Press, 1988)

[7]Pierre Bourdieu, *Outline of a Theory of Practice* (Cambridge: Cambridge University Press, 1977); Idem, *The Logic of Practice* (Stanford: Stanford University Press, 1990)

subjectivism) notions of objects and the self. He maintains that social life must be construed in a framework that recognizes the constitutive role of both objective material and social and cultural structures, as well as the constituting practices and experiences of individuals and groups. Moreover, recognizing science and scientists as a product of their social universe, Bourdieu advances a reflexive sociology, similar to Clifford and Foucault.[8]

Bourdieu's project consists of three fundamental concepts: "habitus," "capital," and "field." Habitus is a set of socially constructed generative schemes that functions in unconsciousness but takes place within a life space of possibilities. Capital, somewhat similar to Foucault's notion of power, is the capacity to exercise control over one's own future and that of others. Field is the space of possible positions and the position taking of agents.[9] Utilizing these concepts, Bourdieu conceptualizes social practice in terms of the relationship between habitus, capital, and field. In this scheme, the habitus produces the capital in the field of concrete time and history. Important to his argument is the role of habitus because its self-reflexivity encounters itself both as embodied and as objectified history, thus, constructing the self, and gradually, the society.[10] Bourdieu's approach is helpful in explicating the social and cultural reproduction of inequality that is inevitably created by social practice. One of the ways to analyze this reproduction and its influence on the self may be by investigating the habitus of and the conditions of the subordinated groups.

Soundings of Sociocultural Constructionism in the Discipline of Psychology

The first modern psychological treatise on the concept of the self can be traced back to William James who made a distinction between the self-as-knower (the self as subject) and the self-as-known (or the self as

---

[8]Michel Foucault, "Preface to The History of Sexuality, Volume II" in Paul Rabinow, ed., *The Foucault Reader* (New York: Pantheon Books, 1984), 333-339.

[9]Pierre Bourdieu and Loic Wacquant, "Interest, Habitus, Rationality" in *An Invitation to Reflexive Sociology* (Chicago: University of Chicago Press, 1992), 115-140.

[10]Ibid., 139.

object).[11] Thus, while the *"I"* observes and experiences self, the *"Me"* involves all that a person considers to be his or her own. According to James, the *Me* consists of three aspects: the *material Me*, the *social Me*, and the *spiritual Me*. The material Me is comprised of the person's body, possessions, and family members. The social Me involves the person's understandings of recognition he or she gets from other people. The spiritual Me refers to the entire collection of the person's own understandings of herself as the person who thinks, feels, acts, and experiences life.[12] However, James did not explicitly make connections between the impact of the social world with the development of the material and spiritual components of the *Me*.

James Baldwin, Charles Cooley, and George Herbert Mead, profoundly influenced by James, advanced the study of the self with emphasis on how the whole *Me* is formulated in the context of social relationships.[13] Baldwin asserts that the *Me* develops as a function of the interaction between the child and the social world. This process involves mutual imitation of self and other. For instance, the child's self grows by imitating his or her mother. As a result, the child's understanding of his or her mother grows, paralleling the development of the self.[14] Cooley likens the "other" to a social mirror in which the *Me* is reflected in the "other;" thus he devises the term "looking glass self." The self is formed as the person comes to imagine how other people observe and understand him or her. Elaborating on the themes articulated by Baldwin and Cooley, Mead maintains that the development of the *Me* involves the ability to take the role of the

---

[11]William James, *Psychology* (Greenwich, CT: Fawcett, 1892/1963), 166-197.

[12]For James, this distinction between *I* and *Me* does not further dichotomize the person as in the mind-body dualism advocated by the Cartesian *Cogito*. Instead, it embraces the intrinsic relatedness of *I* and (material) *Me*. The distinction, also, espouses the relatedness of *I* and (social) *Me*, while it debunks the notion of self-other dualism. For a helpful critique of the Cartesian *Cogito*, see Hubert J. Hermans and Harry Kempen, *The Dialogical Self: Meaning as Movement* (San Diego: Academic Press, 1993), 1-10.

[13]R. Hogan, Personality Theory: The Personalogical Tradition (Englewood Cliffs: Prentice-Hall, 1976); James Baldwin, Mental Development in the Child and Race (New York: Macmillan, 1897), Charles Cooley, Human Nature and the Social Order (New York: Scribners, 1902), George Herbert Mead, *Mind, Self, and Society* (Chicago: University of Chicago Press, 1934).

[14]Baldwin, and Jean Valsiner, *Human Development and Culture* (Lexington, MA: D.C. Heath, 1989).

"other". He argues that as a child matures, through experience in games and other complex social interactions, he or she formulates the concept of a "generalized other"--a personal conception of the general "audience" or "observer" of one's behavior. Thus, he or she imagines how others see the *Me* in general.[15]

Lev Vygotsky adequately articulates both the theoretical framework as well as the actual process of how the mind (mental functions) develops socioculturally, which is a crucial aspect of the development of the socially constructed self.[16] Profoundly influenced by Marxist theory, Vygotsky asserts that "humans' psychological nature represents the aggregate of internalized social relations that have become functions for the individual and form the individual's structure."[17] In other words, mental composition, genetic structure, and means of action or forms of mediation are, in their nature, social and entirely of social origin.

In describing the "general genetic law of cultural development," Vygotsky explicates the process through which any forms of learning take place between self and other, and are then internalized within the self. Vygotsky writes:

> Any function in the child's cultural development appears twice, or on two planes. First it appears on the social plane, and then on the psychological plane. First it appears between people as an interpsychological category, and then within the child as an intrapsychological category.[18]

Moreover, internal mental processes remain quasi-social as human beings maintain the functions of social interaction.[19] In that sense, Vygotsky refers to consciousness as the "fiction of interaction," that is,

---

[15]Mead, Mind, Self, and Society, 140.

[16]Lev Vygotsky, *Mind in Society: Development of Higher Psychological Processes* (Cambridge: Harvard University Press, 1978); Idem, *Thought and Language* (Cambridge: The MIT Press, 1986).

[17]Lev Vygotsky, "The Genesis of Higher Mental Functions" in James Wertsch, ed., *The Concept of Activity in Soviet Psychology* (Armonk, N.Y.: M. E. Sharpe, 1981), 164.

[18]Ibid., 163.

[19]James Wertsch, "A Sociocultural Approach to Mind" in *Voices of the Mind: A Sociocultural Approach to mediated Action* (Cambridge: Harvard University Press, 1991), 18-45.

and are thus instrumental in "the affirmation and defense of the 'now' self."[37]

By introducing the theory of possible selves, Markus and Nurius replace the earlier conceptualization of the self as only the generalized or "average" self, questioning labels such as "positive" and "negative"

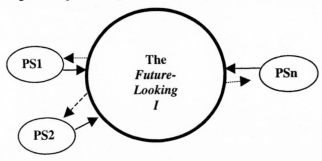

Figure 2-1: The *Future-Looking I* examines and internalizes a possible self(s) of who s/he wishes to be and lives his/her life toward realizing that possible self(s). PS denotes a Possible self.

self-concept, which refer to a person's self as a whole.[38] The theory of possible selves views the self as a multifaceted phenomenon, as a set of images, prototypes, goals, or tasks that are constructed creatively and selectively from an individual's past experiences. Possible selves, thus, may or may not be anchored in social reality. In other words, they consist of the self-knowledge that is socioculturally vulnerable and responsive to changes in the environment.

The theory of possible selves contributes to the "fluidity or malleability of the self because they are differentially activated by the social situation and determine the nature of the working self-concept."[39] While providing a complex and variable self-concept, the possible selves are authentic in the sense that they represent the persistent hopes and fears of the individual.

Thus, in the formulation of the approach to possible selves, Markus and Nurius make a rather obvious, but important, connection in

---

[37]S. Cross and Hazel Markus, "Possible selves across the life span" in *Human Development*, 34 (1991), 230-253.

[38]H. Hermans and H. Kempen, *The Dialogical Self: Meaning as Movement* (San Diego: Academic Press, 1993).

[39]Markus and Nurius, "Possible Selves", 956.

asserting that the individual's possible selves, i.e., hopes and fears, goals and threats, are defining features of the self-concept. Their assertion indeed provides compelling evidence of continuity of identity across time. As postulated by Markus and Nurius, possible selves function as motivating forces for the present action and as the interpretative framework for the present experience.

On the one hand, for persons who are conscientious about their lifestyles and vocations for the future, the theory of possible selves may provide a framework to construct the self. On the other hand, the theory of possible selves could become a source of anxiety and shame for those who are overly introspective. There is a sense in which possible selves take over the self and become an obsession for the unrealistic self. Instead of serving as goals for the future, possible selves can also be utilized as standards to measure self-worth in the present. Depending on how the present measures up in relation to the possible selves, the person's concept can vary significantly. Thus, the concept of possible selves entertains the possibility of multiple states of mind, according to a variety of performance levels within various times, spaces and other variables.

Another concern regarding utilization of the concept of possible selves in construction and organization of the self is that the concept does not take into account the potentially oppressive effect of internalized voices, authorities, and ideologies that might hinder the individuals from fully exercising their agenticity. Some may strive to become the possible selves they envision. Others may strive toward possible selves that are not their own, but are shaped by the wishes and expectations of their internalized voices, authorities, and ideologies. Despite these cautions, the concept of possible selves can be utilized as a tool with which persons can explore their selves.

Imaginary Social Worlds

John Caughey[40] contends that the dichotomy between a "private" world and "public" world is erroneous because each world is populated with imaginary and real people. Based on fifteen years of ethnographic research on imaginary social worlds, Caughey asserts not only that

---

[40]John Caughey *Imaginary Social Worlds* (Lincoln: University of Nebraska Press, 1984).

imaginary worlds exist in people's lives, but that they are an important, powerful, and pervasive aspect of contemporary American life. In American society, intense imaginary relationships through media, dreams, fantasy, and the stream of consciousness are characteristic of those he interviewed.

According to Caughey, when an individual enters an imaginary realm, he or she typically finds a place where he or she is not alone— rather, he or she usually meets other beings and engages in social interactions with them. Thus, imaginary worlds, like actual worlds, are social worlds. For Caughey, this means that, by applying ethnographic methods, he can consider "the kinds of beings who appear, the kinds of roles and identities they play, the values and goals they pursue, and the social satisfactions and frustrations they endure."[41]   In short, he analyzes the patterns governing social interactions in imaginary worlds.

Caughey maintains that in contemporary American society, media consumption serves as an important "socialization" mechanism where media figures do not simply remain on the screen or the printed page. They invade the individual's personal
imaginary systems. Moreover, "media effects," as well as actual and imaginary figures, become part of dreams, fantasy, and the stream of consciousness.

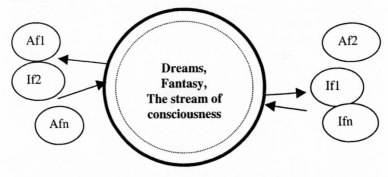

Figure 2-2: The *Actual* as a Product of *Imaginary* I. The actual social order of I, having internalized actual & imaginary figures, becomes a product of imaginary social relationships. Af and If denote actual figure and imaginary figure respectively.

---

[41]Ibid., 29.

Caughey asserts that these imaginary social worlds are significant because of the important effects they have on actual behavior. For instance, imaginary relationships with media figures influence the conduct of actual interactions because people often use these figures as mentors and role models. Dreams also affect actual social relationships because dreams about certain people color one's emotional orientations to them, and waking interpretations of dreams affect the decision-making process. Through stream of consciousness processes, much of a person's actual social conduct is scripted out beforehand during anticipations. Fantasies, too, are socially significant in that they may acquire considerable motivating force by providing vivid pseudo-social experiences of value realization. Through all such cases, "the actual social order becomes a product of imaginary social relationships."[42]

According to Caughey, as the individual makes his or her imaginary processes the subject of personal observation, he or she can significantly increase understanding of himself or herself and awareness of cultural conditioning. He argues that American culture often categorizes people in one of two ways. One category is those who deal with problems actively by trying to affect the external environment (the so-called problem solving approach). The other category is those who deal with problems through "intrapsychic" or "emotion-focused" methods—that is, by trying to accomplish shifts in their own state of mind. American culture has tended to "assume that healthy people use problem-focused modes and that sick people use emotion-focused methods."[43]

In contrast, Caughey maintains that people have the power to become aware of their own imaginary worlds and the ability to modify their experiences in the actual world. For instance, he contends that people can increase the effectiveness of intrapsychic methods by the cultivation of deliberate internal strategies, such as stream of consciousness, which include an extensive amount of critical self-talk.[44]

Caughey's findings thus indicate that imaginary dialogues and interactions exist side by side with real interactions between people and imaginary persons (i.e., parents, friends, family members, media figures and imaginary figures produced in dreams and fantasies, as if

---

[42]Ibid., 244.
[43]Ibid., 252.
[44]Ibid.

they were really present). However, he falls short of suggesting adequate steps to implement his theories. His approach is an ethnographic and descriptive account of how people function smoothly in both imaginary and actual social worlds. He shows the mutual influence of these two social worlds that are populated with imaginary and actual people.

Invisible Guests and the Development of Imaginal Dialogue

Mary Watkins takes an interdisciplinary approach to developing the theory of invisible guests or imaginal others in her conceptualization of the multivoiced self.[45] She contends that there exist dialogues within the imaginal social worlds of the self and that these dialogues influence the daily lives of people in a significant manner. These dialogues exist alongside actual dialogues with real others, and are "interwoven with actual interactions, and an essential part of our narrative construction of the world."[46]

Watkins' contribution to the theory of invisible guests is her creative argument for imaginal dialogues among the (actual and invisible) selves. By distinguishing the "imaginary" and the "imaginal," Watkins undercuts the real-unreal distinction, and she proposes that the imaginal be reckoned in terms not of a narrow conception of "objective" reality, but "a broader one which gives credence to the reality of the imaginal."[47] Furthermore, Watkins argues that, despite their invisible quality, imaginal others and imaginal dialogues must be conceptualized to have autonomous and creative space where they can exist with integrity.

Arguing against Mead's assertion that only adults converse in thought with a "generalized other," Watkins maintains that imaginal dialogues do not disappear in adulthood. Instead, imaginal dialogues continue to be present in their diversity and multiformity. Watkins does not dismiss, however, the existence of Mead's notion of the dialogue with the generalized other. She contends that the two forms of dialogues are not mutually contradictory but rather mutually dependent. In Watkins'

---

[45]Mary Watkins, *Invisible guests: The Development of Imaginal Dialogues* (Hillsdale, NJ: Erlbaum Associates, 1986).

[46]Hermans and Kempen, *The Dialogical Self*, 70.

[47]Watkins, Invisible guests, 4

judgment, Mead's generalized other symbolizes an absent-actual-others where the imaginal is an internalization of social reality. The purpose of the imaginal, then, is adaptation to and preparation for "actual" social reality.

Watkins asserts that imaginal dialogues do not merely reflect reality for a while and then become one unified voice of the generalized other. Instead, Imaginal dialogues create reality where

> the real is not necessarily antithetical to the imaginal, but can be conceived of more broadly to include the imaginal; and that personifying is not an activity symptomatic of the primitivity of mind, but is expressive of its dramatic and poetic nature.[48]

Watkins continues:

> For us the virtue of the system he (Corbin) describes is that it begins with the experience of the imaginal other and illustrates how, when this experience is engaged, there can develop a metaphorical way of thinking, a reflection between mundane and imaginal realities that enriches them both. . . If one lingers with the experience of the figures' autonomy, development is seen in terms of the manner of relating to the figures, rather than the gradual reabsorption and disappearance of the figures suggested by the psychological theories we have discussed . . . Instead of proposing a single line of development for imaginal dialogues, we are suggesting that there are several; which one is observed will depend on the chosen telos.[49]

She is concerned with the development of the imaginal other from an extension of the ego (whether a passive recipient of the imaginer's or the actual other's intention) to an autonomous and animate agency in its own right. The development involves the deepening characterization of many imaginal others, and with how the self develops through *both* the experience of being in dialogue with imaginal others who are felt as autonomous, *and* the experience of even the "I" as being in flux between various characterizations.[50]

---

[48]Ibid., 58.
[49]Ibid., 76-77, 86.
[50]Ibid., 86.

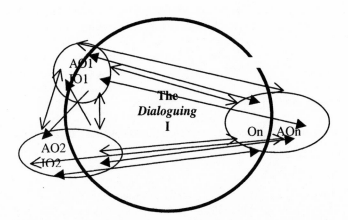

Figure 2-3: The *Dialoguing* I interacts with both actual others and imaginal others as in a round table discussion. AO and IO denote actual other and imaginal other (invisible guest) respectively.

Watkins maintains that only when people value the dramatic quality of mind which gives rise to imaginal worlds can the building of relationships in dialogue between the imaginal guest (other) and the "I" (self) take place. In the process of mutual articulation, invisible guests or characters become not only more autonomous but also more highly specified and discrete in their identities. Watkins conceptualizes four aspects of character development: animation of each character, articulation of psychological properties of the character, clarification of the perspective of the character, and specification of identity of the character.

The *telos* of Watkins' approach is wholeness within the self, where multiple imaginal characters become mutually respectful, listening to one another and learning to work with one another. In other words, it seeks the multiplicity of characters to co-exist and converse harmoniously, as in the imagery of actual persons coexisting and conversing harmoniously at a roundtable.[51] It is not about uniformity,

---

[51]See Justo L. Gonzalez, *Out of every Tribe and Nation: Christian Theology at the Ethnic Roundtable* (Nashville: Abingdon, 1992). The image of roundtable dialog among invisible guests provides a possibility where multiplicity of internalized themes in the lives of human beings can coexist together.

as in Mead's generalized other" where the multiplicity of internalized voices, authorities, and values lose their uniqueness in hopes of creating the "coherent self."[52]

Parenthetically, Watkins' theory of invisible guests is categorically different from a pathological state of multiple personality. For the person with multiple personality disorder, there is no imaginal dialogue. Instead, only sequential monologue exists in which "the person identifies with or is taken over by various characters in a sequential fashion" and "the ego is most often unaware of the other voices."[53]

By likening imaginal dialogues to a sacred process as in Martin Buber's "I-Thou" relation and Erich Fromm's notion of "the being mode," Watkins offers a very promising approach to organizing and constructing the self. Watkins' approach provides ways to understand and engage in the process of defining selves as agentic human beings in their action, in a respectful and mutual manner, with both internalized and actual authorities, voices, and ideologies.

Watkins' concept of invisible guests and the development of imaginal dialogues have much in common with Belanky, Clinchy, Goldberger, and Tarule's[54] notion of constructed knowledge. The process of reclaiming the self by attempting to integrate all forms of knowledge[55] is similar to Watkins' process of mutually respectful and harmonious coexistence of the multiplicity of characters. Another important similarity is that they both recognize the confluence of "real" or imaginal characters. They also assert that all knowledge is constructed in a sociocultural context, and that persons, as knowers and as agents of action, are intimate and dialectical beings found in a variety of contexts.

---

[52]McAdams, *Stories We Live By*; Idem, *The Person*, 745-768.

[53]Watkins, *Invisible guests*, 104.

[54]M. Belenky, B. Clinchy, N. Goldberger, and J. Tarule, *Women's Ways of Knowing: The Development of Self, Voice, and Mind* (New York: Basic Books, 1986).

[55]Ibid. The ways of knowing involve silence; received knowledge—listening to the voices of others; subjective knowledge—the inner voice; subjective knowledge—the quest for self; procedural knowledge—the voice of reason; procedural knowledge—separate and connected knowing; and constructed knowledge—integrating the voices.

The Dialogical Self

Hubert J. Hermans and Harry Kempen have introduced a theory of the dialogical self in their conceptualization of the multivoiced self.[56] Drawing from Vico's challenge against Descartes' notion of *Cogito*, Hermans and Kempen contend that the multiplicity of voices, authorities, and values are nothing less than multiple selves that are embodied within the individual. Appropriating Bakhtin's notion of the multivoicedness of meaning and the heterogeneity of voices[57], they contend that within the self exists the polyphonic narrative of embodied selves.[58]

These selves are not merely archetypal patterns, but *"I"* positions which are discernible from other *"I"* positions. In this notion of the self, the individual can live in a multiplicity of worlds, with each world having its own author or self telling a story and leading life in a given world, relatively independent of the selves of the other worlds.

Thus, *"I"* is able to move, as in a space, from one position to the other with changes in situation and time. Moreover, *"I"* is considered not as a coherent whole in the individual, but as multiple *"I"* positions that can be occupied by the same individual. These *"I"* positions, according to Hermans and Kempen, engage in dialogue with other *"I"* positions as interacting characters in a story. However, these distinct *"I"* positions are formulated as authentic selves embodied in the physical body at a given time in a given world.

In other words, the physical body functions as a conduit for various *"I"* positions (thus, embodied self) that are engaged in constant dialogue (thus, dialogical self) with other "authentic" *"I"* positions (thus, social self). Therefore, *"I"* (*"I"* positions) or the self (selves) is highly decentralized and relatively autonomous "individuals" with highly decentralized *"Me's"* in an individual. Commenting on one of

---

[56]Hermans and Kempen, *The Dialogical Self*; Hubert J. Hermans, Harry Kempen, and Rens Van Loon, "The Dialogical Self: Beyond Individualism and Rationalism" in *American Psychologist* 47, 1 (1992), 23-33.

[57]Bakhtin, *The Dialogical Imagination*; Michael Holquist, *Dialogism: Bakhtin and his world* (New York: Routledge, 1990); James Wertsch, *Voices of the Mind.*

[58]For a helpful discussion on the socially constructed embodied self, see Allison Weir, *Sacrificial Logics: Feminist theory and the Critique of Identity* (New York: Routledge, 1996), especially the chapter called "toward a Theory of Self and social Identity: Julia Kristeva," 145-183.

the aspects of the modern self, Hermans and Kempen argue that the centralization concept of the coherent self presents "serious limitations on the relations among the different characters of the self-narrative as a field of possibilities."[59]

In their postmodern view of the self, it is fluid and ever evolving as it encounters the unknowns of future and of the immediately preceding time and space of the present reality. Moreover, the individual with multiple narratives will likely have multiple goals that are not necessarily related to one another. These goals, however, constantly interact and are negotiated among the multiple selves. The theory of the dialogical self allows multiple narratives from multiple voices—multiple I-positions creating multiple me's—which result in a complex, narratively structured self.

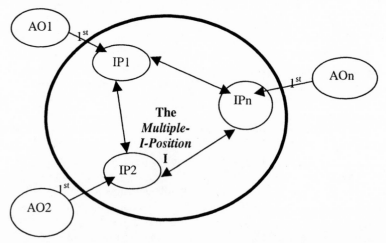

Figure 2-4: Having internalized actual others, the multiple I positions of The *Multiple-I-position* I negotiates which I position (or a combination of I positions) should be in charge of the *Multiple-I-Position* I at a particular time and space. AO and IP denote actual other and internalized I position, respectively.

As a multiplicity of voices, authorities, and values are internalized within the self, they reside in the self as multivoiced selves, and they

---

[59]Hubert J. Hermans and Harry Kempen, "The Dialogical Self: Beyond Individualism and Rationalism" in *American Psychologist* 47, 1 (1992), 29.

attempt to co-exist mutually for the benefit of the self. However, Hermans and Kempen contend that there exist "suppressed voices" and other issues of dominance within dialogical relations. In other words, there exist asymmetrical relationships among the multiple selves, especially when the dialogue is between an imaginal adult and an imaginal child, whether it is interactional dominance, topic dominance, amount of talk, or strategic moves.[60] They theorize that the notion of suppressed voices is a possibility for investigation into the inner-workings of the multivoiced self.

The Saturated Self

Kenneth Gergen argues that destabilization of the self is one of the characteristics of postmodernity.[61] Among many of the societal influences involved in the social construction of the self, Gergen asserts that the media plays a crucial role in enabling the human being to encounter many diverse peoples representing different social enclaves and ethnic or religious backgrounds. In his scheme, the self is opened to become multivocal as the human being carries a number of voices

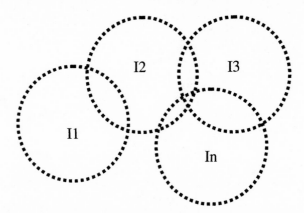

Figure 2-5: The *Saturated, Distributed*, and *Protean Self.* I denotes various I-positions that hang together loosely to form (and reform) the self.

---

[60]Hermans and Kempen, *The Dialogical Self*, 75.
[61]Kenneth Gergen, *The Saturated Self* (San Francisco: Basic Books, 1991).

and identities within him or her. In the process, s/he finds that s/he no longer has a central core with which to evaluate and act. Instead, s/he finds himself or herself decentered in the way the self may be mobilized and dispersed. Essentially, Gergen argues for the interaction between face-to-face connections and the symbolic community, which both constitute self. Gergen's focus on the influence of the media in the construction of the multivoiced self informs one of the significant influences on the construction and narration of self.

Conclusion

Through this chapter, current notions of self-construction and narration, which understand the self as having a singular essence, traveling linearly towards a projected goal are set aside. Instead, a new concept of the self is introduced, as responsive to multiple factors, which include but are not limited to the salient voices, values and authorities which are present in one's sociocultural context. Understanding this model of self sheds light on the project of self construction and narration in the lives of second-generation Korean Americans, whose lives are influenced by often conflicting norms and a multiplicity of authorities, values and voices. The next several chapters will revisit the ideas presented in this chapter, particularly in regard to the research methodology outlined in chapter three and the adaptation patterns for Korean Americans described in chapter four.

Chapter 3

Reflections on Methodology

The research tradition employed in this study is that of qualitative research, primarily utilizing ethnographic interviews and participant observation. The study sought to observe the insights and patterns of thought, action, and reflection on a variety of issues ranging from life decisions to self-understanding and view of church.

Research Paradigm

The research paradigm employed in this study is the constructionist paradigm.[1] In general, constructionists contend that knowledge and truth are created, as opposed to discovered by the mind, and mediated through symbol and language systems. However, at a deeper level, the constructionist paradigm can be construed in several different ways, depending on the nature of reality and the emphases of inquiry.[2]

While both constructionism and constructivism emphasize the role of human construction in what human beings take to "be real,"

---

[1]Yvonna S. Lincoln and Norman K. Denzin, "Competing Paradigms in Qualitative Research" in Norman K. Denzin and Yvonna S. Lincoln, eds., *The Landscape of Qualitative Research: Theories and Issues* (Thousand Oaks: Sage, 1998), 195-220; Thomas A. Schwandt, "Constructivist, Interpretivist Approaches to Human Inquiry" in Norman K. Denzin and Yvonna S. Lincoln, eds., *The Landscape of Qualitative Research: Theories and Issues* (Thousand Oaks: Sage, 1998), 221-259.

[2]Ibid., 235-245.

constructivism asserts that the process of world construction is psychological in that human beings mentally construct the world of experience as individuals.[3] The constructionism view, presented here, asserts that what is or becomes real is an outcome of social relationships. Meanings are generated through coordinations among persons. Thus, relationships function as antecedents for any meaning-making processes and, in fact, give rise to all that is intelligible. However, this social constructionist framework does not simply treat relationships as human endeavors that can be abstracted out of context or environment. Gergen contends that

> In effect, all understandings of relationship are themselves limited by culture and history. In the end we are left with a profound sense of relatedness—of all with all—that we cannot adequately comprehend.[4]

The constructionist framework, then, assumes that reality consists of the meanings people imbue into their experience within their particular sociocultural contexts. Reality is then context-based and constructed through human perceptions. Thus, reality is construed in multiplicity and the constructions of reality are alterable. However, no claims are made on the nature of reality in this study.

This study presupposes that the research and the researcher are inseparably and interactively linked. There is no way the process of research does not impact the nature of reality itself. The findings are *literally created* as the investigation proceeds. In a sense, the distinction between ontology and epistemology is blurred.

Thus, the aim of the research is to develop a unique, in-depth understanding of persons in a specific category and context, namely second-generation Korean American young adults. Research findings may transfer to other groups, people, and contexts, but this research does not make that claim. This research is value-bound in two aspects. First, I, the researcher, select and impose what is deemed the most appropriate research paradigm to guide the study. Second, I am intentional in promoting values of altruism and empowerment in the process of research.

This research attempts to construct a new consensus of perspectives through mutual understanding of many voices, including my own.

---

[3]Gergen, An Invitation to social Construction, 236-237.
[4]Ibid., 48.

Thus, I am construed as a "passionate participant" a facilitator of multivoiced reconstruction. The research is also intended as the setting of an extended conversation in which everyone involved is impacted and his or her perspectives changed.

Research Procedures

My Role and Observation: A Participant as Observer

The initial study design began by identifying my own interest areas and commitment toward studying the lives of second-generation Korean American young adults. The nature of my relationship with the young adults is characterized by my prolonged engagement with various aspects of these people's lives.

I can be considered in many ways as a *full participant* who is "simultaneously a functioning member of the community undergoing investigation and an investigator."[5] However, having been born in Korea and immigrated to the U.S. at the age of 13, I also consider myself more of a *participant-as-observer* who, in addition to sharing many common experiences with the second-generation young adults, attempted to enter into the lives of these people more fully. Glesne discusses the paradoxical dilemma often faced by a participant-as-observer in the course of research when she says:

> A paradox develops as you become more of a participant and less of an observer. The more you function as a member of the everyday world of the researched, the more you risk losing the eye of the uninvolved outsider; yet, the more you participate, the greater your opportunity to learn.[6]

As a participant-as-observer, I engaged in a prolonged period of observing the everyday life of second-generation Korean American young adults for several reasons. First, participating as an observer in their lives aided me in experiencing the various spheres of life in which the young adults are involved, while understanding the importance of

---

[5]Corrine Glesne, *Becoming Qualitative Researchers, 2nd edition* (New York: Longman, 1999), 44.
[6]Ibid.

the contexts in which they live. Second, the prolonged engagement gave opportunities for me to gain first-hand impressions of their lives in order to formulate questions for personal interviews for the study. Third, the data obtained from the prolonged engagement was used to triangulate data with the perceptions of the young adults on common experiences shared by both the researched subjects and myself. Moreover, the observation data was used to triangulate the data obtained from the interviews with the young adults.   Fourth, the prolonged engagement provided opportunities to view aspects of their lives that may escape their conscious attention. Fifth, I was able to discern some aspects of their lives about which the young adults were unwilling to talk.

I employed several observational strategies and lived out certain dispositions in his prolonged engagement with the young adults. I assumed the role of detective, being curious and open-minded, and ready to ask probing, yet non-threatening questions. I also attempted to exercise patience and was expectant during some of the mundane aspects of their lives. Occasionally, I appropriately tested my hypotheses and observed patterns by sharing these hypotheses and soliciting the responses of some of the young adults. At all times, I attempted to delineate the difference between descriptions and inferences during the prolonged engagement with the young adults.[7]

As I assumed a role of evaluator, I increasingly noticed patterns in my participants about which I jotted down evaluatory remarks before returning to observation. I usually recorded a scene or episode in my mind by recording a word or phrase that would help me bring back the episode in its entirety. Then, usually in a day or two, I tried to discern the importance of my evaluatory remarks or generalization in the whole schema of study.

I approached the young adults as a subjective inquirer, looking for meaning and posing questions for myself and looking for significance in terms of the aims, beliefs, sentiments, and convictions of the young adults regarding themselves and their lives. I was then, in a sense, both observing and constructing the events simultaneously.

I was able to assume the role of insider, looking for internal logics, order of things, and rules that make relationships and community

---

[7]Robert Boostrom, "Learning to Pay Attention" *Qualitative Studies in Education*, 7:1, 1994, 51-64.

function. I understand rules as the aspects of life that express the thoughts of a community imagining itself into being. These rules embody an order because the participants see the sense of them. I moved into the role of reflexive interpreter, evaluating the interplay of the insider and subjective personal views, as if becoming inducted into another way of life and seeing the world from their perspective.

Selecting the Participants for Interviews

The selection of participants for the study is a purposive sampling strategy, combining various sampling strategies.[8] First and foremost, homogeneous sampling was employed at the outset of the study to delimit the scope of the study based on the research focus. All the chosen participants were persons between the ages of 25 to 31, who either were born in the US or immigrated to the U.S. at the age of 5 or younger. All of them had been involved in the Korean American church for a significant part of their childhood, early adolescence, and adolescence. They all resided in the metropolitan area of Chicago and attended a Korean American church at the time interviews were conducted.

However, within the homogeneous sample maximum variation sampling was utilized to document as many unique variations as possible within their lives. While the sample was representative in the sense that most of the participants grew up in the major metropolitan areas of the U.S., those who were born in Korea and those who grew up in smaller cities in the U.S. were included, as well. Although they were not representative of second-generation Korean American young adults, young adults raised by a single parent and those who attended a large church were included to insure maximum variation.

Lastly, opportunistic sampling strategies were utilized to allow new leads during fieldwork, taking advantage of unexpected turns of events. The initial selection of the potential interviewees was made based on recommendations of church leaders of the second-generation Korean American young adults and on leaders of Christian ministry organizations in the Chicago area. The recommendations were based on who the leaders viewed as "typical" of the young adults they have in

---

[8]David A. Erlandson, Edward L. Harris, Barbara L. Skipper, and Steve D. Allen, *Doing Naturalistic Inquiry* (Newbury Park: Sage, 1993), 82-84.

their congregations and on the ability of the persons to reflexively articulate various issues concerning their lives. While formulating a provisionary list of interviewees employing the first two strategies, I was prepared to seek out potential interviewees *serially* and/or *contingently*, based on unexpected recommendations by the interviewees.[9]

Letters describing the nature of the study and a follow-up phone call were made to contact potential interviewees. The letter included the discussion on how I obtained the information of the potential interviewee, the focus of study, how the data was intended for use, guarantee of the protection of the interviewee's identity at all stages of the research, voluntary participation, and consent form. The phone calls generally involved a brief introduction of myself, answering any questions about the interview, and making an appointment for the interview.

Utilizing the saturation principle[10], I interviewed 24 second-generation Korean American young adults. However, 2 interviews had to be discarded for analysis due to the technical difficulty of transcribing the audiotapes of the interviews. Table 6-1 provides the information of those who were interviewed.

Name Sex	Age/Marital Status	Education	Occupation	Church Involvement
Isabella F	26 Married	BA/Journal-ism - private university; MA/Clinical-Psychology-private college	Family/children psychotherapist in Chicago suburb	Lay leader
Sam M	28 Married	BA/Psychology - private university; MA/Clinical Psychology	Financial aid counselor-private college	Deacon

[9]Glesne, Becoming Qualitative Researchers, 28-30; Michael Q. Pattern, Qualitative Evaluation and Research Methods, 2nd ed. (Newbury Park: Sage, 1990), 182-183.

[10]Lincoln and Guba, *Naturalistic Inquiry*, 233.

Name Sex	Age/Marital Status	Education	Occupation	Church Involvement
Albert M	26 Single	Private university; Law school	Lawyer in general practice in suburb	Sunday School teacher
Nick M	30 Single	Private university; Medical school	Medical doctor in family practice	Deacon
Julia F	28 Single	BA/Psychology - private university; MA/Counseling Psychology-Seminary	Psychotherapist for youth and families	High involvement in her church
Michelle F	26 Single	BS/Chemistry Private college	Physical therapist in hospital in suburb	Life-long church attendee
Kris F	27 Married	BA/Psychology-state school; MA/Education-Accepted in Pharmacy School	Elementary School teacher three years	Regular church attendee
Kelly F	26 Married	BA/Journalism - private university	Newspaper reporter-One child	Regular church attendee
Paul M	33 Married	State school; Dental school	Dentist	Regular church attendee
Georgia F	24 Single	State school	In transition	Regular church attendee
Joel M	25 Single	State school; planning to go to seminary	Quality control chemist for a dental company	High church involvement
Elissa F	27 Single	BA private college	Collector for household retail service	Regular church attendee

Name Sex	Age/Marital Status	Education	Occupation	Church Involvement
Betsy F	24 Single	Accounting major - State school; MAT/State school	Accepted to teach	High church involvement
Rose F	24 Single	BA/Chemistry-Seeking to go to medical school	At Youth & Family Services	Attends a Caucasian Bible church
Dilan M	26 Single	Finance major-State school yrs.	Systems programmer; computer technology	Youth leader
Daniel M	30 Married	State School; MAT/State school	High school math teacher in suburb	Sunday School Superintendent
Molly F	23 Single	BA/Elem.Ed. Teachers' college	Teacher for 2 years in uptown Chicago	High church involvement
Mark M	28 Single	BA/Finance degree-private university	Category management specialist for food company	Regular church attendee
Abigail F	28 Single	BA private college	Graphic designer	Worship leader
Luke M	25 Single	BA State university; Grad courses; Seeks medical degree	Rehabilitation Technician in a hospital	High church involvement
Brian M	32 Single	BA State university	Freelance artist	High church involvement
Melinda F	24 Single	BA Early Childhood Education-State	Job in transition; Accepted to teach	Core member of a para-

		university; Intercultural studies with certificate in ESL/Graduate school at private college		Asian American church

Table 3-1 Brief descriptions of interviewees

Interview

The interview methodology employed in the study was a combination of structured and semi-structured interview formats. While questions and order were predetermined, questions were open-ended and, when appropriate, the order of the interview was altered. All the interviews were audio taped and fully transcribed.

The interview guide was designed in such a way that the content (the areas of exploration), wording (the ways of exploration) and order (the sequence of exploration) would provide the maximum opportunity to obtain compatible information from interviewees. In the process of designing the interview guide, I avoided *multiple, leading,* and *yes/no* questions while including *open-ended, singular, clear* questions. The interview guide was also designed in light of the holistic nature of human beings and their experiences. In that light, questions were designed to inquire about the interviewee's background/demographic information, experience/behavior, sensor/feeling, knowledge/cognition, and opinion/values in his or her life.

The interview guide was designed for the study to obtain, first, "here-and-now constructions" of decisions, actions, feelings, motivations, concerns and other issues that help identify the internalized voices, authorities, and values that are operative in the life of the interviewee. Second, the interview provided an opportunity for the interviewee to engage in "reconstructions" of the above issues as experienced in the past. This process further guided the interviewee to observe more insights and patterns in which the internalized voices, authorities, and values function in the self. Lastly, I invited the interviewee to engage in "projections" of how the above issues and the internalized multiplicity of voices, authorities, and values would impact the interviewee's future. The interview guide used for this study is displayed in Appendix 1.

As discussed above, the first set of questions (Questions 1 & 2) is a series of open-ended questions that provides the interviewee the opportunity to identify "here-and-now constructions." Question 1 invites the interviewee to reflect on his/her decision-making strategies in order to draw out the influence of any internalized voices, authorities, and values. Question 2 channels the interviewee to reflect on his or her parents' decision-making patterns in order for the interviewee to talk about any parental influences on the interviewee's decision-making style.

The second set of questions (Questions 3, 4, 5, and 6) provides an opportunity for the interviewee to engage in "reconstructions" of the possible loci of sociocultural factors that s/he has experienced in his or her life. Question 3 is a broad, general question about the influence of the interviewee's culture (however s/he defines it) and of the American society (again, however s/he defines it). Question 4 gets at the influence of two more specific sociocultural tools, namely, media and education. The question also seeks to address the influence of the Korean American church and its religious education as an important sociocultural institution and its educational process, respectively. The question gets at the role of religion, particularly Christianity, in the life of the interviewee. Question 6 deals with the role of parents and a few significant others in the interviewee's life.

The final set of questions (Questions 7 and 8) is formulated to bring understanding of how the internalized multiplicity functions in the construction and narration of the self in terms of the participants' decision-making process and self-identification. Question 9 invites the interviewee to be reflexive about his or her responses in the interview and to devise any plans for the continuation of his or her construction and narration of the self. Moreover, it asks the interviewee to entertain some thoughts about creating appropriate religious education approaches to the ministry of second-generation Korean American young adults. The last question invites the participants to reflect on the interview process itself.

Utilizing this interview guide, I sought to conduct the interview in the spirit of naturalistic inquiry[11] by: stressing the interviewee's

---

[11]Lincoln and Guba, *Naturalistic Inquiry.* I take Lincoln and Guba's notion of "naturalistic inquiry" in which no manipulation on the part of the inquirer is implied, and no a priori units on the part of the inquirer are imposed on the

definition of the situation; encouraging the interviewee to structure the account of the situation; and letting the interviewee introduce to a considerable extent his/her notions of what she/he regards as relevant, instead of relying upon my notion of relevance.[12]   I conducted the interviews as if I were creating art. I made every effort to listen actively and non-judgmentally. In asking questions, I used at least two alternate ways to ask the same question for the interviewee's sake. I attempted to be sensitive to my role, avoiding the use of academic terms or citation of studies, for instance. I engaged in some self-disclosure when appropriate. My responses were generally short and affirming. I also utilized a summarizing technique after each section of the interview in order to raise the quality of data. I engaged in gentle probing when follow-up questions were necessary. I also wrote down significant ideas or themes on a notepad.

Insuring the Quality of Data: Establishing Trustworthiness

In this study, various naturalistic techniques were utilized to establish the trustworthiness of data. For credibility, prolonged engagement and persistent observation of second-generation young adults were employed throughout the study. When appropriate, member checks were utilized such that participants and interviewees had opportunities to either verify or correct the data that involved their lives or stories. Moreover, the data obtained from prolonged engagement and interviews were triangulated in every stage of the study. In terms of transferability, the widest possible range of information of participants and interviewees was included to compile thick description. As discussed above, purposive sampling strategies were used to bring together the sample as approximately representative of the second-generation Korean American young adults.

In the area of dependability, efforts were made to reduce researcher error and acknowledge the design-induced changes in the study. For those purposes, field-notes were written and kept throughout the study.

---

outcome. Margaret Ann Crain maintains that naturalistic inquiry presupposes that "voices need to be heard and honored." (Jack L. Seymour, Margaret Ann Crain, and Joseph V. Crockett, *Educating Christians* (Nashville: Abingdon, 1993), 14.

[12]Lincoln and Guba, *Naturalistic Inquiry*, 268.

I was vigilant in keeping methodological and analytic comments in the course of the research.

For the purpose of insuring confirmability, decisions for data collection, interpretations, and conclusions were kept. This allows others to be able to trace back through the entire research process.

Analysis of Data

Analysis of data entails investigation and formal identification of salient themes/codes that emerge from both ordinary and critical readings of the data from prolonged observation and interviews. It also involves a construction of hypotheses[13] or generalizations that can be verified through the triangulation process among the various strands of the data. These findings were further refined by any participants' critical comments and by the theories that are employed in the study. In the end, the study attempts to demonstrate support for those themes and hypotheses.

Data reduction or coding is a process of looking for ways to reduce the data from interviews, observation, and artifacts. It is done with *anticipation* according to a conceptual framework and the research question. Developing coding categories involves several steps. The first step was to go through all the files and get them in order. I used The Ethnography v5.0 by Qualis Research for the initial stages of data analysis.[14]

Secondly, I took long and undisturbed periods and carefully read the data at least twice. While I was reading the data, I developed a preliminary list of possible coding categories. In developing codes, I was mindful of words and phrases interviewees and participants used that were unfamiliar to me or were used in ways to which I was unaccustomed. A typical family of codes for the data coding process in the study was informed by the recommendation of coding categories developed by Bogdan and Biklen.[15] They are setting/context codes,

---

[13]Robert Bogdan, and Steven J. Taylor, Introduction to Qualitative Research Methods: A Phenomenological Approach to the Social Sciences (New York: John Wiley & Sons, Inc., 1975), 79-94.

[14]This researcher found Ethnograph v5.0 to be inefficient and laborious for the purpose of this current research.

[15]Bogdan and Biklen, Qualitative Research in Education, 170-186.

definition of the situation codes, subjects' ways of thinking about people and objects study, process codes, activity codes, events codes, strategy codes, relationship and social structure codes, and methods codes.

Thirdly, after generating preliminary coding categories, I formulated and assigned abbreviations of codes to the units of data for corresponding paragraphs or a group of sentences. This task involved scrutinizing sentences carefully and judging what best codes the material pertained. At times, some units of data were assigned multiple codes, and coding segments overlapped with each other. Some of the coding categories were modified, new categories were developed, and others discarded during this process. Finally, the units of data for each of the codes were delineated and printed for further analysis.

The next step, data display, is an organized, compressed assembly of information that permits conclusion drawing and/or action taking. While data coding organizes data into manageable units, the coded data provides no clues about the *interrelationships* within them. In other words, data displays assist in the process of making connections by presenting a reduced set of data upon which to reflect.

The final step involved conclusion drawing and verification. I interpret or draw meaning from displayed data. The process may involve comparison/contrast, noting of patterns and themes, clustering, use of metaphors, confirmatory tactics such as triangulation, looking for negative cases, following up on surprises, and checking results with respondents.

The following chapters will incorporate the findings of my research into my study of the history of Korean Americans, various adaptation and identity formation models, the Korean American family, the present lives of second- generation Korean American young adults, and their experience with the Korean American church.

Chapter 4

A Portrait of Americans of Korean Descent

This chapter paints a portrait of Korean Americans. Fragments of salient information on the Korean American immigrant experience are brought together from various, though somewhat limited, sources of literature on Koreans in America. The history and demographics of Koreans in America are briefly examined in order to inform an understanding of the second generation. Then several models of adaptation for immigrant groups and their descendants are outlined. By evaluating the dominant assimilation model that has been widely utilized to describe the integration of Americans of Asian descent into the host society, this chapter examines how the reception of the host society has influenced the reality of Americans of Korean descent. Then the factors that have shaped the adaptation process of first generation immigrants are delineated, based upon the particular sociocultural contexts. This chapter concludes by examining some critical issues that pertain to the shaping and functioning of the second generation in its unique sociocultural context, such as Korean American values, the Korean American family, and the Korean American church.

The Brief History and Demographics of Koreans in America

Three distinct phases of Korean immigration to the U.S. divide the history of Koreans in America. According to Won Moo Hurh, these distinct phases have been directly related to the changes in the U.S.

immigration policies.[1] The first period involved the predominantly male plantation workers immigrating to the Hawaiian islands in the first decade of the twentieth century.[2] Until 1924, these men brought their "picture brides" from Korea to the U.S.[3] The nuclear families created by these marriages eventually either settled in Hawaii or migrated to the west coast of the North American mainland.

In the years following the Korean War, 1953 and onward, the population of Koreans in America changed considerably. This second phase of immigration was comprised of young Korean women who were married to American servicemen and brought into the U.S. by their husbands. American families also adopted a substantial number of Korean War orphans. Many of the orphans were Amerasians fathered by American servicemen who participated in the war.[4] The whereabouts of these two groups of people of Korean descent have been difficult to monitor, resulting in a virtual absence of studies on these populations. During this second phase, a small number of students and professional workers came over and were allowed to settle in the U.S. The second wave of migration from Korea became the seed for the exponential growth of the Korean population in the U.S. that occurred after 1965.

The third phase of Korean immigration is said to be a direct result of the change in the U.S. Immigration Act made in 1965. This policy deliberately favored family reunion, according to Hurh and Min, granting preferential treatment to immediate family members of

---

[1] Won Moo Hurh, *The Korean Americans* (Westport: Greenwood Publishing, 1998), 31-47.

[2] Chan, *Asian Americans: An Interpretive History*, 194. Pyong Gap Min asserts that these 7,200 men came not as immigrants, but as contract laborers (a practice outlawed in the U.S. at that time) forced to accept low wages and poor working conditions offered by plantation owners. See Pyong Gap Min, "Korean Americans," in *Asian Americans: Contemporary Trends and Issues,* ed. Pyong Gap Min (Thousands Oaks: Sage Publication, 1995).

[3] Hurh, *The Korean Americans*, 38-39. Picture brides refer to Korean women brought to the U.S. by marriages arranged through the exchange of pictures. The immigration of 1924 prohibited entry of any Asians to the U.S., resulting in 3000 men living as bachelors.

[4] This segment of the Asian American population is called a "minority among minorities." M. Motoyoshi, "The Experience of Mixed-race People: Some Thoughts and Theories," *Journal of Ethnic Studies* 18 (1990): 77-94.

permanent residents or U.S. citizens. Extending Reimer's[5] analysis of the immigration policy, Hurh asserts that

> Preferential treatment for the purpose of family reunion was in fact originally intended to encourage immigration from European countries. Unexpectedly, however, immigration from Europe fell by the mid-1970s, while Asian immigration increased about six fold. The U.S. Congress and immigration reformers certainly did not foresee the potential effect of chain immigration under the family preference system, especially the fifth preference (brothers and sisters).[6]

Moreover, the new immigration policy provided opportunities for professionals and their family members to immigrate to the U.S. For example, about 13,000 Korean medical professionals immigrated to the U.S. between 1966 and 1979. Additionally, Korean students came who were later able to change their residency status upon obtaining employment in the U.S. business sector. They, in turn, exercised their privilege as official immigrants:

> Once an immigrant, he uses the second preference to bring over his spouse and children. A few years later the new immigrant, and his spouse, become citizens and are eligible to sponsor their brothers and sisters under the fifth, the largest and most popular preference, or to bring in their spouses and children and expand the immigrant kin network still further when they become citizens.[7]

According to the 1970, 1980, and 1990 U.S. censuses, the Korean population in the U.S. increased in dramatic proportions from 69,155 to 354,593 and to 798,849 respectively.[8] While the key pull factor for this increase has been attributed to the change in immigration policy[9], there are two major push factors that further influenced Korean immigration to the U.S. in these years.

One of the push factors involved a change in the Korean government's policy towards the emigration of its people in the mid 1960's and onward. As the Korean government scrambled to find

[5]D. M. Reimers, *Still the Golden Door* (New York: Columbia University Press, 1985).

[6]Hurh, The Korean Americans, 39.

[7]Ibid., 41.

[8]Min, Asian Americans: Contemporary Trends and Issues, 16, 204.

[9]Hurh, The Korean Americans.

policies to improve difficult socioeconomic conditions of the war-torn nation, it adopted and actively supported emigration of its people as one such policy. At one level, the government saw emigration as part of the country's population control program[10], especially welcoming the U.S. policy favoring family immigration. At another level, the government concluded that emigration would contribute to the economic stability of the nation, viewing the immigrants as strategic partners in the distribution and consumption of various Korean exported products.

Perhaps the more important push factor that contributed to the dramatic increase in the Korean immigration rate was the cumulative consequences of military dictatorship and its policy of "guided capitalism" in Korea from the early 1960's and onward. As the government established a symbiotic relationship with business conglomerates, it allowed many inequitable practices of these conglomerates to go unchallenged and unpunished. In return, the military elite received enormous sums in bribes. While this form of guided capitalism put the nation on the economic map of the world, it was largely done at the expense of the lower and middle classes of the Korean population.[11] Hurh contends that the guided industrialization resulted in:

> weakening of small and medium-size indigenous enterprises, impoverishment of the rural population, a ban on labor activities, political oppression, blatant violation of human rights, career frustration for a large proportion of white-collar workers, polarization of the rich and poor, and social and geographic dislocation of various strata of the population. These conditions brought an acute state of normlessness to Korean society as a whole.[12]

Thus, the stage was set, and in 1965 when the U.S. immigration policy changed, many Koreans took advantage by starting their lives over in the land of opportunity. But, while those who wished to immigrate to the U.S. from the urban and middle classes had the resources and family connections to do so, most blue-collar workers and peasant farmers had no such advantage.

---

[10]Chan, Asian Americans: An Interpretive History, 150-151.
[11]Hurh, The Korean Americans, 41.
[12]Ibid.

When a sample of U.S. visa applicants in Seoul was interviewed in 1986, they expressed their preferences in choosing the U.S. over Korea. Four principal preferences were higher wages, rewards for hard work and ability, a more favorable political environment, and a good education for their children.[13] Once these Koreans immigrated and settled in the U.S., the preferences listed above became their expectations and life-goals. Kitano and Daniels concur stating that "economic success in the majority culture, retention of aspects of Korean culture, rapid flight to more desirable housing in the suburbs, and the development of ethnic business districts. . . (and) a good education for their children"[14] have been the primary goals and patterns of adjustment for the Koreans in the U.S.

The 1990 census indicates that Korean Americans settled in the various communities surrounding major cities of the U.S. Four concentrated pockets were the surrounding communities of Los Angeles, New York City, Washington D.C., and Chicago, listed in the diminishing order of population size. These four pockets comprised approximately two thirds of the Korean American population in the U.S., with 44% residing in West Coast states. These statistics showed that Korean Americans, as an ethnic group, were more diversely dispersed than any other Asian ethnic group.[15]

The average household size for Korean Americans, as reported in the 1990 census was 3.86 persons, whereas the average household size for all other Asian Americans and for all Americans were 3.5 and 2.63 respectively. Hurh estimates that based on the 1980 and 1990 censuses, roughly one third of the Korean American population was born in the States.[16] However, Hurh's appraisal does not factor in the number of the "knee high" group of Korean Americans who came to the U.S. at or before five years of age.[17]

From 1965 to 1996, an average of 23,300 Koreans immigrated to the U.S. per year. During the peak period of 1974 to 1990, an average of

---

[13]Harry Kitano and Roger Daniels, *Asian Americans: Emerging Minorities,* 2nd ed. (Englewood Cliffs, NJ: Prentice Hall, 1995), 119.

[14]Ibid.

[15]Min, *Asian Americans: Contemporary Trends and Issues,* 206-208. For example, compare with 76% of Japanese Americans and 68% of Filipino Americans settled in the West.

[16]Hurh, Korean Americans, 52.

[17]Lee C. Lee and Nolan Zane, eds., *Handbook of Asian American sychology* (Thousand Oaks: Sage, 1998), 241.

32,226 Koreans settled in the U.S. per year. In recent years, however, there has been a steady decline in the influx of Korean immigrants to the U.S. In the years between 1991 and 1996, the average went down to 19,024 persons per year, and in 1994 a low of 16,011 Koreans immigrated. Moreover, in 1993, an average of 3,026 Korean Americans returned to Korea, whereas 6,487 of them left in 1992.[18]

The Models of Adaptation of Immigrant
(and Their Descendent) Groups

At a popular level, the portrayal of the diversity among people in American society has often taken on the form of metaphors such as the melting pot, salad bowl, and mosaic. These different ideas indicate the effect of both centripetal (the pull toward) and centrifugal (the pull against) forces that are operative on immigrants in respect to American culture. The effect of the centripetal force can be described as assimilation, the process that leads to greater homogeneity in society, and the effect of the centrifugal force as pluralism, the condition that produces sustained ethnic differentiation and continued heterogeneity.[19] This chapter proceeds to discuss five sociological models that explain how immigrants and their descendants adapt, as ethnic groups, into American society. The chapter concludes by examining perspectives that explain how immigrants and their descendents adapt to American society as individuals.

The "Anglo-Conformity" Assimilation Model

In exploring the extent and scope of the integration of immigrants and their descendants into American society, many sociologists have approached the phenomenon from an assimilation perspective. Robert Park and Ernest Burgess, two influential sociologists of the century, defined assimilation as:

---

[18]These calculations have been done by this researcher based on the multiple sources appeared on Hurh, *Korean Americans*, 33.

[19]Harold Abramson, "Assimilation and Pluralism," in *Harvard Encyclopedia of American Groups,* ed. Stephen Thernstrom (Cambridge: Harvard University Press, 1980), 150.

a process of interpenetration and fusion in which persons and groups acquire the memories, sentiments, and attitudes of other persons or groups, and, by sharing their experience and history, are incorporated with them in a common cultural life.[20]

Assimilation, then, is a multi-dimensional phenomenon that occurs at many levels and stages in the lives of immigrants and their descendants, as both individuals and groups. The rate at which these changes take place varies for individuals and groups depending on their perception and response to experiences in America. Milton Gordon has delineated the variables that an individual encounters in the assimilation process:[21]

Sub-process or Condition	**Type or Stage of Assimilation**
Change of cultural patterns to those of host society	Cultural or behavioral assimilation (Acculturation)
Large-scale entrance into cliques, clubs, and institutions of host society, on primary group level	Structural assimilation
Large-scale intermarriage	Marital assimilation (Amalgamation)
Development of sense of people-hood based exclusively on host society	Identification assimilation
Absence of prejudice	Attitude receptional assimilation
Absence of discrimination	Behavior receptional assimilation
Absence of value and power conflict	Civic assimilation

Table 4-1: Milton Gordon's Assimilation Process

These variables are by no means sequential or invariant, but they are simply possible variables an individual might experience in the assimilation process. Each of the above stages or sub-processes in the

---

[20]Robert E. Park and Ernest W. Burgess, *Introduction to the Science of Sociology* (Chicago: University of Chicago Press, 1921), 736-737.

[21]Milton M. Gordon, *Assimilation in American Life* (New York: Oxford University Press, 1964), 71.

assimilation process takes place in varying degrees. These variables suggest that assimilation is a complicated phenomenon that is potentially influenced by such factors as the strength of the immigrant's substructure and subculture, as well as the extent of the host society's resistance to absorbing the immigrants.

Based on the assimilation variables, certain hypotheses about the relationship of these variables can be advanced. First, in majority-minority group contact, cultural assimilation or acculturation on the part of the minority will occur before any of the other variables can occur. Second, acculturation may take place even when none of the other types of assimilation has occurred and this situation of "acculturation only" may continue indefinitely. Third, if structural assimilation occurs along with or subsequent to acculturation, all the other types of assimilation will inevitably follow under this model.[22]

Gordon's hypotheses presuppose the existence of a "host society" or "core group" in America prior to the arrival of the immigrant group. This core group denotes the dominant power and status system of the community that provides the master cultural mold or meta-narrative for the class system of the other groups in the society. The dominant sub-society then provides the standard for the assimilation process to which other groups adjust or measure their relative degree of adjustment.

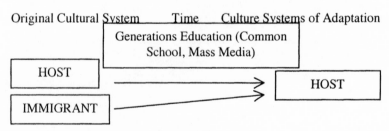

Figure 4-1: Anglo conformity perspective[23]

The direction of this assimilation approach has been used predominantly in understanding the various aspects of integration of

[22]Ibid., 77-81; Milton M. Gordon, "Toward a general theory of racial and ethnic group relations," in Ethnicity: Theory and experience, ed. Nathan Glazer and Daniel P. Moynihan (Cambridge: Harvard University Press, 1975), 84.
[23]Andrew M. Greeley, Ethnicity in the United States (New York: John Wiley & Sons, 1974), 304.

immigrants to America. It argues that the immigrant group will want to yield its attachment and commitment to the origins of its cultural and social distinctiveness in order to assimilate into the dominant culture, which is the Anglo-European culture in America. According to this perspective, the different ethnic groups will eventually become an integral part of the Anglo- European society in culture, structure, and identity. In 1909, Ellwood Patterson Cubberley, the famed educational leader, cast a vision for the common schools:

> Everywhere these people (immigrants) tend to settle in groups or settlements, and to set up here their national manners, customs, and observances. Our task is to break up these groups or settlements, to assimilate and amalgamate these people as part of our American race, and to implant in their children, as far as can be done, the Anglo-Saxon conception of righteousness, law and order, and popular government, and to awaken in them a reverence for our democratic institutions and for those things in our national life which we as a people hold to be of abiding worth.[24]

Furthermore, complete assimilation would mean a change from a minority ethnicity to a dominant ethnicity.[25] In the meantime, the dominant group would not change but would be large enough to embrace others into the ethnic background. This has become the predominant way of defining Americanization.[26]

This theory of white-conformity, then, resonates well with the two-category system of superordination and subordination where white ethnic American culture always dominates, while the non-white Americans either voluntarily or involuntarily take the lesser role.[27]

The Melting Pot Model

While the Anglo-conformity perspective to assimilation has dominated the study of immigrant integration into American society,

---

[24]Ellwood Patterson Cubberley, *Changing Conceptions of Education* (Boston: Houghton Mifflin, 1909), 15-16.

[25]Abramson, "Assimilation and Pluralism," 151.

[26]Michael Walzer, "What does it mean to be an 'American'?," *Social Research* 57:3 (Fall 1990): 595-596.

[27]Michael Banton, *Race Relations* (London: Tavistock Publications, 1967), 71; Harry Kitano, *Race Relations* (Englewood Cliffs: Prentice-Hall, 1974), 46.

the melting pot model is an alternative perspective. This perspective advocates the assimilation of truly mixed backgrounds into a new ethnicity or character. This so-called "melting-pot theory" envisions an ethnogenesis in America where a new ethnicity emerges through evolution of, and assimilation to all cultures, rather than the conformity of immigrant cultures to the preexisting dominant Anglo culture. This ethnogenesis becomes reality as all ethnic backgrounds, including the dominant Anglo-Saxons and the various minority ethnic groups, are

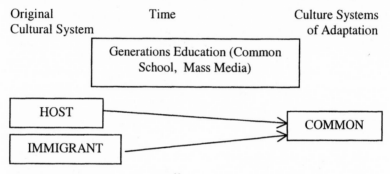

Figure 4-2: Melting pot perspective[28]

integrated into a new creation, a new breed of humanity, with its own ethnic culture, structure, and identity in a still diverse world.

In the 18th and 19th centuries, the debate was between those who advocated the assimilation of diverse cultures (mostly of northern and western European origin) into the hegemony of Anglo Americans and those who argued for the integration of such diversity into a unique American national character.[29] With the increase of ethnic diversity, especially in the large cities of the U.S, the melting pot ideal regained its momentum for a brief period at the beginning of the 20th century. This surmounting acceptance was due to the 1908 production of a play entitled "Melting Pot," written by an English Jew, Israel Zangwill. The egalitarian and universal nature of the melting pot was construed to be the ideal destiny for the U.S. While the overall response to the romantic play demonstrated the persistence of Anglo-conformity, the possibility of an idealistic society merging not only diverse white

[28]Greeley, Ethnicity in the United States, 305.
[29]Abramson, "Assimilation and Pluralism," 152.

European groups, but the African and Asian groups, was portrayed as well.[30]

However, as the influx of new immigrants from southern and eastern Europe and Asia in the first quarter of the 20th century increased, anxiety and hostility increased among white Americans. Critics of the new immigrants held them to be beneath Anglo-Americans. The new immigrants were by and large poor, visibly different, and predominantly non-Protestant. In the ensuing years, the Anglo-conformity of assimilation, now called Americanization, prevailed and took on a distinct character among the white majority. The majority of white Americans came to believe that Anglo-conformity was "the best 'solution' to what they saw as crime, poverty, and deprivation among the immigrant masses."[31]

Classical Cultural Pluralism Model

Both Anglo-conformity and melting pot perspectives presuppose three issues: the inevitability of assimilation among immigrants and their descendents, the loss of former ethnic distinctiveness, and the mutually exclusive nature of the Americanization and ethnic attachment processes. These theories entertain a linear notion of adaptation. The positive trajectory for all Americans in the Anglo-conformity perspective is Anglo-American society. In the melting pot perspective, a newly created ethnicity is the goal. Both theories share two common requirements for immigrants and their descendents: assimilation and loss of former ethnic distinctions. Moreover, both theories inevitably denigrate the other end of the spectrum, or negative trajectory of adaptation, which is cultural pluralism.

The classical cultural pluralism perspective takes into account the persistence of the ethnic, social and cultural ties of immigrants' descendents to their former heritage while living among immigrants and their descendents. Horace Kallen contends that while immigrants and their descendents do to some extent embrace the social conditions

---

[30]Ibid., 153.
[31]Ibid.

of the host culture, they also maintain much of their own culture.[32] According to this perspective, they become U.S. citizens, commit themselves to American political values, learn the English language, and enjoy the common mass media while also indulging in the media of their own cultural group.[33] Yet these people maintain their own communities where their former heritages are strictly followed, as is still done in many ethnic enclaves in large cities in the U.S. (See Figure 4-3).

Original   Time   Culture Systems
Cultural System   of Adaptation

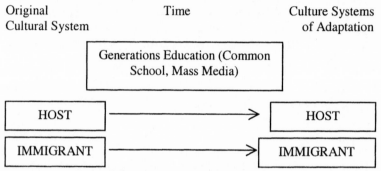

Figure 4-3: Classic cultural pluralism perspective[34]

"Acculturation but Not Assimilation" Model

However, the cultural pluralism that is more readily embraced by its defenders is perhaps Milton Gordon's view of "acculturation but not assimilation."[35]   In this model, immigrants and their descendents embrace many cultural traits of the host society, while the host simultaneously absorbs a few traits from the immigrant groups, as well. In the process, there emerges a common culture that the two groups both share (see Figure 4-4).

This model, however, carefully acknowledges the apparent existence of distinguishing features between the hosts and the immigrants. At a cultural level, Greeley observes, the two groups

---

[32]Horace M. Kallen, *Cultural Pluralism and the American Idea*
(Philadelphia: University of Pennsylvania Press, 1956); idem, *People of Paradox* (New York: Alfred A. Knopf, 1972).

[33]Greeley, Ethnicity in the United States, 305.

[34]Ibid., 306

[35]Gordon, *Assimilation in American Life*; idem, "Toward a general theory of racial and ethnic group relations."

maintain some distance from one another in the private spheres of their lives. Intermarriage does occur, of course, but at a substantially lower rate than if the choice of marriage partner occurred independent of ethnic background. Similarly, close friends, recreation partners, and informal associates are far more likely to be chosen from one's own ethnic community than from the common pool of society. Put quite simply, when people are free to choose they tend to choose from their own kind – even though they share large numbers of cultural traits with other groups in the society.[36]

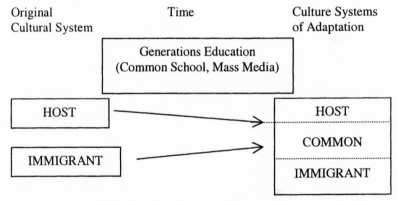

Figure 4-4: Acculturation but not assimilation perspective[37]

At a societal level, the structural features that preserve the cultural heritage and privilege of the host have historically produced systemic barriers preventing immigrants and their descendents from becoming fuller participants in American society.

Ethnogenesis Model

Figure 4-5 presents a variation from the "Acculturation but not assimilation perspective." Greeley names it the "ethnogenesis" perspective. In this perspective, ethnogenesis refers to, not an ethnogenesis of all Americans into a new homogenized ethnicity (as in

---

[36]Ibid., 306-307.
[37]Ibid., 306.

the melting pot perspective), but a more local phenomenon that takes place within a given immigrant group and its descendents, and possibly among a given racial group and its descendents.

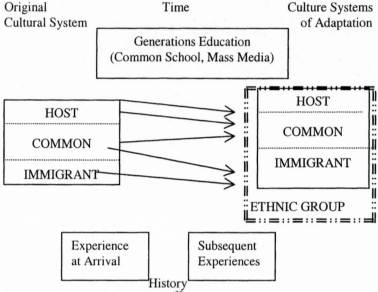

Figure 4-5: Ethnogenesis perspective[38]

The most important distinguishing feature of this perspective is the creation of an ethnic group through the dialogical interaction between the host culture and immigrants and their descendents. The new ethnic group develops a cultural system that is an admixture of traits of the common culture and traits that are distinctive to its own group. In the process, the characteristics of the newly formed ethnic group differ from those of their immigrant predecessors. Greeley asserts that the newly formed people "share more with the common culture than they did to begin with, but in some respects they also may be more different from the descendants of the hosts than their ancestors were from their hosts."[39] This approach also opens up creative possibilities to conceptualize further developments as newly formed ethnic groups

---

[38]Greeley, *Ethnicity in the United States*, 309.
[39]Ibid., 309.

interact with one another. One such possibility is the development of a pan-ethnicity where various ethnic groups within the same race interact closely together to form a new ethnicity.

These five models above are different perspectives through which not only immigrants and their descendents, but also American society, are evaluated. If these five models contain utilities and limitations of their own, and if there persists ethnic pluralism in American society, Greeley argues for the multiplicity of perspectives for considering "the phenomena of unity and diversity within that society."[40]

Adaptation Conditions Experienced by Immigrants and Their Descendents

The models of adaptation examine how immigrants and their descendents adapt to American society as a group. They are instructive in building an understanding of the broad picture of the adaptation strategies employed by immigrant groups and their descendents upon entrance into a new social context. However, the number of adaptation models entertains the possibility that some individuals' experience may not correspond to the group experience of which they are a part. In fact, the experience of individuals in the group may differ widely depending on the various sociocultural factors they have encountered.

Abramson maintains that one way to assess the adaptation conditions that different individuals experience is to examine two salient variables involved in the adaptation process, namely, symbolic ethnicity and relational ethnicity.[41] Symbolic ethnicity refers to the ethnic root one believes to be one's own and consequently responds to as one's own by birth or experience. Relational ethnicity refers to the kind of ethnic people with which one relates. These two variables provide four possible sociocultural conditions of ethnicity for the individual.

The first and most common condition is that of an unmistakable presence of both symbolic and relational ethnicities. The presence of symbolic ethnicity involves forms of ethnic traditionalism, religioethnic movements, and any other practices that contribute to a shared awareness of a somewhat distinctive origin and way of life. The ethnic enclaves of large cities, for example, are perhaps where such

---

[40]Ibid., 307.
[41]Abramson, "Assimilation and Pluralism," 155-156.

persistence is most visible. Regionalism also "offers the possibilities of differentiated ethnic or quasi-ethnic cultures and structures."[42]

Moreover, in this condition, symbolic ethnicity is shared with contemporaries beyond kinship or locality. It often involves membership in ethnic and religio-ethnic organizations. This membership, in turn, becomes part of one's group identity. The "hyphenated" Americans, usually the first generation, are considered to be in this condition. Abramson asserts that many hyphenated Americans have been successful in coalescing both a loyalty to America with a historic loyalty to the ethnic past.[43]

The second and the next most frequent condition is that of "beginning ethnic change, away from the anchors of traditionalism."[44] Those who are in this condition, the "converts," are certain about the ethnic structure into which they have been received, which is different from the one into which they were born or raised. Converted ethnicity is essentially relational in nature in that the immigrants' sense of belonging comes through social interactions with the people they've joined.

While immigrants are considered structurally assimilated into the culture of the new ethnicity, their ambivalence comes from the uncertainty of the symbols of the new culture. In this process, there always remains

> some degree of confusion between the old and the new, between the ethnic culture taken for granted by those born and raised in it, and the assumptions about that culture made by those who come to it from outside. . . The distinction between the traditionalist and the convert is the difference between *being* and *becoming*.[45]

The third and less common condition is where "the memories and symbols of an ethnic culture exist, but there are no primary networks and structural attachments."[46] The psychological condition of those in this situation mirrors that of refugees or displaced people who are isolated from a past identification. However, the key difference is that those in this condition are in an individual, as opposed to collective,

---

[42]Ibid., 157.
[43]Ibid., 155-156.
[44]Ibid.
[45]Ibid.
[46]Ibid.

sociocultural exile where their ethnicity cannot be made part of an ongoing structure.[47]

The fourth and least common condition is where no ethnic culture or structure exists. Those who are in this condition mainly involve children who were pulled away from the upbringing of their family's enculturation, with no apparent replacements for those lack of influences. They usually have no symbolic or relational resources to address these deficiencies. In discussing some possible trajectories for this condition, Abramson contrasts it with the other three categories:

> The ethnic exile may be able to "go home again" or at least convert and assimilate, the ethnic convert is able to reciprocate group connections, and the ethnic traditionalist is moored to an entity of belonging. But without symbols and group relations, there is little for the isolated individual to build on.[48]

Adaptation Patterns of First-generation Korean Americans

Won Moo Hurh and Kwang Chung Kim, two prominent first-generation sociologists contend that the theory of assimilation has not provided an adequate framework to understand the adaptation patterns of first-generation Korean Americans.[49] They argue that the theory is based on the mutually exclusive and linear nature of the two processes, namely Americanization and ethnic attachment.

Instead, based on their extensive research with Korean immigrants in Chicago, Hurh and Kim proposed a "syncretic socio-cultural adaptation" or "adhesive adjustment" in understanding the immigrant experience. Their model incorporates both assimilation and retention of ethnic cultural ties as the two dimensions of the immigrant experience. This model opens up "a new avenue for a realistic understanding of their complex adaptation experiences."[50]

---

[47]Ibid.
[48]Ibid.
[49]Won Moo Hurh and Kwang Chung Kim, *Korean Immigrants in America* (Cranbury, N.J.: Associated University Press, 1984); Department of Sociology and Anthropology, Western Illinois University, August 1991. Unpublished document.
[50]Ibid., 3. Where "Blending" refers to the mode of adaptation which combines the two response patterns, "acceptance" and "retention" or

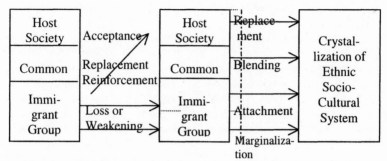

Figure 4-6 Hurh & Kim's syncretic socio-cultural adaptation
The Persistence of Korean Cultural Values

Hurh and Kim report the persistence of strong attachment to Korean sociocultural values and attitudes among the first generation regardless of the length of residence in the U.S. Values such as filial piety, family interest over individual interest, and perpetuation of Korean cultural heritage among posterity remain especially strong. Moreover, attitudes such as a negative perception of racial intermarriage, conservative gender ideology, and a preference for Korean churches continue to be pervasive among the first generation.[51]

They also maintain close ties with their relatives and their fellow first-generation friends. According to Hurh, Korean Americans have the strongest social and cultural ties among all Asian American ethnic groups.[52] These ties function as both social and emotional support in critical times. Moreover, homogenous groups function as a socioeconomic welfare network of first-generation Korean Americans through which ideas, resources, and help are exchanged.

The first generation has kept much of its traditional value systems and has only selectively embraced American values and attitudes. One such change is the belief in raising children equally, regardless of gender. Also, the idea of a wife working outside of the home is

---

"reinforcement," but when the immigrants' prolonged experience of acceptance and retention eventually results in a new way of life, such a hybrid nature of ethnic life may be called a "blending" or "synthesis" type of adaptation. In contrast, "marginalization" refers to the process of "loss" or "weakening" with little experience of "retention" or "acceptance."

[51]Hurh, The Korean Americans, 70-79.
[52]Ibid., 105.

accepted more readily although most first-generation Korean Americans still believe that a woman's place is at home. Chan argues that Korean American women are obliged to work outside of the home because "the male members of their families earn such low wages."[53] Another dimension of Americanization among the first generation is the value placed on individual achievement, self-reliance, and self-actualization. They also deem social interactions with white Americans to be important.[54]

Occupational Adjustment of First-Generation Korean Americans

In terms of occupational adjustment, the first generation has often had to settle for employment that is less than what they desire. This kind of downward mobility is a direct result of language barriers. Even after years of residence in the U.S., many first-generation Korean Americans express great difficulty communicating in English.[55] This difficulty, as well as other difficulties in cultural adjustments, comes perhaps from the monolingual and mono-cultural Korean society in which they were raised before coming to the U.S. Thus, although about 35% of the immigrant adults are college graduates in Korea and a significant number received further education in the U.S., many have not been able to work in professions that reflect the education they received. Many professionals, in fact, despite holding proper U.S. licenses, work with predominantly Korean-speaking people around the Korean population centers in major U.S. cities.

Moreover, there is a significant shift from the occupational involvement in Korea to that in the U.S. Consequently, a substantial number of the first generation turns either to owning or operating small businesses. [56] While the American public generally portrays small

---

[53]Chan, Asian Americans: An Interpretive History, 169.
[54]Ibid., 73.
[55]Ibid., 70-71.
[56]Ibid., 42-43.

	In Korea (%)	In U.S. (%)
Administrative/Managerial	4.0	1.9
Professional/Technical	45.5	26.3
Small Business Owners	13.8	30.2
Sales & Administrative Support	27.8	13.0

business ownership as an immigrant success story, Sucheng Chan accurately unveils the true story behind the Korean American small business owner when she says:

> Many of them operate only small mom-and-pop stores with no paid employees and very low gross earnings. Unlike journalists who tout Korean entrepreneurship as a sign of success, scholars who have examined the situation argue that the kind of business Korean immigrants engage in is, in fact, a disguised form of cheap labor: owners of small business run a high risk of failure and work long hours. Many of them could not stay afloat were it not for the unpaid labor they extract from their spouses, children, and other relatives.[57]

Many of the businesses are located in low-income neighborhoods of the major cities of the U.S. The Korean American owners of these businesses fit the classic profile of the middleman minority who provides goods largely supplied by the dominant group to underclass minorities. The middleman minority often becomes the scapegoat in times of economic and political distress, as was evident during the Los Angeles riots in 1992. Analyzing the riots, Pyung Gap Min asserts that the "middleman proposition helps us understand hostility toward Korean merchants in African American neighborhoods as well as government inaction in protecting Korean merchants during the Los Angeles riots."[58] While the riots were widely depicted as the outcome of racial conflict between Korean Americans, Hispanics and African Americans, they reflected the even more deeply rooted racial and economic inequalities that exist in the United States. Korean American merchants typified for poor African Americans and Hispanics the concrete and symbolic otherness.[59]

Service Occupations	1.7	4.6
Precision Production, Craft, & Repair	4.0	7.0
Operators, Fabricators, Laborers	3.2	17.0
Total	100.0	100.0

[57]Chan, Asian Americans: An Interpretive History, 169-170.

[58]Pyung Gap Min, Caught In the Middle (Berkeley: University of California Press, 1996), 26.

[59]Karnow and Yoshihara, Asian Americans in Transition, 4.

Although in less magnitude, Korean American merchants in the major cities of the U.S. have been subjected to similar difficulties with other racial minorities, especially African Americans. Again, Min maintains:

> One view interprets hostility toward Korean merchants in African American neighborhoods as nativist reactions to immigrants' economic activities; the other emphasizes sociopsychological factors, such as cultural differences, language barriers, and mutual prejudice, as contributing to Korean-Black conflicts."[60]

Then why do many first-generation Korean Americans continue to own and operate small businesses despite the hard work and tensions? They still perceive that small business is "an important channel of upward mobility open to nonwhite immigrants who face obstacles in obtaining well-paying and secure jobs."[61] It affords freedom of ownership and opportunity to move up to bigger business. In comparing the occupational patterns of Korean Americans with that of Chinese and Japanese Americans, Kitano and Daniels contend that Korean Americans have a more individualistic outlook than the group-oriented outlook of the latter groups.[62]

Moreover, the ownership of small business requires a less sophisticated knowledge of English. Family members and spouses can be easily recruited and utilized free of charge or at a very low cost. There is still enough inflow of newly immigrated Korean Americans who need work that requires virtually no conversational English skills. Again, past skills and education are not factors of occupational decision for these people. These jobs are mostly low-paying jobs in unfavorable working conditions. More often than not, female and youth segments of the new immigrant population have had better opportunities for employment. Observing this phenomenon, Kitano and Daniels comment:

> Families that in Korea would never think of wives and children working now find that such opportunities, though low paying are readily available. . . The effect on family dynamics can be stressful. The temptation to make

---

[60]Ibid.

[61]Chan, Asian Americans: An Interpretive History, 170.

[62]Kitano and Daniels, Asian Americans: Emerging Minorities, 120-121.

money is difficult to restrain, and problems of childcare, latchkey children, and obsession with earning a living are difficult to avoid.[63]

The occupational patterns of the first-generation generally indicate segregation from the mainstream society for various reasons. Many first-generation Korean Americans are isolated and have limited exposure to mainstream white America. While the concept of the Korean ghetto can be conceived of geographically, the real Korean ghetto lies in the elaborate, almost self-sustaining networks of first-generation Korean Americans. This phenomenon can be seen not only in terms of economic survival but in their social relationships as well.

The Role of the Church in the Korean American Community

In fact, Hurh asserts that Korean Americans' social ties with their own ethnic group have been strengthened as the direct result of immigration and the length of time as U. S. residents.[64]   They frequently maintain close contact with their relatives. Most of their friends are Koreans. Many of them say that they spend their time with only Korean Americans in their neighborhood. They belong to small voluntary organizations that have origin in Korea, such as high school alumni organizations and town meetings based on their Korean birthplace.[65]

However, the most significant network and social institution for first-generation Korean Americans is their Korean American church. According to the research data on Korean Americans, church affiliation seems to be extremely high. In major cities such as Los Angeles and Chicago, for example, 69.9% and 76.7% of Korean Americans in the respective cities were affiliated with Korean ethnic churches. 84% and 78% of these groups, respectively, attend church at least once a week.[66]

The Christian legacy in Korean American history can be traced back to the first group of settlers in Hawaii. These settlers maintained close

---

[63]Ibid., 121.

[64]Hurh, The Korean Americans, 77.

[65]Ibid., 78.

[66]Ibid., 42, 78, 107-114; Kitano and Daniels, *Asian Americans: Emerging Minorities*, 122-123; Ho-Youn Kwon and Shin Kim, eds., *The Emerging Generation of Korean-Americans* (Seoul, Korea: Kyung Hee University Press, 1993).

relationships with American missionaries who encouraged them to move to Hawaii, as previously mentioned. Many Korean American churches were founded in Hawaii soon after their arrival. A similar phenomenon took place in the Pacific Coast.[67] This legacy has continued among the second[68] and third waves of Korean immigrants. In 1991, there were approximately 700 Korean churches in the Los Angeles area alone.[69] Presently, there are more than 250 Korean churches in the Chicago area.[70] These figures resonate well with a popular saying in Korean:

> When the Chinese go abroad, they open a restaurant.
> When the Japanese go abroad, they open a factory.
> When the Koreans go abroad, they start a church.[71]

It is estimated about half of the immigrants were Christians before coming to the U.S. Upon immigration, the need for Christian fellowship heightened. The increase in church attendance by those who were not previously affiliated with the church is due, in part, to the role the immigrant church has played in providing services to meet a variety of the needs encountered by new immigrants.

As the sociocultural center for Koreans in the U.S., the Korean ethnic church has provided an opportunity for the first generation to search for "the meaning of their uprooting and existential alienation in the new country."[72] As the most inclusive and accessible social institution for

---

[67]Chan, *Asian Americans: An Interpretive History*, 72-73. In first 15 years from 1903 to 1918, there were 39 Korean Protestant churches and an estimated 3,000 Korean Christians in Hawaii. During that time, more than a dozen churches were established in the Pacific Coast where only about 1,000 Koreans living there.

[68]The establishment of churches can be documented only among the Korean student segment of the second wave of immigration. This Christian legacy cannot be supported or denied for the wives of the U.S. servicemen or for the adoptees that make up the second wave.

[69]Jung Ha Kim, *Bridge-Makers and Cross-Bearers* (Atlanta: Scholars Press, 1997), 8.

[70]Hurh, The Korean Americans, 108.

[71]Karen J. Chai, "Competing for the Second Generation" in R. Stephen Warner and Judith G. Wittner, eds. *Gatherings in Diaspora: Religious Communities and the New Immigration* (Philadelphia: Temple University Press, 1998).

[72]Ibid., 109.

Koreans in the U.S., the church has also provided a sense of belonging and psychological comfort for the first generation. Moreover, it has functioned as the most valuable network for dealing with a variety of issues in the community.[73] Furthermore, the Korean American church has functioned as an extension of the Korean immigrant family. The church has been the center of the socialization into Korean culture for the second generation, reinforcing family expectations.[74]

---

[73]Ibid., 110-111.
[74]Sang Hyun Lee and John Moore, eds., *Korean American Ministry* (Louisville: General Assembly Council-Presbyterian Church U.S.A., 1993).

Chapter 5

The Second-Generation Korean American Experience in the Context of the Asian American Experience

As the descendents of first-generation Korean Americans, second-generation Korean Americans have shared some common experiences. In fact, in their growing up years, much of their time is spent in interactions with their first-generation parents, grandparents, extended family members and other adults at the Korean American church. Moreover, the second generation spends a significant amount of time with their Korean American peers who shared similar values in the church and their neighborhoods. However, their existential reality as a whole includes broader segments of the society than that of the first generation's. The second generation has had much more first-hand experience with mainstream America, including friends, schooling, media, and work. In this sense, the second-generation Korean Americans have more in common with Americanized Asian Americans than with their first-generation parents and other adults.[1]

A survey of theories of identity formation as they specifically relate to the experiences of minority persons in society allows for construction of an adaptation for Asian Americans. The narratives of the Korean American study participants reveal the sundry tensions in this process of identity formation. Next, the experience of

---

[1]All the Asian ethnic American groups have been grouped together for mainly political purposes in the U.S. Asian Americans have been considered as one of the ethno-racial pentagon in the U.S. Korean Americans is then a sub-set of Asian Americans. See David A. Hollinger, *Postethnic America* (New York: Basic Books, 1995) for excellent treatment of this concept and its implications.

Americanized Asian Americans sheds light on the experience of second-generation Korean Americans. Perception and reception of second-generation Korean American mainstream American society crystallizes in this context.

Ethnic Identity Formation

Several theories of identity development have been proposed in recent years in an attempt to understand the identity development of minority Americans in the context of mainstream American society. Most of the theories have utilized James Marcia's identity status paradigm as the point of departure for theoretical conceptualization.[2] Marcia's model is based largely on Erik Erikson's work[3] on identity development within his psychosocial development theory. Following Erikson and Marcia, these theorists contend that an achieved identity is the outcome of a crisis or awakening, which leads to a period of exploration or experimentation, and finally to a commitment or incorporation of one's ethnicity. Although these models provide important conceptualizations, there is relatively little research to validate them.

Cross proposed a descriptive model on "the Negro-to-Black Conversion Experience" that consists of five stages (see table 4-1). This model places considerable importance on understanding the dynamics of the Negro personality and worldview, and on the need for temporary withdrawal into Blackness. This model, with only one "transition" stage (Immersion-Emersion), concludes with internalization-commitment.[4] Kim, according to Phinney, also formulated a descriptive model on Asian American identity

---

[2]James Marcia, "Development and Validation of Ego Identity Status," *Journal of Personality and Social Psychology* 3(5) (1966): 551-558.

[3]Erik H. Erikson, *Childhood and Society* (New York: W.W. Norton & Company, 1950); idem, *Identity: Youth and Crisis* (New York: W.W. Norton & Company, 1968); idem, *Identity and the Life Cycle* (New York: W.W. Norton & Company, 1959); idem, *The Life Cycle Completed* (New York: W.W. Norton & Company, 1982).

[4]W. Cross, "The Negro to Black Conversion Experience," *Black World*, 20, (1971): 13-27

development in a group of young adult Asian American women. Unfortunately, this study is not published.[5]

Atkinson, Morten, and Sue constructed a model that is called the Minority Identity Development Model(MID). The MID model identifies five stages of development describing how oppressed people struggle to understand themselves under the confluence of their own culture, the dominant culture, and the oppressive relationship that exists between the two.[6]

Jean Phinney proposed a three-stage model of ethnic identity formation. This three-stage progressive model encapsulates well the various issues considered by other theorists.[7]

Marcia (1966, 1980)	Identity diffusion	Identity foreclosure	Identity crisis*	Moratorium	Identity achievement
Cross (1971)		Pre-encounter	Encounter	Immersion /Emersion	Internali - zation
Kim (1981)		White-identified	Awakening to social political awareness	redirection to Asian American Consciousness	Incorporation
Atkinson Morten, & Sue (1983)		Conformity: Preference for values of dominant culture	Dissonance Questioning and Challeng-ing old attitudes	Resistance and immersion: Rejection of dominant culture	Synergetic articulation and awareness

[5]Jean Phinney, "Stages of Ethnic Identity in Minority Group Adolescents," *Journal of Early Adolescence*, 9 (1989): 34-49.

[6]D. Atkinson, G. Morten, and D. Sue, *Counseling American minorities* (Dubuque, IA: W. Brown, 1983).

[7]Jean Phinney, "Ethnic Identity in Adolescents and Adults: Review of Research," *Psychological Bulletin*, 108, no.3 (1990): 499-514.

Phinney (1989)	Unexamined Identity Lack of exploration of ethnicity		Ethnic Identity Search (Moratorium) Involvement in exploring and seeking to understand meaning of ethnicity for oneself	*Achieved Ethnic Identity* Clear, confid-ent sense of own ethnicity
	A. Diffuse: Lack of Interest in or concern with ethnicity	B. Fore-closed: Views of ethnicity based on opinions of others		

Table 5-1: Models of Ethnic Identity Development and Ego Identity Status
* Identity crisis can be seen as an initial experience(s), force(s), or event(s) that set forth the moratorium status. Identity crisis is not one of Marcia's original four statuses.

The first stage of Phinney's model is characterized by the lack of ethnic exploration. Persons from minority groups, especially from infancy to mid-late childhood or early adolescence, initially accept the values and attitudes of the majority white culture, often including an internalized negative view of their own ethnic group that is shaped by the majority's prejudice. This stage might be compared to identity foreclosure discussed by Erikson and Marcia.[8] Foreclosure represents the absence of exploration of issues, accompanied by commitments based on attitudes and opinions adopted from others without question. In this case, it is American society's values, not necessarily those of their parents or members of an ethnic group, that are being accepted and internalized. However, adolescents whose parents have provided positive models of ethnicity may be foreclosed, without having examined the issues for themselves. These adolescents may have a positive view of their own ethnic group.

The second stage generally begins when adolescents encounter a situation that initiates exploration of their ethnic identity. The situation, or series of such situations, can become a turning point. The child voluntarily or involuntarily engages in an exploration to understand the meaning of their own ethnicity, as opposed simply to accepting the teaching presented to them by their parents. This stage may be highly emotional because it usually coincides with an identity

---

[8]Erikson, *Identity and the Life Cycle*; Marcia, "Development and Validation of Ego Identity Status."

crisis. Adolescents may feel anger and outrage directed towards the majority white society for its racism and the racial prejudice exhibited against their particular minority group or minority groups as a whole. Erikson acknowledged that a transitory "negative identity" or rejection of appropriate roles might be a necessary precondition for a positive identity.[9]

In the final stage, ethnic identity achievement is characterized by a confident sense of one's own ethnicity. At this point one is finally able to accept and internalize his or her own ethnicity. This stage can be compared to an identity achievement where a person has resolved some of the uncertainties about his or her future direction and has, in turn, made commitments to his or her ethnic identity that will aid in guiding future action.

Phinney and the above models of ethnic identity development suggest that these stages are sequential, with an individual's progress to higher stages occurring over time[10]. However, contextual factors may influence the extent and rate to which individuals through these stages develop. Furthermore, major crises and ethnic encounters could compel persons to revisit previous stages, especially the ethnic identity search (moratorium), and reformulate their ethnic identity multiple times throughout a lifetime.

While the theories of ethnic identity formation provide an informative perspective in understanding the identity formation of an ethnic American person such as an Asian American, these models are usually silent about the constitutive role of race in one's identity formation. Race, being neither a mere illusion nor an essence, is

an unstable 'decentered' complex of social meanings constantly being transformed by political struggle. . . Race is a concept that signifies and symbolizes social conflicts and interests by referring to different types of human bodies. . . The concept of race continues to play a fundamental role in structuring and representing the social world.[11]

Racial formation is thus a process of historically situated *projects* in which human bodies and social structures are represented and

---

[9]Erikson, Identity: Youth and Crisis.

[10]Phinney, "Stages of Ethnic Identity in Minority Group Adolescents"; idem, "Ethnic Identity in Adolescents and Adults: Review of Research."

[11]Michael Omi and Howard Winant, Racial Formation in the United States: From the 1960's to the 1990s, 2nd. (New York: Routledge, 1994), 54-55.

organized.   Omi and Winant contend that a *racial project* is "simultaneously an interpretation, representation, or explanation of racial dynamics, and an effort to reorganize and redistribute resources along particular racial lines."[12]

An Asian American Model

Harry Kitano and Roger Daniels proposed an adaptation model of Asians to the U.S. based on their extensive research of Asian immigrants and their descendents.[13] Using two variables, assimilation and ethnic identity, they proposed an orthogonal model.

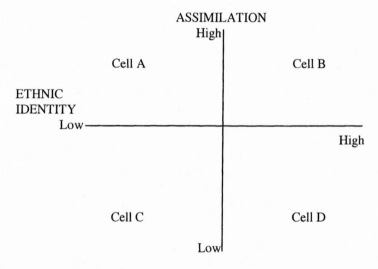

Figure 5-1 Kitano and Daniels's adaptation model of Asians to the U.S.

Cell A: High assimilation, low ethnic identity
Persons in this category see themselves as more American than ethnic. Many Asian Americans of second to fifth generation and Asian Americans separated from ethnic communities comprise this category.

---

[12]Ibid., 56.
[13]Kitano and Daniels, Asian Americans: Emerging Minorities, 199-201.

Persons who wish to become the stereotypical "American" regardless of the generation also fit into this category. English is their primary language, the traditional ethnic language having long since been forgotten. Life styles and expectations are American. Marital patterns indicate a higher rate of marriage to non-Asian Americans. More females than males are in this category.

Social patterns and interactions of those in this cell exhibit a higher proportion of non-Asian contacts than usual. Many of their friends and their organizational affiliations are with non-Asians. Ethnic identification for these people is usually through the partaking of ethnic foods and occasionally celebrating ethnic holidays. However, for Asian Americans in this cell, "the one inescapable fact is ethnic visibility, and reactions from the outside world force the retention of an ethnic identity, no matter how slight."[14]

Cell B: High assimilation, High ethnic identity

Persons in this category exhibit similar patterns of assimilation as those in Cell A. The difference for the persons in Cell B is that they retain a strong ethnic identity. The social patterns and interactions of those in this cell are usually bicultural in nature. They are fluid and comfortable functioning in both cultures.

Ethnicity is an integral part of identity for the people in this category. Many of them have been nurtured or educated by people with a multicultural perspective. Thus, they are often knowledgeable about ethnicity and ethnic culture, and committed to social justice issues.[15]

Cell C: Low assimilation, low ethnic identity

A small segment of Asian Americans fall under this category. Those in this category are those who are either alienated or disillusioned by both the American culture and the markers for their ethnic identity.

Cell D: Low assimilation, high ethnic identity

The persons who fit into this category are either newly arrived immigrants or those who have spent much of their lives in ethnic enclaves. Included in this category, also, are members of the first generation who may have achieved a "'functional level' of adaptation

---

[14]Ibid., 200.
[15]Ibid.

to the American culture but are more comfortable within ethnic enclaves"[16] and consistently maintain their ethnic culture in daily living. Asian Americans who see or have experience of the U.S. as a racist society may opt for this kind of adaptation.[17]

Some of the pressures outlined in the Asian American Model are validated by the voices of second generation Korean Americans who speak of the struggle they feel in attempting to achieve both high ethnic identity and high assimilation to mainstream society. Below are some of their responses to the multiple demands of their particular sociocultural environment.

Voice of Assimilation

The voice of assimilation has been one of the core internalized values among the young adults interviewed. Their desire to be accepted by the mainstream society has moved them to employ several strategies. First, these study participants avoided anything that might accentuate their cultural difference from Caucasian American peers during their growing up years. Second, they were eager to eliminate cultural inadequacies (in their own perception, most of the time) by actively embracing American values and ways of living. Third, although they experience various forms of racism in everyday life, they choose not to speak out against the practices of racism. Fourth, instead of submerging their Korean cultural heritage, the young adults seek to maintain it in the private sphere of their lives.

High Ethnicity and High Assimilation Valued

Desire to be American During growing up years
    Without exceptions, all of these second-generation Korean American young adults shared a desire to be assimilated into mainstream society as Americans, especially during their growing-up years. They did not want to be differentiated as the other by the majority. They shared about their wish to look different and to be born into a Caucasian family. These young adults talked about their attempts to avoid

---

[16]Ibid.
[17]Ibid.

association with anything resembling Korean culture when they were in public settings, such as when they were with peers at school. Sam describes his desire to be white during his growing up years:

> Where I grew up, there was not a good racial mix, mostly white, Polish blue-collar people. My Asianness or my Koreanness was always backward and it was always pointed out to me. And so it was always very prominent and growing up during that time you just want to fit in and the fact was that I couldn't because I looked different. It was making me want to be white, and I think probably most Asians go through that at some point in their life, but during that time I think I really wanted to be white, and that's probably one of those defining experiences in my life as I look back.

Paul concurs with Sam when he says that when he was "growing up, I resented it (being a Korean American). I didn't want to be different. I wanted to fit in." Brian shares about his ethnic journey from his high school to college years:

> Because there weren't any other Korean kids around (growing up), you don't even look at yourself as a Korean. You kind of try to blend in with other people and obviously it's very difficult to try to fit in. After a while when other Korean families moved in, I just totally disassociated with any Koreans. I couldn't even say hi to them because it was so awkward for me to like even acknowledge it (that I was a Korean American). It would mean like "well, maybe I am Korean." . . . I worked so hard to disassociate myself from being Korean—like simple things like not wanting to use chopsticks in a restaurant. So I feel I didn't do a good job of handling myself until I got to college. I thought that in college at least people were diverse. So thought maybe I could find a niche composed of not only Caucasians but also different ethnic backgrounds.

Perhaps an exception to other young adults is Kelly. Kelly talks about how learning and maintaining Korean culture has helped her ethnic identity and self-esteem. She shares about how she was able to cultivate the Korean side of her identity:

> Somehow my parents managed to reinforce the Korean language throughout the years, especially summers . . . I was involved in young Korean traditional dance for a long-time and Korean image classes . . . And I think the way I survived in the suburbs, especially in grade school and junior high, was to kind of flaunt

my differences, to let them know that I knew where I was from. If you tell me to go   back from where I came from, I could point to one country and I'd be there. And I learned the bad words in Korean and the other kids would get into trouble for swearing and I'd be getting away with murder because I was speaking another language . . . They would have culture days and I would beg my mother, "Please cook some mandu (Korean dumplings)." And do some Korean folk dance for them, I'd bring in my Hanbokk (Korean traditional dress). So I think in a way I was kind of desperate to show them I was very proud of my culture even though they were making fun of it.

Persistent desire to be American?

For many, the desire to fully assimilate into mainstream society continues to manifest in various ways, even in the young adult years. While many feel comfortable with the degree of assimilation they have been able to achieve, some are still hard at work. Several young adults share that they wanted to either date or marry a Caucasian American. In their eyes, Caucasians were more attractive and nicer than Korean Americans they have known. Joel shares his wish that he were a Caucasian:

I think there were a couple of times when I wished I were a Caucasian for dating purposes. I know my parents wanted me to marry a Korean and at that time I really didn't like Korean girls because for some reason they're not the nicest people I've met. And I got along with Caucasians girls a lot better than I did with Korean girls, and I wished that I wasn't Korean so I could marry a Caucasian.

Brian shares how his inner shame about being a Korean American led him to think seriously about erasing his ethnic descent as a Korean American:

I felt inferior being Korean, just the fact that I was a minority in every sense of the word. (Interviewer: Have you ever wished that you were a Caucasian?) Yeah, pretty much and even in college, I always thought that I would marry a Caucasian. If I can turn myself into a Caucasian, gradually I'll change my descendents into Caucasian.

Inadequate preparation for life in the mainstream America

Reflecting on their growing-up years in the Korean American family, some of the young adults believe they were not adequately prepared for life in mainstream America, in comparison to the mainstream Americans. For them, their college years were a humbling time in their lives, especially academically and socially. They felt keenly their lack of study habits, cultural capital in general, and general disciplines in life, especially in the absence of their parents. Abigail talks about her experience:

> I didn't have a stable family like my college roommates. It was just such a contrast for me. Like my roommates were so connected to their families. Like my sophomore roommate, she would talk to them every week, like consulting about every decision that she made. For me and I looked at that and thought "you're really queer" because for me, my mom would call me once every like two or three months and say "How are you? Are you alive?" It just felt like there were a lot of assumptions about life, the children, like giving to their parents and yet me feeling like I never received anything from my parents. I grew up as a latch key kid and I stayed home. My mom would never let me go outside to play, to be friends with people . . . A lot of those years were kind of like washing away a lot of the garbage, like my anger, how I was raised and then on top of that like my inability to perform in very practical ways, and just feeling so frustrated with myself and hating myself, and like suffering consequences for my own inabilities.

Michelle, who was able to attend one the most prestigious colleges in the U.S., talks about her humiliating experience during her college years:

> College was a very humbling experience for me. Throughout high school I did very well and I used to think that school was not big deal, no problem. When I went to (the college), I was amongst very, very smart and intellectual people. I realized how much I didn't know, and how much work I actually had to do. And probably it was one of the few times where I had to study all the time, and still not coming out with very good results from that. So I think college was a very humbling experience, it really taught me how to be disciplined and taught me how to work hard and taught me not to take things for granted.

Korean American Identity

Exposure to fellow Korean Americans in college

For many Korean Americans, college years mark a pivotal period in reassessing and embracing their Korean American heritage. The college years for these study participants were the first time they could actually explore what it means to live as second-generation Korean Americans. As they had freedom to decide about their life style on college campuses, many opted to live with their fellow Korean American peers and develop significant relationships with them. In the process, they were able to embrace their Korean American heritage by associating with their cohorts, not necessarily by acquiring Korean language or other particularities of the culture.

Many of the interviewees felt for the first time that they no longer had to fit into the mainstream society. They felt that the general climate on the campuses allowed them to hang around with fellow Korean Americans, and they took full advantage of that. They report a high level of comfort and understanding as they spent the significant part of their college years with their fellow Korean Americans. Don shares his college experience:

> When I got to college, I joined a Korean Christian college group there. Then I think my Koreanness came out more, and then started watching like Korean comedy videos and went out with Korean Americans. I really liked Korean food once I started getting it in college. So, going to the Korean American church and all, I think college really brought out more of my Koreanness.

Betsy also shares about her college experience, "I liked Korean Americans in college because they understood me and you just feel close to them because they're Korean.

Voluntarily acquisition of Korean culture

The young adults are, in general, eager to articulate their Korean American identity. However, they are quick to point out that they do not possess enough Korean culture to back up their claim in their life style. Moreover, they have not been active in acquiring some of the aspects of the culture. Nick talks about this irony:

Yes, I am Korean and have a strong sense of that identity . . . a kind of inside thing, Korean. Unfortunately, I don't have a deeper appreciation. Sometimes I feel kind of badly about that, some of the more deeper roots of being Korean, like the Korean language, of course, not being able to speak the language as well . . . I have to deal with the conflicts in terms of reconciling the two—being Korean and not being completely American—whatever that is and trying to figure that out.

Michelle echoes Nick's observation when she talks about her identity issues:

I don't know much about the traditions, but I really do think of myself as Korean. And I think part of it is just my upbringing and I really appreciate being Korean because I feel like my parents have really tried to instill in us just how to preserve the culture. We try and carry on a lot of the traditions, like every New Year's we always have a memorial service for my grandparents and we set up a table and we do the bowing and pay our respect, having all the pictures of them. He does things with all the food and I don't even know exactly what all of it means. But he is trying to teach my brother so that my brother can do it when my parents pass on and so we do that. And just little things like when my sister got married this past May and they set up the whole traditional bowing ceremonies for my sister and her husband, even though he's a Caucasian. And my mom actually flew to Korea and bought the traditional gowns for both of them, he even wore like the boots and the hat and everything, and so we did that. And I just appreciate having the food—I think that is part of my identity of knowing that I have that in me.

She expresses her desire to learn the Korean language more:

I'm really hoping that before I'm married and before I have kids I can learn how to speak Korean more fluently because I would want my children to speak a little bit. But I don't know, maybe my goals or expectations are too high, but that would be my wish.

Luke talks about his efforts to learn the Korean language:

I remember being in the high school and my parents told me you should learn Korean. I used to say, "Forget that." But now I feel like I need to learn Korean, I want to learn Korean. I have been hypocritical about that, haven't been studying it as much as I should. I've got tons of flash cards and I'm working on it.

Luke also shares about his appreciation for Korean music:

> Some people feel like Korean music is very boring. (Interviewer: What kinds of music?). The old classical Korean music, like 1950's music, yeah, I like that kind of stuff. My dad used to play it a lot on the piano, so I started enjoying it . . . My parents have karaoke in their house, so it's fun to enjoy that kind of music.

A definite preference in marriage

Many of the young adults want to marry a Korean spouse in hopes of keeping their Korean American culture alive. Julia shares her desire to marry a Korean American man and raise her children to be Korean Americans:

> Well, he (my future husband) would have to be Korean. You know I feel like I have my own values in the sense that I want to keep my culture. I don't want to be a "defector" if you marry, you know, go outside of your race and then that's it,
> as far as culture . . . I love Korean food (laughter) and I really want to speak, I can get by with Korean but I really want to take classes. I took classes in undergrad, Korean classes. And that's something my parents really regret, like, forcing me not to speak, because they speak English very well and so they speak Korean to me. And I understand it, but that's something I want to teach my kids, how to speak Korean . . .

She continues to share her reasons for her preference for a Korean man:

> Well, I just think that Caucasians—they don't really understand (laughter). They don't understand what it is like being a minority in this country and they don't understand the Korean culture . . . With Koreans I don't like I have to explain myself, or like explaining cultural things. And I realize that marriage is not only with me but it's with my family. It really is not just an individual decision—that it is a family thing, too, and that it impacts my own family.

The voices of assimilation and high ethnicity produce tension in the self-narratives of second generation Korean American young adults. The following section critiques the assimilation model for its assumption that all immigrants will eventually meld into the mainstream, dominant culture. It emphasizes the many factors that have affected the assimilation of immigrants and their descendents, beyond just the pull of the two cultures.

Critique of the Assimilation Model from an Asian American Perspective

The assimilation model has enriched the understanding of the acculturation process of immigrants and their descendants into American society. A general consensus among sociologists has been that the majority of descendents of immigrants assimilate well into American society. Especially, the assimilation studies of Asian Americans have presented data showing a healthy and promising rate of acculturation. These studies have described and also predicted the general direction of the behavioral changes of Asian Americans in accepting the American way of life. In recent years, Asian Americans have earned the reputation of "model minorities" and are often cited as an example of a healthy assimilation and good race relations in America.[18]

The 1990 U.S. Census report shows that Asian Americans are not only successfully entering the American middle-class, but they are enjoying the highest median family income, as an ethnic American group, even surpassing that of non-Hispanic whites.[19] Over 40% of

---

[18]Harry Kitano and Stanley Sue, "The model minorities," *Journal of Social Issues* 29 (1973): 1-9; Martin Kasindorf and Daniel Shapiro, "Asian Americans: A 'model minority'," *Newsweek*, 6 December 1982, 39-42; Timothy P. Fong, *The Contemporary Asian American Experience: Beyond The Model Minority* (Upper Saddle River, NJ: Prentice-Hall, 1998).

[19]The median income levels for white, Japanese, Asian Indian, Filipino, and Chinese Americans were $37,102, $51,550, $49,309, $46,698, and $41,316 respectively. The median for the income for Korean Americans was considerably lower than most other Asian American ethnic groups with 33,909. However, Min argues that census data does not provide an accurate picture of the income level of Korean Americans. By arguing from the studies on the income reporting patterns of self-employed workers, he maintains that Korean Americans, who have had the highest self-employment rate than any other ethnic/immigrant group, have grossly underreported their incomes. See Min, *Asian Americans: Contemporary Trends and Issues*, 211-212; Hurh, *Korean Americans, 54-56.* 16.9% and 2.6% of Korean Americans in the labor force are self-employed and unpaid family workers, compared to 7.0% and 0.4% for the total U.S. population, respectively. Moreover, many Korean Americans in the

Asian Americans hold college degrees compared to 23% for non-Hispanic whites.[20]   Other studies report that Asian Americans are achieving high rates of upward social mobility[21] and that there has been a continued increase in interracial marriage.[22]

In short, according to the assimilation model, Asian Americans are well engaged in the assimilation process, reaping the enormous benefit of assimilation into the mainstream society.   The above and other studies that investigate the reasons for the success of Asian Americans subscribe to a cultural explanation that adheres to the assimilation perspective.   Thus, on the one hand, these studies contend that the assimilation of Asian Americans into the mainstream white culture is a self-completing process in hope of fulfilling the American Dream.   On the other hand, these studies designate those who do not assimilate into the American mainstream to be the new immigrants, the foreign-born, the unskilled, those with personal deficiencies, and those who have not been able to acculturate into American society.[23]

The assimilation model has been relatively less productive in specifying the factors that have been operative in hampering the process of structural assimilation of Asian Americans into the American society.   While the importance of assimilation studies, especially those describing the historical white European immigrant experience in the U.S., should not be discounted, the assimilation

---

labor force are employed by these self-employed businesses, giving ample opportunities for the underreporting.

[20]Stanley Karnow and Nancy Yoshihara, *Asian Americans in Transition* (New York: The Asia Society, 1992), 26, 40. However, compared to other Asian American ethnic groups, the education achievement for the Korean Americans was below the average for Asian Americans with 34.5% who have obtained bachelor's degree or higher among the 25 years of age and up. The percentages of bachelor's degree or higher for Asian Indian, Chinese, and Filipino were 58.1%, 40.7%, and 39.2% respectively. See Hurh, *Korean Americans*, 52-55.

[21]Gene N. Levine and Darrell Montero, "Socioeconomic Mobility Among Three Generations of Japanese Americans," *The Journal of Social Issues* 29 (1973): 33-48.

[22]Fong, The Contemporary Asian American Experience, 224-238.

[23]Wen H. Kuo, "On the Study of Asian Americans: Its Current State and Agenda," *The Sociological Quarterly* 20 (Spring 1979): 281; Don Nakanishi and Tina Yamano Nishida, eds., *The Asian American Educational Experience* (New York: Routledge, 1995).

model has been known for its conservative flavor and its "blame the victim" approach.[24]

The major premise of this model accepts American society as a just society, offering all citizens equal opportunities. Thus, the problems of poverty, underemployment, unemployment, and social disorganization prevailing among ethnic and racial minorities are often attributed to their lack of assimilation or inadequate socialization into modern American industrial society. Moreover, successful assimilation has been considered to be synonymous with attainment of equal opportunity and upward mobility for the members of ethnic minority groups. An opportunity, in this system, is the "opportunity to discard one's ethnicity and to partake fully in the 'American Way of Life'; in this sense, assimilation is viewed as the embodiment of the democratic ethos."[25]

Furthermore, the assimilation model has been based largely upon the ethnocentric optimism of an earlier generation of sociologists who envisioned the inevitable assimilation of American minority groups into some common framework, namely the white culture. Unfortunately, the power struggle and conflict that exists in America between the minority groups and the majority group, and even within the minority groups themselves, have been largely ignored in the model. Another issue that the model ignores is the degree of access to societal rewards - economic, political, institutional, and so on - for the minority groups in comparison with those available to the majority group.[26] These concepts can be seen in the forms of racial prejudice and discrimination.

Racial Prejudice and Discrimination against Asian Americans in the Past One Hundred Fifty Years of U.S. History

Asian Americans have endured their share of racial prejudice and discrimination as immigrants to America, the so-called "free" and "democratic" nation. In the late 1870's, as America experienced

---

[24]Kuo, "On the Study of Asian Americans: Its Current State and Agenda," 279.

[25]Paul L. Metzger, "American Sociology and Black Assimilation: Conflicting Perspectives," *American Journal of Sociology* 76 (January, 1971): 628.

[26]Gordon, "Toward a general theory of racial and ethnic group relations," 86.

economic depression and as the numbers of Chinese immigrants increased into the thousands, the Chinese became the first ethnic group to be banned from entering America. In 1924, the Oriental Exclusion Act banned all immigration from Asia. Portraying the Chinese-American experience, Larke Huang and Yu-Wen Ying write:

> During the period from 1890 to 1945, more Chinese left than entered the United States. Those remaining lived under the oppression of the exclusion laws, suffering innumerable humiliations, racial violence, loss of property and livelihood, and sometimes loss of life.[27]

For Japanese-Americans, World War II virtually destroyed their livelihood. Shortly after the attack on Pearl Harbor, all the West Coast Japanese and Japanese Americans were incarcerated in concentration camps because of their Japanese ancestry.[28] The identity of Korean Americans has been often misunderstood as either Chinese or Japanese Americans, and they were subjected to similar harsh treatments.

The U.S. Congress and government were instrumental in legally legitimizing many of these discriminatory practices. However, while cases of institutional racism were apparent, those practices were largely the consequence of negative stereotypes of Asian Americans held by

---

[27]Larke Hahme Huang and Yu-Wen Ying, "Chinese American Children and Adolescents," in *Children of Color: Psychological Interventions with Minority Youth,* ed. J. T. Gibbs and L. Huang and Associates (Unknown, 1980), 33-34.

[28]Stephen S. Fugita and David J. O'Brien, *Japanese American Ethnicity* (Seattle: University of Washington Press, 1991), 9. Fugita and O'Brien comment: "One immediate effect on the structure of the ethnic community was to replace the authority of the *Issei* (first generation Japanese Americans), which was suspect according to military officials, with that of youthful English-speaking *Nisei* (second generation Japanese Americans) leaders. Japanese-Americans also were physically removed from their isolated ethnic enclaves and rural settings. After the war, a large number of them did not return to these areas. It should be noted that official government policy encouraged the geographic dispersal of Japanese-Americans, ostensibly to reduce the likelihood of arousing prejudices and discrimination by the white majority." Yet, neither German-Americans nor Italian-Americans had to experience anything remotely similar to the experience that Japanese-Americans went through during the WWII.

the majority of American society.[29]   Discussing the Asian-American
experience in American history, Won Moo Hurh and Kwang Chung

Approximate Period	Verbal Stereotype	Actual Consequences
1850-1940	unassimilable inscrutable, tricky, immoral, heathens	Chinese Exclusion Act (1882) Gentlemen's Agreement (1908) Alien Land Act (1913) Immigration Act of 1924
1941-1945	cruel, disloyal, enemy aliens, faithful ally (only Chinese)	Japanese evacuation (1942-1945) Eligibility for naturalization (1943, only for Chinese)
1946-1965	industrious, quiet, law-abiding	Cultural assimilation and emergence of Chinese/Japanese American middle class
1966-	successful, intelligent, hard-working model minority	Disguised underemployment; Exclusion from minority programs; False consciousness among Asian Americans (assimilation & mobility myth); Legitimization of the "open" society and downgrading of other less "successful" minorities
1982-	Overachieving, insular, threatening	Glass-ceiling effect; bigotry, resentment, and anti-Asian violence

Table 4-2 Vicissitude of the American Image of Asians in the U.S.

Kim observe the American majority's image of Asian Americans and
the actual consequences of such images:[30]

---

[29] Won Moo Hurh, Won Moo, "The 1.5 Generation: A Cornerstone of the
Korean-American Ethnic Community," in *The Emerging Generation of
Korean-Americans*, Ho-Youn Kwon and Shin, eds. (Seoul, Korea: Kyoung Hee
University Press, 1993), 62.

[30] Won Moo Hurh and Kwang Chung Kim, "The 'Success' Image of Asian
Americans: Its Validity, Practical and Theoretical Implications," *Ethnic and*

Oriental and Media Portrayal of Asian Americans

The majority of Americans' image of Asian Americans, or "Orientals" as they have been commonly identified, has fluctuated in accordance with the changing socioeconomic and political conditions of America. Robert Lee argues that an analysis of American popular culture reveals the history of portrayal of Asian Americans as the eternal "other." Among others, six images—the pollutant, the coolie worker, the deviant, the yellow peril, the model minority, and the gook—represent the Oriental as an alien body and "a threat to the American national family."[31] Lee maintains that

> Each of these representations was constructed in a specific historical moment, marked by a shift in class relations accompanied by cultural crisis. At such times American nationality—who the "real Americans" are—is redefined in terms of class, gender, race, and sexuality.[32]

These representations of Asian Americans have been especially shaped by and reflected in mass media. Discussing the media portrayal of Asian Americans over the century, Kitano and Daniels assert that:

> Starting with the villainous stereotypes in early movies, progress can be measured only in inches. The evil Jap of World War II and the communist gooks in Korea, China, and Vietnam – faceless, fanatic, maniacal, willing to die because life is not valued – are endlessly recycled with changes in nationality as our foreign policy changes. A recent flurry of Hollywood films with a favorable approach to Asian Americans, the most notable of which was the adaptation of Amy Tan's popular novel, *Joy Luck Club*, may change the pattern, but unfavorable images still predominate.[33]

When Asian American filmmakers attempted to portray Asian Americans in a more realistic manner, they have achieved a limited

---

Racial Studies 12 (1989): 515; Won Moo Hurh, "Majority Americans' Perception of Koreans in the United States" in Ho-Youn Kwon, ed., *Korean Americans: Conflict and harmony* (Chicago: Covenant Publications, 1994).

[31] Robert G. Lee, *Orientals: Asian Americans in Popular Culture* (Philadelphia: Temple University Press, 1999), 8.

[32] Ibid., 8-9.

[33] Kitano and Daniels, Asian Americans: Emerging Minorities, 186.

success.[34] This is probably due, in part, to limited public appeal and to Asian Americans, themselves, because of the lack of material addressing their authentic experiences. Some Asian Americans in the film industry try to "shun the Asian American label and wish to be judged solely on their merits."[35] Asian American actors and actresses are rarely seen, unless they appear as exotic martial arts experts or in often degrading supporting roles.

In recent years, Asian American females have experienced limited success in securing news anchor roles in major U.S. cities. What is noticeable about this success is the equally noticeable absence of Asian American males in similarly visible positions.[36] Commenting on how the media has dealt with hate crimes against Asian Americans, the U.S. Commission on Civil Rights noted that the media gave

> little attention to hate crimes against Asian Americans, thereby hindering the formation of a national sense of outrage about bigotry and violence against Asian Americans, a critical ingredient for social change."[37]

During the Los Angeles riot, the media singled out Korean Americans as the primary group against which African Americans in the area held issues and hatred. The media conveniently disregarded the enormous part of the riot that included white, black, and Hispanic Americans, choosing rather to singularly portray Korean Americans as the oppressors to the poor in the inner city of Los Angeles. This naïve or hegemonic media portrayal constructed, in the mind of African Americans and other Americans all over in the U.S., a viewpoint that indeed dismissed the persistence of multiethnic and socioeconomic problems in the U.S.[38] Korean Americans were made the scapegoat for all of the economic injustices of the inner city.

---

[34]Such movies as Dim Sum, Chan Is Missing, and Hito Hita.

[35]Kitano and Daniels, Asian Americans: Emerging Minorities, 186.

[36]Ibid.

[37]U.S. Commission on Civil Rights, "Civil Rights Issues Facing Asian Americans in the 1990s," Executive Summary (Washington, D.C., February 28, 1992), 1 as cited in Hurh, The Korean Americans, 126.

[38]Edward Chang, "Los Angeles 'Riots' and the Korean American Community," in Korean Americans: Conflict and Harmony, ed. Ho-Youn Kwon (Chicago: Covenant Publication, 1994).

The "Model Minority" Myth

Since the 1960's, as more Asian Americans have entered the American middle-class and achieved an upward social mobility, the American majority's image of Asian Americans has begun to change in a more positive direction.[39] Asian Americans were referred to as the model minority with high educational levels, high median family incomes, low crime rates, and the absence of juvenile delinquency and mental health problems.[40] However, this success image of Asian Americans is still a dubious one. Many studies portraying Asian Americans as a successful minority have relied on raw data (level of education, occupation, and earnings) in estimating the socioeconomic status of Asian Americans.

In terms of median family income, level of higher education, and occupational prestige scores, Asian Americans have surpassed all other ethnic American groups, including non-Hispanic whites[41]. In reality, however, this data does not tell the whole story. In order to more accurately simulate the socioeconomic status of Asian Americans, the data should be combined to show the composite picture of socioeconomic status. Only when the rate of return (namely median family income and occupational prestige scores) and investment (level of education) is calculated properly (rate of return divided by investment) does the measure of socioeconomic status become a valid one.

Hurh and Kim report that Asian Americans earn less than white Americans under the equivalent condition of investment.[42]   Hurh argues:

Overqualification for their jobs or underutilization of their education (underemployment) has been the most serious occupational problem for both native- and foreign-born Asian Americans. . . Our analysis of individual earnings demonstrates that regardless of their race-ethnic status,

---

[39]Hurh, "The 1.5 Generation: A Cornerstone of the Korean-American Ethnic Community," 62-64.

[40]Chen, Asian Americans: An Interpretive History, 167.

[41]Karnow and Yoshihara, *Asian Americans in Transition*, 26, 40; Hurh, "The 1.5 Generation: A Cornerstone of the Korean-American Ethnic Community," 64-65.

[42]Hurh and Kim, "The 'Success' Image of Asian Americans: Its Validity, Practical and Theoretical Implications."

place of birth, and sex, Asian Americans suffer from earnings inequity. As long as this inequity exists, the success image of Asian Americans remains largely a myth.[43]

The study also shows that there are more members per household working in Asian-American families than in white American households. The consequences, sacrifices and strains that, undoubtedly, a multi-wage earner household must face need to be considered as well. Chan articulates a more contextualized critical analysis from the Asian American perspective in an attempt to debunk the model minority myth:

More than half of the Asian/Pacific American population in the United States lives in only five metropolitan areas – Honolulu, San Francisco, Los Angeles, Chicago, and New York – and of these, more than nine-tenths are found in urban centers. These cities are not only high-income areas but also high-cost-of-living areas. . . The low unemployment rate of Asian Americans . . . merely camouflages high underemployment. With regard to the educational attainment of Asian Americans, the sizable influx of highly educated professionals after 1965 has inflated the average the average years of schooling completed. . . For Asian Americans, even in 1980, these returns (returns to education as opposed to educational level) were still not on a par with those received by white men.[44]

Asian Americans have also experienced "glass ceiling" effects and other forms of racism in higher education. In terms of the admission and enrollment of Asian-American applicants to some of the country's most selective public and private colleges, Asian Americans encounter informal quotas and higher standards for admissions because of their ethnic background.[45]
On the one hand, some prestigious schools have changed their admission policies in an elaborate manner to admit more non-Asian American students, such as children of the schools' alumni, who are

---

[43]Hurh, "The 1.5 Generation: A Cornerstone of the Korean-American Ethnic Community," 66.

[44]Chan, *Asian Americans: An Interpretive History*, 168-170.

[45]Don Nakanishi, "A Quota on Excellence?," *Change* (November/ December 1989): 39; Nakanishi and Nishida, *The Asian American Educational Experience*.

mostly white Americans.[46] Some schools admit students with athletic affiliations that favor those from families with more sociocultural capital.[47] On the other hand, Asian Americans are no longer considered a minority to be considered for affirmative action. The new term that is created for affirmative action, the *underrepresented* minority, excludes Asian Americans from benefiting from the practices. As a result, the social vehicle that had been construed to be the most equitable for upward mobility and advancement in American society can no longer be taken for granted by Asian Americans.

Parenthetically, according to Laurence Steinberg, while Asian American adolescents feel the pressure from their parents to excel in academics, their peers and teachers at school socialize these adolescents to pursue academics. He argues that Asian Americans do not have access to various social groups in American high schools. Instead, Asian American students are "permitted to join intellectual crowds, like the 'brains,' but the more socially oriented crowds – the 'populars,' 'jocks,' and 'partyers' – are far less open to them."[48] Thus, Steinberg is arguing that the academic success of Asian American students is "at least partly a by-product" of two ways in which they get categorized by their peers. First, although many Asian American adolescents long to be members of more socially-oriented crowds, their peers do not often welcome them.[49] Second, Asian Americans are expected to maintain the image of "brains" or "nerds."

This glass-ceiling effect experienced by Asian Americans in higher education disappears when they enter the workplace. It is estimated that Asian Americans have an average of one and a half years more education for the same professional positions held by white Americans. Yet, Asian American professionals are still routinely passed over for promotions.[50] They are often perceived as unassertive and passive, deemed as having neither leadership qualities nor social skills, and are typed as "detailed" or technically oriented.[51]

---

[46]Chan, *Asian Americans: An Interpretive History*, 179-181.

[47]Hurh, The Korean Americans, 96-101; Takagi, The Retreat from Race.

[48]Laurence Steinberg, "Ethnicity and Adolescent Achievement," *American Educator* (Summer, 1996): 46.

[49]Ibid.

[50]Leon E. Wynter and Jolie Solomon, "A New Push to Break the 'Glass Ceiling,'" *Wall Street Journal,* 15 November 1989, B1.

[51]Fong, The Contemporary Asian American Experience, 109.

The myth of model minority breaks down the solidarity of Asian Americans in two ways. First, people believe that they can "make it on their own" without paying heed to their communities. Also, restrained by quota, there is a sense of growing competition among Asian Americans as they climb the success ladder of society. Second, Asian Americans refuse to be associated with members of their ethnic group for fear of being "stereotyped."

The implications of such stereotyping and its long-term effects have been documented.[52] The model minority stereotyping oversimplifies the issues faced by Asian Americans and obscures important realities in the community. It fails to take into account the variety of Asian American experiences resulting from the different time periods and circumstances in which immigrants arrived to America. The diversity of Asian American experiences, the results of varying interactions with sociocultural differences such as geographical regions, socioeconomic status, gender, and generations, often get lost in the stereotyping.

Some Asian Americans have indeed been highly successful as many studies have shown. However, there are also many immigrants and their descendants who have been less fortunate in their American experience. Both the benefit and the cost of Asian American experience must be evaluated in understanding the second-generation Korean experience.

Again, the model-minority is a characterization that has been imposed on Asian Americans from without. It is not something with which many Asian Americans can identify. A more cynical view of the labeling is that Asian Americans are compared with the "unruly" minorities who are adapting with much less quietness and conformity.[53] This view claims that the model minority myth was created during an era of racial unrest when the black population was increasing and demanding equal citizenship.[54]

---

[52]Stacey J. Lee, *Unraveling the "Model Minority" Stereotype* (New York: Teachers College Press, 1996).

[53]Kitano, *Race Relations*, 193.

[54]Labeling the Asian-American community as a model eased the conscience of white Americans when accusations of racism, prejudice and discrimination permeated the atmosphere. Asian Americans are either used to prove the non-existence of institutional racism or to prove the benign nature of racism as an element that has no social consequences in American society. The idea of one minority far exceeding the others is used to create an illusionary hierarchy of

**Effects on Family and Self: An Asian American
Bicultural Dilemma**

While Asian American families vary greatly depending on factors
such as the rate of acculturation, the level of ethnic adherence, and
family of origin, they are constantly in negotiation with traditional
Asian values in the functioning of the Asian American family. This
negotiation process is at work in many forms that will be discussed
later.

The point of departure for this intense negotiation is the view of
person. Whereas in Western cultures the independence and autonomy
of the individual is the source of personhood, the family unit takes the
center-stage in construing personhood in traditional Asian American
cultures.

The person is construed as the product of all the generations of his or
her extended family both present and past. The person is also
understood as a link for the future of the family. Hence, a person's
action and life are not just his or her own, but they both represent and
reflect his or her extended family and ancestors. In this view, where
the person consists of a web of extended family members of both the
present and the past, two principal vehicles of socialization, obligation
and shame, are used to maintain sociocultural norms and expectations.
The person is expected to function according to the societally defined
roles and positions, such as age, gender, social class, and hierarchies, in
various aspects of the society. Thus, the esteemed values are
"harmonious interpersonal relationships, interdependence, and mutual
obligations or loyalty for achieving a state of psychological
homeostasis or peaceful coexistence with family or other fellow
beings."[55]

---

success among ethnic minorities. In pitting one ethnic group against the other,
divisions among various minority groups may be forever insured.

[55]Evelyn Lee, "Asian American Families: An Overview" in Monica
McGoldrick, Joe Giordano, and John K. Pearce, *Ethnicity and Family Therapy*,
2nd ed. (New York: The Guilford Press, 1996), 231.

The View of Family: Another Asian American Dilemma

While there exist three subsystems in Asian nuclear families just as in an ordinary nuclear family in the U.S., the salience of these three subsystems is different.

In terms of marital subsystem, the husband takes on the role of authority and the wife the homemaker. The wife has to submit to her father and her in-laws, as well. In the marriage, physical and verbal expressions of love are rare. The dominant subsystem in the family is that of the parent-child, rather than the husband-wife dyad.[56] The mother is responsible to provide nurturance, while the father is to complement her by disciplining the children. According to Lee, "the strongest emotional attachment for a woman is sometimes not her husband, but her children (especially her sons)."[57] In the sibling subsystem, siblings are expected to cooperate and share with one another. Oftentimes, older siblings (especially the eldest daughter) are to carry on the bulk of the child-care responsibility of younger siblings. However, in many extended families, a wide range of adults raises children.[58]

Depending on how the above values are negotiated and synthesized with American values in various spheres of sociocultural contexts in the U.S., Asian American families can be categorized into five hypothetical constructs: traditional families, "cultural conflict" families, bicultural families, "Americanized" families, and interracial families.[59] These constructs resemble the four cells of the orthogonal scheme of assimilation and ethnic identity among Asian Americans discussed above.[60] These five constructs can also be construed as sequential steps toward greater assimilation.

In the first construct, traditional families have limited exposure and interactions with American mainstream society. Traditional Asian values typically dictate their decisions and behaviors in life. They maintain their Asian culture and converse mainly in their native languages.

---

[56]Ibid.
[57]Ibid.
[58]Ibid.
[59]Ibid., 232-233.
[60]Ibid., 231-233.

The second construct involves "cultural conflict," families that are comprised of members who are both very acculturated and those who hold to traditional Asian values. Often, the more acculturated are the children who were either born in the U.S. or who came to the U.S. at an early age, and the more traditional are the parents and grandparents. There may be considerable intergenerational conflicts and role confusion in these families. The language barrier between the parents and children often exacerbate such conflicts.

Bicultural families, the third construct, are the families where both parents and children are bicultural in their interactions. Many of these parents immigrated with their parents in their elementary years or early teenage years. Some of the parents in bicultural families were born in the U.S. but grew up in traditional families. They are usually professionals who come from a middle or upper-middle class background. These families tend to be more egalitarian in marital interactions. They often function as a nuclear family and reside in the suburbs of major cities.

Finally, in the fourth construct, "Americanized" families are usually comprised of parents and children born and raised in the U.S. With the passing of each generation, members and their subsequent families tend to lose their Asian cultures and choose not to make a conscious effort to retain their ethnic heritages. These families often operate entirely on American values. However, while the third-generation Japanese Americans are more highly acculturated to mainstream American culture than the first and second generations, the resurgence and persistence of Japanese culture within them has been reported, especially in comparison with their Caucasian American peers.[61]

While interracial families, the last construct, may be construed as a part of the fourth construct, where there is integration of an Asian American and other American cultures, some of these families experience intercultural conflicts as well as conflicts that are unique to interracial families. The interracial marriages have largely involved Asian American women marrying Caucasian American men. Interracial marriages among Asian Americans have been on the rise in recent years. Some of the problems faced in these families may be

---

[61]S. S. Fugita and D. J. O'Brien, *Japanese American Ethnicity: The Persistence of Community* (Seattle: University of Washington Press, 1991).

conflicts in values, communication style, child-rearing issues, and in-law problems.[62]

Mental Health Issues among Asian Americans

Predictors of mental illness for the general population in the U.S.—employment/financial status, gender, old age, and social isolation—serve as predictors for Asian Americans, as well. Asian Americans who are in financial distress, female, elderly, and isolated from society tend to have higher rates of mental illnesses. While these predictors are useful for both Asian Americans and the general U.S. population, some of the underlying reasons for illnesses may be different for Asian Americans and their families. A predictor unique to Asian Americans is relatively recent immigration. Another predictor unique to Asian Americans, especially Americans of Southwest Asian decent, is refugee pre-migration experience/post-migration adjustment.[63]

Common mental illnesses for Asian Americans include "somatization, depression and anxiety, adjustment disorder, schizophrenia, alcoholism, drug addiction, gambling, and suicide."[64] Problems that originate from Asian American families are usually "parent-child conflicts, martial discord, in-law problems, and domestic violence."[65] Half of Asian Americans seeking psychological help deal with issues as varied as depression, low self-concept, and relationship conflicts. Problems with parent-child relationship, acculturation, somatic complaints, and isolation are some other major reasons for seeking professional help among Asian Americans.[66] Uba and others demonstrate a high rate of mental illness among Asian Americans as a result of value conflicts, conflict with parental generations, and assimilation.[67] Studies also show that many Asian Americans suffer

[62]Lee, "Asian American Families: An Overview," 233; Fong, *The Contemporary Asian American Experience*, 224-238.

[63]Uba, Asian Americans: Personality Patterns, Identity, and Mental Health, 175.

[64]Lee, "Asian American Families: An Overview," 234.

[65]Ibid.

[66]Lee, "Asian American Families: An Overview," 234.

[67]Uba, *Asian Americans: Personality Patterns, Identity, and Mental Health;* Stanley Sue and Derald Sue, "Chinese American Personality and Mental

from marginal personality, self-hatred, and identity crisis.[68]   At least two studies suggest that the nature of psychological problems tend to be more severe for Asian Americans than European Americans. Based on their analysis of the MMPI of Asian and European American samples, Stanley Sue and Derald Sue report that Asian Americans have more somatic complaints than European Americans. Stanley Sue and H. McKinney maintain that Asian Americans who seek mental health services exhibit more severe disturbance than non-Asian counterparts.[69] Moreover, the suicide rates of Chinese Americans and Japanese American young adults (20-30 years) have been reported to be 36% and 54% higher, respectively, than that of all Americans of that age group.[70]

After looking at the experience of second-generation Korean Americans, we will look in this section at some of the ways these study participants have negotiated the multiple tensions and pressures around them. They share here some of the values and voices they have internalized to help them negotiate the process of identity formation, including appreciation for a multicultural environment, and recognition

---

Health," *Amerasia Journal* 1 (1971): 36-49; Sharlene Furuto, Renuka Diswas, Douglas K. Chung, Kenji Murase and Fariyal Ross-Sheriff, *Social Work Practice With Asian Americans* (Newbury Park: Sage, 1992).

[68]Ron Low, "A Brief Biographical Sketch of a Newly Found Asian Male," in *Roots: An Asian American Reader*, eds. Amy Tachiki, Eddie Wong, Franklin Odo, and Buck Wong (Los Angeles: UCLA Asian American Studies Center, 1971), 105-108; Irvin Paik, "That Oriental Feeling," in *Roots*, 30-36; Donna K. Nagata, "Japanese American Children and Adolescents," in *Children of Color: Psychological Interventions with Minority Youth*, eds. J. T. Gibbs and L. N. Huang and Associates (Unknown 1989), 67-113; Tong-He Koh, "Ethnic Identity: The Impact of The Two cultures on The Psychological Development of Korean-American Adolescents," in *The Emerging Generation of Korean-Americans*, eds. Ho-Youn Kwon and Shin Kim (Seoul, Korea: Kyoung Hee University Press, 1993), 29-46.

[69]Lee, "Asian American Families: An Overview," 234; Stanley Sue and Derald W. Sue, "MMPI Comparisons Between Asian Americans and Non-Asian Students Utilizing a Student Health Psychiatric Clinic," *Journal of Counseling Psychology*, 21 (1974): 423-427; Stanley Sue and H. McKinney, "Asian Americans in the Community Health Care System," *American Journal of Orthopsychiatry*, 45 (1975): 111-118.

[70]Joan E. Rigdon, "Exploding Myth: Asian-American Youth Suffer a Rising Toll from Heavy Pressures," *The Wall Street Journal*, 10 July 1991, sec.1, p. 4.

of some of the faults of mainstream America (their concerns for America).

Multiculturalism Valued

Appreciation for the city life compared to the life in the suburbs

Many of the young adults share that growing up in Chicago gave them a sense of confidence about being Korean American. However, when they moved to the suburbs of Chicago, they remember the difficulties that they encountered as an ethnic minority. They talk about their struggles to fit into the mainstream culture or at least to not stick out as someone different. Kelly shares her experience:

> I remember spending time in the Chicago public schools where it didn't matter what you were. My best friends were: one was Indian, one was Greek, and one was I think he was Philippino . . . So, it (my ethnicity) really didn't matter until I got to the suburbs in the second grade. Boy, things got changed quickly!

Molly also talks about the kinds of cultural adjustment she had to make during her high school years in the suburb after growing up in the city. She says:

> We went to Elmhurst at that time and it was a rotten two years. I had a really hard time. First of all, I had never felt like an outsider because in the Chicago public schools everything is so culturally diverse. When I went to York High School, that's the first time I ever felt like I stuck out like a sore thumb kind of a thing. And it was a really difficult two years. I didn't make many close friends, I was very closed off. I think which is why when I went to UIC it was really nice. . . Although I didn't like the school much, at least I fit in with all kinds of people.

In discussing her experiences in both the city and the suburb, Molly makes an interesting observation about Caucasian Americans. She speaks of a rather clear distinction between those who live in the city and in the suburbs. When she was asked about whether she has regrets moving from Chicago to the suburb, Molly says:

> No, I don't think I ever regretted it—I think if anything the pride (of Caucasian Americans) made me cynical of Caucasians to a degree. It

made me think like, "They just like to hang among themselves." . . . But
then I've come to realize, I have had several Caucasian friends (living in
Chicago), that there is a distinct difference between Chicago Caucasians
and suburban Caucasians. I find a very big difference. I think Caucasians
in Chicago are much more open and they are much more accepting. And
you know we've already embraced their culture—obviously just by
moving here. And a lot of my (Caucasian American) friends (in Chicago)
were very wanting to know about my culture and they made me feel like
it's cool, it's nice, and you should be proud of it, to be different. Whereas
here (in the suburb), it's like you have to completely assimilate or fit or
else.

Concerns for mainstream America

Notwithstanding their appreciation for the freedom and opportunity
for success in American society, many of the young adults express their
concern for the disinterest and insensitivity toward various people
groups in the U.S., as well as in the world. Paul, who was born and
raised in the U.S., talks about his experience with many Caucasian
Americans.

"I have to ask you where did you learn your English because you have
absolutely no accent?" I think if I had met Kelly before I would have said
something rude or like "Where did *you* learn your English?" But I just
merely say, "Oh, I was born in Chicago" so immediately he knew where I
learned my English. And I kept hearing stories of people, other doctors
who would talk to me later on, saying, "Oh, I assigned a patient to you."
And then again I suffered because they (the patients) thought I wouldn't
be able to understand them or they wouldn't be able to understand me, just
by virtue of my last name. I laugh about it but I remember one of the
dentists, like told them I had a sister in Green Bay, and there was an Asian
reporter who was working up there and immediately he said "Oh, you
mean Cindy Shu?" And I said "No," so immediately they think -- I think
they have the impression that if you're Asian, you are related somehow, to
know each other. . . But as far as I could tell, it was nothing malicious, it's
just cultural ignorance, I guess.

This kind of experience, according to the young adults, is a very
common occurrence in their everyday life.
    Some of the young adults are concerned about many Americans
being myopic about what's going on in the world and in the country,
especially the urban settings. Albert, again American-born and raised,

talks about the narrow-mindedness he observes in many Caucasian Americans, in that they only know their own little world:

> I deal with suburban DuPage, upper middle class. Many of these people have a very limited view of what their world is. I find it even more entrenched in the Christian community and there are some people who are very prejudiced . . . But my general impression is that they have a very narrow view of the world and that's tough to deal with, especially when I come from a different perspective and a different view of the world.

Joel recalls his experience with racism that reminded him of how insensitive and prejudicial majority people can be. He talks about one of his many experiences where he was hanging out with his African American roommate during his freshman year:

> My roommate was an African American. So when we went places, a lot of people would stare at us, whether going into Wal-Mart or to a grocery store. I remember people were looking at us as we were going about our business, which I felt discrimination. They probably thought we were gonna steal something.

The Signs of the Persistence of Ethnocentrism Among Korean Americans

In the young adults' minds, Korean Americans do not fare much better concerning the myopic outlook on the world around them. Melinda states:

> I think Korean Americans are very ethnocentric. They think that Korea is the best, and that Koreans have the best way of doing things. And I see that, from my parents, that's the way they were raised and they grew up prejudiced—you know, going along with that ethnocentricness, very nationalistic.

Georgia observes that Koreans in the U.S. have become entrenched in Korean culture. She also thinks that they are more traditional and perhaps more backward than Koreans living in Korea. Georgia shares:

> Actually I think the Korean Americans are more traditional in the States than they were in Korea. They are more Korean than Koreans in Korea because people change, but our parents have not changed. And they insist

on keeping those same patterns, beliefs and behaviors from before. And I think they really need to change some of that.

Michelle reflects that the ethnic pride and identity are somehow intertwined for the first generation. She hopes that the second generation will be different. Michelle says:

Korean American people have a lot of pride, especially in their culture, in their identity as Koreans. And I see a lot of pride in my parents and other Korean parents that I know. And that's always bothered me a little bit . . . Especially trying to be a good Christian, we have to learn how to humble ourselves. At least in our generation, we have to be different.

Preference for a Multicultural Society in Life and in Vision

Many of the young adults prefer working in a more multiethnic context, rather than in the suburbs, which consist mostly of Caucasian Americans. They presuppose they will feel more comfortable and more accepted for who they are in such a context. Betsy talks about her preference for working in a more multicultural context from her personal biographic perspective:

I really liked Niles North a lot because there were a lot more people that could understand where I'm coming from because there were a lot of Asian Americans and other kinds of people . . . I felt very comfortable with my Indian (American) roommate too. I feel a lot more comfortable around non-whites—it's weird, like at my work they weren't Asian Americans but they are black and Hispanic at UIC. I really felt just very comfortable and I don't know what it is.

Betsy continues:

On the whole, I would prefer working with minorities, and maybe that's why I even want to work more in the city, as I think about it . . . I was telling somebody (a Korean American girl) about that . . . It's really weird that she said "yeah, I feel the same way."

However, while their preference is to work in a multicultural context, they are adamant about marrying a Korean American. Moreover, although they desire to see their English-speaking congregations in the Korean American church or their independent English-speaking Korean

American churches become more multiethnic, they seldom think about attending a non-Korean American church. Michelle is perhaps one of a few exceptions who articulates her vision for a multiethnic and multicultural church, when she shares about her experience at her sister's inter-racial wedding. She uses her experience at the wedding as an analogy or metaphor for what the church ought to strive for. Michelle starts with how both sides were able to get along, when she says:

> Once, because she became engaged, they made an effort to get to know him and know his family and just by God's Georgia they got along very well. I think because his father is 100% German, he emigrated from Germany and his mother and her whole family is Syrian and so what my parents share with them is this cultural barrier that they are all having in America. . .

Michelle talks about how she felt blessed:

> I just remember at the wedding feeling very blessed because I saw all these different cultures with my relatives coming from Korea, not speaking any English, we had relatives from Germany coming and relatives that couldn't speak a lot of English, even the Syrian culture. We had this wedding and reception that was like. There was a Syrian band and they did a traditional Syrian dance. And we had all my relatives and their hymnbooks. And then we had Jason's uncle from Germany giving a speech in German. And I just remember my relatives and some of their relatives. they were all speaking in their native tongues and not understanding anything of what the other person was saying. But all just being happy, hugging each other, kissing each other, shaking their hands and everyone is smiling and just having so much fun. I remember some people in his family would get like my aunts and my grandmother to go up and dance. They were dancing together and it was just wonderful.

Michelle continues:

> It was so odd to me because I used to think oh, they're going to be so uncomfortable because none of them can speak English. And I remember turning to (my pastor who is a Caucasian American) "(Pastor), this is like small version of heaven to me." To see all these different cultures and people of all different tongues coming together, and just having fun, and being in one room, and just having a great time together, and not even caring that they were all speaking different languages and stuff . . . It was just great and God really blessed me through that wedding and I was really

hoping that this would be a kind of stepping stone for my sister and Jason, to realize a little bit more what God wants us to be. Because (my pastor) did a great job of trying to center the ceremony around God and God's blessings, I was even very pleasantly surprised to see that my sister and Jason allowed her to mention these things at the wedding since they both are not Christian. And there was actually like scripture readings and two prayer times, and everyone recited the Lord's Prayer and so there were blessings in that.

Voices from Multicultural Environment

Growing up in the city of Chicago has provided some of these study participants with a healthy sense of their ethnic identity. Through multicultural interactions, they were able to view themselves as part of the mosaic of the U.S. They recall that their peers or the people in their neighborhoods were not color blind. Instead, these people lived their lives in light of their own cultural heritages, as legitimate citizens of the U.S. They were also eager to share their own cultural heritages with fellow Americans from different ethnic and cultural backgrounds. It is in this kind of context some of the young adults grew up and were able to accept their Korean American heritage, perhaps more easily than those who grew up in the suburbs of Chicago.

Having grown up in the city of Chicago, Dylan believes that he has a healthy sense of who he is, especially when it comes to his ethnic identity. He reflects on this:

I think I was one of the first Asians in our neighborhood and one of the first days I met someone right away and there was no problem. We became friends and we used to play with all the kids in the neighborhood. And when we got mad at each other, I don't remember getting down to the point of where he insulted me for being a certain race, instead he insulted me how dumb I was or something . . . In high school, you think you're older and more mature or more tolerant . . . (Interviewer: Was the makeup of the high school pretty much multi-ethnic?) Oh, yes, absolutely. And that's one thing you have to or the school definitely tried to push. You know, the diverse city because they had to, it was the melting pot.

Chapter 6

An Inside Look at the Second-Generation in the Context of the Korean American Family

Despite the valiant efforts made by the first-generation Korean Americans in various spheres of their lives, adapting to life in a new country has proven to be difficult. Kitano and Daniels observe the existential reality of first-generation Korean Americans who find themselves:

> contending with a multitude of issues, including cultural and linguistic differences, parent-child stresses, changes in roles, conflicts in norms and values, achieving a healthy identity in a predominantly white society, and varied levels of acceptance by both the majority and other minorities already living here.[1]

My research found many common dynamics within Korean American families as they have responded to these difficult issues. The influence these family dynamics have on second-generation Korean American young adults is crucial in understanding their construction of self.

Family Valued as Mixed Blessing: Commitment to Family

"Traditional family" Valued

The young adults have internalized the value of having a traditional family arrangement. They want to marry well, have children, and have a good family. For many, the value of having the traditional family arrangement has factored in and continues to do so in major decisions

---

[1]Kitano and Daniels, Asian Americans: Emerging Minorities, 119.

of their lives. Julia shares her desire to marry well and have a good family. She takes marriage so seriously that she is extremely cautious:

> For me, marriage is a real scary thing for me right now, to be honest with you, because that's probably the most important decision that you will ever make in your life. It's just something I have to trust God with. For me, I guess, I want certainty, and guarantee that things will work out . . . I realize that marriage isn't easy and I realize that it's more complex. It gets more complex when you get married and even like kids, such a huge responsibility. So I think I am realizing all these things but it is a serious thing.

Those who are already married make decisions based on the future needs of the family. Although Kris has been married for a couple of years, she decided where she and her husband would buy a house based on "where we were going to raise our family, our future children."

> Many of the young adults reminisce about how their parents talked about the importance of getting married well and having a good family. However, in reality, the young adults share that they really do not know what it means to have a good family. Again, many of them talk about the empty house they used to come in after school and the scarcity of interactions with their parents.

Close and growing family valued

The young adults place high value on maintaining growing relationships with parents and siblings. Their desire is to have healthily functioning extended families. Many realize that they have a limited set of siblings and relatives in the U.S., and they want to safeguard those relationships. Kelly reflects on the value of maintaining relationships with her mother and sister:

> Maybe we've just come to realize that when all is said and done there are only four of us in the family and we need to be close. So I'm on the phone, as our
> phone bill will attest, with my mother and sister virtually every day. And I drive down on my days off to my parents' house and sometimes once a week they will come up here to visit. And now that we have kids, my sister and I, there is this really strange desire for both kids to know each

other and to know their grandparents. So we spend a lot of time with my family.

Some young adults value their mothers' attempts over the years to maintain relationships with their extended families, as well as that of their husband's side. Daniel talks about his respect for his mother's effort to maintain relationships with her extended family:

> My mom, I really respect my mom because of just the way that she handles being (the wife of the first born son in the family). I know that she had—at times very difficult times but she has done a great job holding the family together. I know that she is the one who always wants to try to get the family together and do things together, and that kind of stuff. So in most of my decisions I think—you know, it's more important that she approves of my decisions than my father.

Thus, Daniel's respect for his mother's nurturing posture toward extended families has spilled over into other realms of his life. He values her advice and wants to please her.

Relationships with siblings valued

Some of the young adults express their appreciation for their siblings. They share that their siblings have had, and continue to have, a significant influence in their lives. Dylan talks about how his brother helped him out financially when he decided to get complete programming training after exhausting job possibilities. Dylan says:

> There was a tuition fee and my brother helped me out with that. He had been working for a few years, I think, and saved up some money so it was like $4000 or $5000 within 3 or 4 months of the program. So I borrowed that and after earning some money I was able to pay him off. (Interviewer: Interest free?) Interest free, of course. That's what brothers are for.

Kris also values her sister who has provided true companionship. She speaks of her sister being there for her, especially during her parents' extended periods of absence:

> We grew up together so I always had somebody to talk to because our parents were never around . . . I feel like I'm pretty well rounded as a result of it, because we always played together, we always talked together

and we always did stuff together. So I felt like just having her there . . . If I didn't have a sister that I could talk to like that, I don't think I'd be the same person.

In light of their appreciation of their siblings, many young adults continue to welcome and treasure their siblings' presence and influence in their lives.

Appreciation of being the youngest one in the family

In reflecting on their family relationships, those young adults who are the youngest ones in the family share fond memories of being the youngest in the family. Dylan says that being the youngest one in the family helped him to have a closer relationship with his parents:

I think I had the best relations with my parents and my whole family . . . And this is because I think being the youngest I got to see all the things my parents used to go through with my brother and my sister, and really just kind of learn from them. And then also I think personality-wise I have my mother's personality that is kind of like "no shame" just no fear at asking questions or whatever. And I think because I'm the youngest it was tolerated by my father and mother as well, now I think because of all of that it turned into a better relationship with my parents. My mom, I think, gave equal love in the sense that she tried to love us equally, but being the youngest I was her favorite, of course.

Melinda also shares how she was able to relate to her father as the youngest girl in the family. As she reminisces about her father's recent death, Melinda is able to celebrate the good times she has had with her father:

. . . I would kind of bring it out in him, but there is no doubt in my mind about his love and care for me. Yeah, I was daddy's little girl, I could get him to do anything or buy me anything (laughter). And I think that's what made his death easier for me. I had no regrets, I had no unsettled business, I knew where he stood and he knew where I stood. And I think he and I are more similar in terms of temperament and personality. And my mom and my dad just always trusted me.

Speaking of her Korean heritage, Julia is very proud of the upbringing in her house. She attributes her possession of Korean heritage to being the youngest one in the family. She says:

> Yeah, actually, out of all the siblings, I was the one who was most Korean, I would say, because I had more Asian friends . . . I wanted to hang around my parents all the time and I think that's why I felt more Korean—that I had more in common with them.

Extended Family Valued

Many of the young adults appreciate the ways in which their extended family members help and support one another in times of need. Betsy talks about how her father took good care of a distant relative:

> What I really like about my dad is that—like this girl has been living with us, and she is not really related, she's an in-law and he is taking care of her like this semester. It's really far in-laws--it's my father's like half brother, whose wife's older sister's granddaughter—it's something like that. She went to high school at Lake Forest Academy, boarding school, during the past three or four years he would make sure that, it was kind of an added hassle for my dad, but he did it because they were still in some way related. And so he would watch out for her. And she lived here this semester as a favor to her parents.

The young adults also talk about their appreciation for their cousins, who served as role models. These cousins lent a hand whenever needed and were a source of encouragement and support. Luke speaks of his cousins, who became more like his brothers:

> When I look back these guys (my cousins) were very positive peers. I mean I've looked up to them at the time and they were good role models in high school . . . I think we are distant cousins, but they treated me like a brother at the time and they took me out to a lot of venues and they were kind of like the older brother that I didn't have, so that was positive.

Rose talks about how one of her cousins, who was younger than she was, had a delightful impact in her life. Rose shares that she feels like the roles have reversed between them because she always thought that she was to help her younger cousin, but her younger cousin helped her in recent years:

> I ended up spending a lot of time with her because she wasn't coming to church and I really wanted to try to be there for her spiritually and help her come back to her relationship with God. But a funny thing happened. She ended up being the person who was there for me, rather than me being there for her. And we became really close and she reinforced what I learned in England about cooperation and about non-competitiveness, about not focusing on name brand or like climbing the ladder stuff, but to look around and know what's important before you do that. And so she became a great support system for me when I was going through my issues with my mom, and when I began my job. She's always there for me.

While reflecting on the value of the support from the extended family, these study participants also feel pressure from familial closeness. The relatives often expect the young adults to succeed and make a name for the family. Although they do not levy the same level of pressure as their own parents, nonetheless it is still added expectation. Rose talks about the mixed blessing of having extended family:

> I've always been really close to my extended family. They have always been a piece of my life that I really enjoyed. But in terms of like getting into medical school I think they added to the pressure that I got from my mom . . . I believe all my aunts and uncles were brought up in a similar fashion that they do push and they do put some pressure. So I felt like my mom was a source of pressure but behind her were this wall of people who also had these expectations of me that did not make it easy for me . . . When they would come to my graduations, "Oh, you're the smart one in the family and you're the doctor" and all this. They always said nice things but those nice things always just made me feel more pressure, more expectations.

For some young adults, the helping hand is also extended inwardly, as well. As previously discussed, Dylan received an interest-free loan from his brother for his educational tuition. Luke talks about helping solve his parents' financial crisis. While he is angered by a series of questionable decisions made by his parents, Luke still feels obligated to relieve them of their financial burdens:

> I have trouble with those issues (my parents' previous financial decisions) because a large percent of my current income is going to support the

family where their problems were based on too much giving to the church beyond their means. I've had some issues with that and so we have had some major difficulty and major fights as a result of that . . . But, I need to help them out.

Voice of Comparison

One of the internalized voices that the young adults report as having had a major influence in their lives is the voice of comparison. The young adults speak of a differing set of expectations the parents had for each of the siblings. The partial treatment of the children has caused envy and a competitive spirit through sibling rivalry. In some cases, the partial treatment has resulted in severed relationships and other disastrous consequences.

Isabella talks about her father's differential treatment toward her, her brother and her sister that caused a lot of friction between her brother and her father, and among the siblings. She says:

> My father is at times really distant and kind of cold, especially with my brother. He had the typical father/son relationship with my brother. There is not very much communication between them. My brother feels very pressured. My dad pushes him to be a doctor, pushing him to succeed. So I think there is a lot more hurt between my brother and my father that I don't totally understand . . . I also think there was some conflict between me and my brother and sister because I was sort of my daddy's little girl. Everybody knew it and he favored me a lot. And I, as a kid, really played on that—just being a kid and "Daddy likes me the best." And so I think that was a source of conflict growing up with my siblings.

In sharing her father's partial treatment toward her and her sister, Elisa talks about how the partial treatment has impacted her life, especially her self-esteem. Elisa inevitably uses comparative statements to describe her sister:

> My father is probably like the typical Korean father who I just don't even want to talk to. But then I see him with my youngest sister, because I have two younger sisters. But I see him with her. And he opens up to her, he talks with her. Obviously, she is his favorite and in his eyes she can do no wrong. She is going to be a junior at U of I and she is an English major. She just decided on her major. And I guess it's because she is more

athletic, she is bigger than us, and she's very smart. And he has always favored her, I think, over us.

Some of the young adults measure their success or lack of it in comparison to that of other young adults in their church. While they know that they should not assess themselves in comparison with others, still they compare themselves through the eyes of their parents. Paul talks about the voice of envy and comparison, when he says:

I know I really am not supposed to envy other people's standing in life, but I think it's the nature to do. My parents do it. All the Koreans do. Well, I'm sure others do too. But I'm not sure how to get away from it.

Elisa shares her feeling of inadequacy as she compares herself with others in the church:

For a while I just felt that I didn't belong (at the church). I guess because when I was new of course, it's a new environment. But I don't know, I guess I just felt inferior to everybody because everyone seemed to be smarter and just a lot smarter—like schools they went to and jobs they have . . . They would just talk about the kinds of classes they were taking in college and stuff they talk about.

Voices of Mediocrity and Inadequacy

Having parents who are first-generation immigrants from Korea, the study participants feel that they were not adequately nurtured for the life in the U.S. When these young adults speak of the voices of mediocrity and inadequacy, they often speak in the voice of comparison with Caucasian Americans. The young adults feel that they needed more guidance and encouragement from their parents. Moreover, they share that they have often felt deprived of cultural capital. Abigail says that, when she went to college, she felt short-changed and blamed her parents for the misfortune:

At (the college), my academic performance wasn't that good, but again, everything was just kind of like heaped on me. I was so unstable, I didn't have a lot of good foundation. And I think all of my life I had felt like I've kind of been short-changed. A lot of people had things better off than myself and I didn't really have the opportunities that other people had. And it was really easy for me to look at another person and feel kind of jealous or just feel like I am so far behind. I'm so far behind, and feeling like my parents were not the best parents at all, not being able to see more good about my rearing experience.

At a more practical level, the young adults recall that their parents were not around for them to get involved in extracurricular activities. They essentially describe the scarcity of both informal and non-formal educational opportunities that culminated in their sense of inadequacy and mediocrity about themselves. Betsy shares her life without her parents after school during her growing-up years:

> I really hated (my parents not being at home) because I could never go to places because I never had a ride. My parents are never home. Like, for example, the park district or go swimming or do like. I wanted to do gymnastics but I couldn't do it because nobody could drive me. It was embarrassing because I would always have to get rides with friends. Like even I did violin, and then we have to go early like every once a week, and I always had to ask my friends—"Oh, my mom can't drive me." . . . They weren't available.

Kris has a different tone. In discussing spiritual issues, Kris talks about the fact that she was simply not impressed with the life of many Korean American Christians during her growing-up years. She says that she resisted becoming Christian because she felt that they were hypocritical and too proud.

> You know, all the Christians I had seen—the only thing that I hesitated about becoming a Christian was because all the Christians I saw in the past, I felt like they had bad character. But then they were saying they were Christians and I would always ask myself "Why do I want to be a Christian?" I felt like I had more integrity than some of those people. So I was really turned off by them. Well, I still feel the same way about many Christians, well Korean Americans. They are hypocritical many times.

The Korean American family has experienced conflicts as a result of the multiple cultural forces to which it is exposed. The following section will address both the strengths and weaknesses of these families through a review of relevant literature and the narratives of the second-generation Korean American study participants. The discussion will trace cultural conflicts and critical issues such as evolving gender roles in the Korean American community, filial piety, family honor, exogamy as a manifestation of familial conflict, enmeshment and familial absence.

Evolving Gender Roles in Marriage as a Source of Conflict

The lives of Korean American Women

While the Korean American family is congratulated as one of the most stable families in the U.S., due to its extremely low divorce rate[2], studies indicate some contradictory signs within the family. As discussed above, more than 75% of Korean American women work outside the home, as compared to the 20% that worked while in Korea. The wife working outside the home is also accepted more readily. Although most first-generation men and women still believe that a woman's place is at home, Korean American women are often obliged to work because their husbands or other male members of the families earn such low wages.

Many of these women work long hours, frequently in inadequate working conditions. Studies show that Korean immigrant wives continue to bear the main responsibility for traditional domestic tasks, whether they work outside the home or not.[3] Min reports that Korean immigrant working wives in New York City spend 75.5 hours a week between their job and their housework.[4] Many of these overworked women suffer from stress, role strain, and other forms of depression.[5] Stress often intensifies with the addition of a role or a role change without adequate preparation. This stress is further exaggerated by the unpreparedness of husbands and other family members trying to cope with the new situation.[6]

Laura Uba reports that the major reason Korean Americans seek counseling is the marital tension brought on by changes in spousal

---

[2]Hurh, The Korean Americans, 85-86. 100
[3]Won Moo Hurh and Kwang Chung Kim, "The Burden of Double Roles: Korean Wives in the U.S.A.," *Ethnic and Racial Studies*, 11 (1988): 151-167; Min, "Korean Americans," 222.
[4]Ibid.
[5]Ibid.
[6]Hurh, The Korean Americans, 91.

roles.[7]   According to her research, as Korean American wives work outside the home they become more Americanized and assertive. Their husbands tend to have difficulty coping with the changes in their wives and their families. They continue to maintain the traditional Korean notion that wives should be responsible for domestic tasks and child rearing, even while working outside the home. In the process, tension builds and marital relationships deteriorate. Hurh reports that many Korean American wives living with marital tension brought on by the double burden develop psychological problems.[8]

According to Young Song, 60% of the 150 immigrant Korean women who were surveyed in Chicago stated that their husbands battered them. Out of the 90 women, 70% reported that their physical abuse resulted in bruises and 57% reported being hit by a closed fist.[9] Joyce Lum, citing Song's findings, summarizes:

> 29% reported that the emotional/mental distress required medical attention. Of the battered women, more than a third reported the frequency of abuse to be at least once a month (37%), and 78% reported greater frequency and severity of abuse within the first 3 to 5 years of residency in the United States as compared to subsequent years in this country. More of these women preferred to allow time to solve the problem of abuse (42%), keep the problem in the family (35%), or pray (27%) rather than to talk to friends and relatives (12%) or seek professional help (5%).[10]

One of the reasons for such abuse might be the downward mobility experienced by the husbands. However, as Jung Ha Kim aptly points out, the centuries-old view and treatment of women as "morally inferior," based on Confucian ideologies, is continually at work in the Korean American family. Moreover, the plight of Korean womanhood is conveniently avoided in the Korean American church. In doing so, the Korean American church perpetuates discriminatory practices that

---

[7]Laura Uba, Asian Americans: Personality Patters, Identity, and Mental Health (New York: Guilford, 1994).

[8]Hurh, The Korean Americans, 91.

[9]Young I. Song, *Battered Women in Korean Immigrant Families* (New York: Garland, 1996).

[10]Joyce L. Jum, "Family Violence" in Lee C. Lee and Nolan W. S. Zane, eds., *Handbook of Asian American Psychology* (Thousand Oaks: Sage, 1998), 506-507.

view women as objects of mistreatment. Kim shares a summative remark from an interview she gathered in her research, which typifies Korean women's experience:

> The [Confucian] ideology had a tremendous impact in Korea. Korean women have been really oppressed by this and have internalized it to a great extent. . . And so many of us who are here in [the U.S.], even though we are not afflicted by the laws of Korea, still have much of the law written in our hearts and it impacts our lives [in the States].[11]

Uba reports that the Korean American women who decide to start their life anew through separation or divorce increase their risk of social alienation and, as a result, often suffer from depression, much more so than their Chinese American and Japanese American counterparts.[12]

Hurh contends that the maintenance of extended families is often a source of stress, leading to other psychosomatic symptoms for women. Hurh reports that women who had relatives living in the Chicago area had a higher degree of psychosomatic symptoms than those without relatives in the area.[13] This is supported by the fact that many Korean American families struggle to live out their filial obligation by taking care of aging parents. Many Korean Americans feel ashamed to let their parents move out or live in a nursing home. If the elderly parents leave home for some reason, it is construed as a public admission of failure to fulfill their obligation.[14] Again, the majority of this burden falls on Korean American women.

---

[11]Kim, Bridge-Makers and Cross-Bearers, 11.

[12]Uba, Asian Americans: Personality Patters, Identity, and Mental Health, 179.

[13]Hurh, The Korean Americans, 92.

[14]Kwang Chung Kim, Shin Kim, and Won Moo Hurh, "Filial Piety and Intergenerational Relationship in Korean Immigrant Families," *The International Journal of Aging and Human Development* 33 (1991): 456-477.

Internalized values of women and men
among second generation Korean Americans

Mother's Double Role

Many of the study participants are sympathetic toward their mothers, who had to take on a double role in the family. Most of these mothers had to work long hours, either at the family business or in some form of full time employment. When at home, the mothers managed every aspect of the household. Moreover, they were quite active in the church, taking care of various affairs, especially preparing Sunday dinner for the whole congregation.

Some young adults say they really started appreciating their mothers once they themselves started working and experiencing how difficult it is to balance work and home life. Tears welled up in his eyes when Dylan talked about his mother's selfless work for the family:

> The time when I really started appreciating my mother was after graduating from college and starting to work because it was hard getting up every day. And then coming home, you had to take care of your kids when they were younger. My mom used to cook dinner and I couldn't believe it. And "ah, now I know why she wanted all those massages" and stuff after dinner and it made a lot of sense.

Molly talked about her mother's death bringing her to appreciate deeply what her mother did for the family. As she herself experiences the interplay of housework and career, Molly reflected on her mother's handling of the two:

> (My father) goes for four months out of the year, and he has been doing that ever since I was maybe like 12. . . . So I guess you could say my mother and my father had a very traditionally Korean marriage. My mom didn't question him very often, he did whatever he pleased . . . Now that my mom has passed away, I have to do a lot of things that she used to do for him, and so that's something I'm not used to, doing his laundry, cooking his meals, keeping the house clean, things like that . . . My brother is another typical male who doesn't pick up after himself.

Concerns for how women are valued

Some of the young adults express their concern for the woman's role in the family and how they are treated in the society. Rose laments the role of women in Korean American culture when she says, "I know there is a typical Asian view that the man is dominant and the woman is submissive, staying at home, doing nothing." While Dylan senses some changes, he points out the need for more intentional changes regarding women's role in Korean American culture:

One of things that I think is changing a little bit is maybe the role of women. I know that is one area that's discussed and joked about quite a bit, but I think there are some valid points as to how to treat a woman that the Western culture does much better.

Luke shares his concern for the lack of freedom wives have:

What troubles me is the control that the husband has over the wife. And I think it's a little too stringent, and I feel that wives need some freedom as well. They need to be given some freedom not just work or stay with the children. They should decide for themselves.

Concerns for Korean American men

Many young adults expressed their concerns for the ways in which male members of the extended family are either detached from the family or chauvinistic. Daniel commented, "I don't like the way that a lot of Korean men don't take part in the family. They just don't know what to do with themselves."

Some of the young adults asserted that male members of the extended families do not talk much or have in-depth conversations. Dylan offered that he enjoys the more intimate atmosphere of his mother's side of family where there are more aunts, than his father's side with more uncles. Dylan shared:

I know my mom's side is really close, like the whole family and maybe it's because it's mainly women. They are very, very close. They talk to each other at least once a week—I think all of them— from whatever country. My father's side is more males and one female. And I don't see a level of closeness but more of kind of like we're family.

He recalled an incident that happened during an extended family gathering on his father's side:

> The most memorable family get together was when we were having a get-together, the power went out. I think we were watching the Sound of Music and the power went out, so basically we were stuck with each other. You know, kind of at a loss as to what to do — so we lit candles and it was very dim in there and we played like a group game. Some people watched but they were part of it by making comments and enjoying what was happening in the game. And then there was about maybe 15 or 20 people playing and we were interacting that way, but it didn't happen before and it has never happened again because basically we had no choice but to resort to something like that.

Some of the female young adults asserted that Korean males can be chauvinistic in the way they treat women. In sharing her feelings toward her father, Elisa revealed her feelings about Korean American males, in general. She said:

> I've given up on my dad. I mean no offense for what I am about to say, but I'm just very turned off by Korean men and right now I'm dating a Chinese man and I would never, ever go back to dating Koreans . . . I think they are very chauvinistic, just their mentality and all . . . I think I see a lot of my father in them and then sometimes I think that they are going to be just like my dad and so I am just like "yuck." They are very demanding, not open-minded, and demeaning.

An Exposé of Cultural Conflict in the Korean American Family

A Widening Gap between Parents and Children

Compounding these stresses on the Korean American woman and family is the ever-widening gap between parents and children. As discussed earlier, Korean American parents state that they came to the U.S. for quality education and a better future for their children. However, due to a variety of stresses in the continual process of adaptation into the U.S., the parents seldom cultivate quality relationships with their children. Korean American fathers were especially socialized to keep a distance from their children and not to express much affection to them. Influenced by Confucian teachings, many believe that intimacy with children undermines the children's respect for their parents. Thus parent-child play or parent-child interaction is limited within the Korean family.[15] Fathers, in particular, are absent for much of the parenting process throughout the life course of the typical Korean American family.

Since children of immigrants become Americanized at a much faster rate than their parents, the communication gap between the generations increases dramatically. Many parents work long hours and do not have time to teach their children the Korean language. As previously discussed, the first generation tends to have great difficulty in acquiring English. Moreover, since many parents work in isolated environments removed from mainstream American society, they remain highly ethnic and with low assimilation. Thus, the communication gap between the first and second generations widens both linguistically and culturally.[16]

The authority of parents

At least six salient themes emerged from the data describing how the study participants recollected their parents' authority.

Transmitting Korean culture and values

The young adults appreciated their parents for transmitting Korean culture and values into their lives. The parents often emphasized the importance of keeping their Korean heritage and reminded their children of their ethnic identity. Michelle spoke of her appreciation toward her parents for instilling her Korean identity. Michelle's father reminded her repeatedly that she would always be labeled as a Korean in American society:

> I remember as a child I thought of myself as American. I didn't think of myself as Korean, and so throughout grade school I thought of myself as American. I don't remember why--what precipitated the conversation--

---

[15]Uba, *Asian Americans: Personality Patters, Identity, and Mental Health*, 52; Robert Strom, S. H. Park, and S. Daniels, "Child Rearing Dilemmas of Korean Immigrants to the United States," *International Journal of Experimental Research in Education* 24 (1987): 91-102.

[16]Ibid, 52.

but I just remember there was one day that my father took me aside and sat me down in my room and gave me a lecture. I remember this incident distinctly because it upset me very much, and he sat me down and he told me, "We are living in America, you were born here, but you're not American." And he said "You might think you're American but when American people see you they don't think that you're an American, they see you as being Oriental. It doesn't matter what you think."

Another approach many of the parents utilized to instill Korean identity was to reiterate to their children the superiority of Korean culture over American culture. The parents also spoke of the superior nature of Korean people because their blood was not mixed with other races. Kelly recollects some of the questionable remarks made by her parents and her grandmother:

I remember growing up my parents and grandmother always saying to me—and it probably wasn't the best thing to say, but it was Ok—"Just remember that you are better than they (Americans) are." A very Korean thing. "You're pureblooded. You're all Korean. You know where you're from.

Julia talked about her father's negative reactions to her older siblings when they were dating Caucasians and discussed what she wants to do with her own marriage:

My dad did not really like it if my siblings were seeing someone that is Caucasian. He wouldn't really tell grandpa (who lives in Korea!) because my grandpa really has a problem with like going outside the race and stuff. They really had a hard time with my sister and my grandparents felt very strongly against it. For me, it's my parents that encouraged me to marry a Korean. I think I want that for myself too.

Many of the young adults spoke of attending Korean language schools for years on Saturdays or Sunday mornings at church. Not many, however, enjoyed their experience. Others took lessons in Tae Kwon Do (The Korean martial art) and Korean fan dance, at the encouragement and/or coercion of their parents.

Dictating the children's career trajectories
Many of the interviewees spoke of the ways in which their parents used their authority to dictate to these young adults the career trajectories of their lives and how they dealt with their parents in

response.   Many of these young adults voiced their discontentment toward their parents for their attempts to dictate career decisions. Betsy recalled her parents pressuring her to be an accountant or get a Ph.D. instead of becoming a schoolteacher:

> They (my parents) wanted me to go into accounting because it was stable. They knew that money isn't bad for a *woman* to be an accountant. They were worried about my future. Even with teaching, they didn't want me to go into it, but finally they changed their mind and let me do it. They're still hoping that I get a Ph.D. instead of *just* being a teacher.

She struggles with the fact that her parents have differing criteria for her career because she is a woman. Moreover, she does not appreciate her parents' hierarchal view of jobs based on arbitrary and incorrect information.

Daniel reported his father simply imploding when he changed his career path.

> We had a major conflict when I decided to change my major from electrical engineering to education. (Interviewer: Didn't you graduate with an engineering degree from college?) I did, but my junior year when I made the decision and I told my parents, my father got very upset. And his way of dealing with frustration is he shuts up. He doesn't talk, just quiet—when he's quiet you know he's angry about something. So for a period of time, I would say almost a year, we didn't talk much. I didn't want to talk to him either. It was so bad that there was a time when I needed some tuition money, he would usually take care of it. I didn't ask him, I just charged it on my Visa, and I was paid for that! But it was that bad.

Dictating much of the children's life affairs

Many of the young adults expressed that their parents have repeatedly dictated much of their life affairs.   Chris spoke of her parents as overly involved in her life, "I wished that they would let me do more stuff because they were very strict and very controlling and stuff like that."

Young reflected on how his life was shaped by his overly protective and zealous parents:

> Throughout my childhood years I was raised to be the responsible one. Being the only son in the family, my parents raised me very cautiously. They always had an eye on me wherever I went, made sure that I always

did the right things and said the right things and that carried on throughout my high school years as well. But I felt like I didn't really have a time where I could really grow up and be my own person. I felt like my parents were living out my life for me, and basically telling me what to do and how to live my life, do this and do that, so I really feel as if I didn't get to formulate my own ideas on my own. I didn't really find out who I was until I went college. And being out in Missouri by myself, I had a lot of time, for four years, I really found out who I was on my own, rather than having my parents there to tell me what to do all the time.

Young believes that his parents wanted to live out their lives through him, and that it was not until he moved out of state for college that he was able to figure out who he was by himself.

Some study participants spoke of the difficulty the parents have in terms of adjusting their parental authority once their children are married. These young adults recalled some major crises they themselves or their siblings experienced with their parents.

Paul says he used to go along with his parents and really did not see his parents as controlling people. He says his perception about his parents all changed when he and his wife had a child:

For Bethany's (their daughter) baptism, we wanted both parents to be present and they insisted that the baptism had to be at their church (which happens to be Paul's home church). But if we did that, Kelly's parents couldn't be there because they have their own church. See Kelly's father is the senior pastor. So in our eyes they (Paul's parents) are just elders of the church. They can just take off a Sunday and go to Kelly's parents' church. Then, everyone could be there and Kelly's grandfather, too . . . Well, we ended up have the baptism at my home church.

Soon after the incident, Paul was convinced that he needed to re-define his relationship with his parents. He came up with some very good reasons to leave his parents' church in order to avoid stirring up controversy. Paul and his family were finally able to leave the church, but his parents were still displeased with the decision. Paul says:

They were very unhappy that we were going to do that. They tried to lay a guilt trip on me. They said, "We stayed in this church through thick and thin, during splits and all. You need to stick with the church too. You shouldn't just leave because things aren't right." I explained to them why we were leaving . . . that we were the only married couple with a child, that there was no nursery system set up there and everyone else was solidly single, except one couple. We just explained them that we needed to be with couples that are in our situations . . . . But they didn't see it that way.

Brian shared about how his father-in-law insisted, among other things, that he and his wife buy a house soon after they got married. Brian said:

Well, the decision to buy a house wasn't really my decision, it was her parents'. Every time I went over there (his in-law's house), he kept on reminding me that renting is like throwing away money, which I don't necessarily agree with. I told him that I spent my last dollar on the wedding and honeymoon, so there is no way I could even come up with ten percent of a down payment . . . When he said he was willing to help with the down payment that's when I started to look for a house.

Brian realizes that he should have confronted his father-in-law for running his life, but he said that he did not have courage to do so:

It was probably my fault not confronting him while we were dating. When I realized that (her father's controlling tendency), I kind of like avoided being with him as much as possible . . . So when he made the offer of helping me with the down payment, I just took it.

Preferential treatment and comparison

The young adults spoke of some of the devastating effects of their parents' preferential treatment and comparison among siblings. The parents often set different standards for their children based on either gender or birth order. In general, male children had many privileges. They enjoyed easier access to the family car and a later curfew. For Betsy and her sisters, sleepovers were forbidden, even if they were church functions. Yet, for her brother, it was an entirely different story.

Moreover, fathers definitely favored the first-borns, especially if they were male, and mothers the youngest, especially if they were male. With favoritism came comparisons among the siblings. Daniel spoke of family dysfunction and detrimental effects on his sister as a result of parental preferential treatment for him and his brother and comparison between them and his sister:

My sister, however, always did something different, and I think part of that was because there was a lot of comparison between my sister and I when we were growing up. And so my sister got very frustrated with that and decided "I'm not going to do what Daniel does because then I will always be compared to him." So she always went her own way and because of that my brother and I, between us and her, we never had anything in common. So we are not as close to her as –at this point we would hope—that we want to be. That's a regret I think that I have, not being close to my sister, and now when we try to, she pulls back, so we are in a difficult situation with my sister right now because she keeps pulling back when we try to get closer to her.

Another form of preferential treatment and comparison is based on the child's academic ability and success. Rose said that her mother would single her out and push her to excel in her studies because her brothers (one had a hearing disability and the other was heavily into golf) were not doing well at school. Rose shared her reaction to the enormous pressure and shame brought on by her mother:

My mom was constantly pushing me succeed because she didn't expect much from my brothers at all. She drove me nuts, and for a long time when I would yell at her about that she would say, "But I'm doing it because I love you, and I'm doing it to make you a better person." So I made myself feel guilty that I would do that. She would say, "Why can't you take it in the loving way that I am trying to give it to you?"

Parental authority and physical absence

Many of these young adults considered parents as crucial role models in the development of children. However, when these young adults considered their own parents as models in their growing up years, they usually spoke of three themes: (1) parental non-involvement; (2) conflicted use of authority in absence; (3) misuse of authority.

Most of these young adults spoke of parents' non-involvement in their lives. Many parents worked long hours and were heavily involved in the Korean church or with other Korean friends. Betsy spoke about her relationship with her parents, who were absent from home because of long work hours:

I don't really spend that much time with them. I don't know if I could handle it, spending like a long, long time with them. And that's kind of bad, but it's just that I'm not used to it. I'm really not used to it because ever since we were little, we, it wasn't their fault, it was just that they had to work, it wasn't a choice for them.

Betsy is one of the few who wants to understand their parents' lack of involvement in their lives by suggesting their parents' obligation to provide for the family. For Luke, he still has a tough time reconciling the absence of his parents in his growing-up years:

> In high school I was on the tennis team, and my senior year I think I got third in the state. And to this day, my parents have yet to see or watch me play tennis, they don't even know what I look like when I play tennis. And so there are other things that I didn't get a lot of support on from my parents. They were never there for me.

Many study participants spoke of the fact that their parents greatly influenced their church attendance pattern. They regularly attended the Korean American church along with their parents, recounting the long lingering at the church every Sunday and some evenings during the week. A crucial point, however, is that they had virtually no interaction with their parents while they were at church.

Parents of these young adults did not spend much time with their children; neither did they fare well in the quality of the time. Michelle spoke of the lack of the quality in her relationship with her parents during her growing up years:

> I don't think I have ever heard my dad speak more than like 5 minutes at a time. The only times he has really talked for a lengthy of amount of time is when he is lecturing—when we've been really bad children. But other than that, I've never heard him speak and so my mom has always been like a liaison or mediator between my dad and us. But even with my mom, we never really shared personal things. It was always focused on financial or education or future. It was never emotion --it was never "How are you doing? How are you feeling? Are you okay?" I used to think that my dad wouldn't love us because he never expressed that, he never said it, and he never showed it. But the way that my dad shows love is that he does a lot of things for us. We pretend like things are ok.

Thus, according to these young adults, their parents did not do very well in terms of quantity or quality time. Moreover, they spoke of their parents making no significant contributions to their lives in terms of proper use of authority. Instead, the young adults talked about the authority of their parents as eroded and stifling to their lives.

Many recalled incidences in which parents, especially mothers, desperately attempted to exercise their authority in absence. The parents would repeatedly call home from their businesses to check up on their children, telling them to refrain from watching television, and to do homework and other chores. The interviewees shared that they disregarded their parents' instructions and did what they wanted to do. These young adults say that they did not appreciate the nagging voices of their mothers and the threats they received from their fathers. Abigail said:

> Since my mom was never home, she used to check up on me . . . I came home from school, I turned the TV on, and I just watched it until ten o'clock at night, started my homework at ten or eleven o'clock and it was always like that. My mom did not have to know.

Reflecting on how she became an independent person, Molly credited her time alone during her growing up years:

> I was a very independent kid. And I was the type who questions authority all the time—"I don't have to listen to you, just because you're older than me doesn't mean I have to listen to you" kind of a thing. And "You don't know better than me." I was really obnoxious and I think that's how I came across with everyone. "You have nothing to offer me." I had a very bad attitude. (Interviewer: Where do you suppose you got that, if I may ask?) Where do I think I got that? I don't know, maybe from being on my own all the time, having to be very independent and self-sufficient, arguing with my mom on the phone all the time . . . .

Many of the young adults felt their fathers did not use authority properly in dealing with the family. They recalled their fathers always doing as they pleased, and the family members were expected to follow those decisions. Abigail reminisced about her struggle to love her father because of the kind of situation into which he put the family:

> My father kind of has usurped his authority in my family because he is very idealistic about his dreams of making it big in business. But the problem was that he didn't really have any practical skills or patience to carry that through. He had opportunities, but his own character lacked patience . . . You can't just think that there is going to be a sweep of success for you, you have to work hard. Because he was so caught up in making it big, he compromised a lot of his resources and kind of came to a point where he became bankrupt, literally bankrupted.

Some of the young adults had traumatic experiences with their fathers in their growing up years. They recalled fathers breaking out in anger, destroying small appliances and dishes, and physically and verbally abusing them.   Young told of his experiences with his alcoholic father:

> He would come home drunk and he would physically abuse me and there were many instances where I did something wrong and I felt like my dad used that against me physically.   So, there were many times where I questioned his love for me.   But there were times where we did have good times.   We would go outside and play catch, throw the ball around and he would laugh.   I remember one instance where we were fixing his car and he was just backing up and I thought he was going away, but I ran after him and said, "Take me, take me with you."   And he said, "I'm not going anywhere, I'm just backing up the car."   And I remember that instance, my dad really meant a lot to me, that I didn't want to be away from him.   But yet as I was growing up I find myself getting away from him, wanting to get away from him, remembering all the past hurts and all the bitterness that I held within me.

The First Generation's Outlook on
Future Generations of Korean Americans

In an attempt to maintain the Korean culture and language, the first generation has often forced the second generation to accept traditional Korean ways and language.   In extrapolating the future of the Korean American community, some first-generation scholars entertain, and thus give credence to, the first-generation parents and suggest that the 1.5[17] and second-generation Korean Americans will continue to employ the adhesive adaptation strategy of the parent generation in their lives. Many of the scholars also insist that future generations will lead lives that are bicultural and bilingual in nature.[18]

Many first-generation parents and their churches also have assumed this general outlook as the normative course of development for the 1.5 and second generations.   Indeed, some 1.5-generation Korean Americans have adopted the adhesive strategy in such a way that they are adequately bicultural and bilingual in their spheres of life.

---

[17]1.5 generation Korean Americans refers to those who immigrated as a family when they were between the ages of 7 to 15 year old.

[18]Hurh, *The Korean Americans*, 80-81.

However, what the first-generation Korean Americans were not able to predict was the rapid rate of the acculturation process among many 1.5 and second-generation
Korean Americans in adapting to the American way of life and internalizing American values. Moreover, these descendents of the first generation have concurrently lost their Korean culture, especially language. As a result, there has been much generational conflict within the Korean American family. The conflict is mainly due to the cultural differences between the two generations and an inability and unwillingness to understand each other.

Vicarious living through children

One root problem of the cultural conflict between the two generations lies in the unrealistic and insatiable expectations the first generation brings to bear on the second generation, as a way of repaying the sacrifice the parents made. This payback rarely involves monetary or any other tangible compensation. Nor do the parents attempt to manipulate their children by threatening to withhold their inheritance, such as small businesses or other assets, for many second-generation young adults show no interest in these goods.[19] The most important payback is through high educational achievements, making the parents proud and their sacrifice worthwhile.

Furthermore, Bok-Lim C. Kim points out the "incongruent demands" parents make on their children in terms of assimilation into mainstream American society, asserting that:

> They (the parents) want them (the children) to be successful in school but to be obedient, respectful, and humble at home, not realizing that the attributes needed to succeed in American schools are assertiveness, initiative, and independent thinking. They want their children to be proficient in English and to retain fluency in Korean. They restrict after-school activities with English-speaking peers but expect them to be socially popular. They profess no prejudice toward other racial and ethnic groups, yet resist interracial dating and marriage and explain this in terms of the importance of compatibility between the two families.[20]

Another source of conflict is the conflict between the first-generation's collectivistic and second-generation's individualistic

---

[19]Hurh, The Korean Americans, 67.
[20]Bok-Lim C. Kim, "Korean Families," 287.

orientations in decision making and problem-solving approaches.[21] First-generation parents manifest their authority over their children by supervising and making unilateral decisions in terms of career choice. The parents' prevalent preferences for occupations involve prestigious professional occupations such as medicine, physical science, and law.[22] Many second-generation Korean Americans indeed choose occupations consistent with parental values of success.[23]   However, strife and conflict often result in the process, especially among those who wish to pursue occupations that are deemed to be less prestigious or "nonacademic."

While some predict that parents will permit a greater number of career choices as they become more Americanized, Korean American families, especially parents, continue to retain major influence over college selection and career decisions for young adults.[24]   Another important power the parents exercise is in the areas of mate-selection for their young adult children and, once they are married, a wide range of family issues.[25]   More of these issues will be discussed in the section below.

Voices of Obligation and Filial Piety: Values for Family Cohesion or Disintegration?

The major source of the generational conflict between parents and children lies in the varied understanding and manifestations of filial piety in the Korean American family. J. Hendricks and C. A. Leedham astutely observe that filial piety is:

---

[21]Yee, et. al., "Families: Life-Span Socialization in a Cultural Context," 94; F. T. L. Leong, "Career Development Attributes and Occupational values of Asian American and White American College Students" Career Development Quarterly, 39 (1991), 221-230.

[22]Uba, Asian Americans: Personality Patterns, Identity, and mental Health.

[23]M. S. Kim, "Culture-Based Interactive Constraints in Explaining Intercultural Strategic Competence" in R. L. Wiseman and J. Koester, eds., Intercultural Communication Competence (Newbury Park: Sage, 1993), 132-150.

[24]Yee, et. al., "Families: Life-Span Socialization in a Cultural Context."

[25]Ibid.

nearly always undergirded by an ironclad control over whatever younger people aspired to. Principles of veneration are likely to result from the leverage older people have to ply.[26]

It is less probable for first-generation parents to control their children with material resources in America since the second generation is less dependent on the first for their livelihood. However, many first-generation Korean Americans, especially the elderly, consider filial piety as the key cultural variable for the functioning of the family.[27] This is manifested in various ways.

Voice of Obligation to Parents and Their Expectations

The internalized voice of obligation to the parents possesses a strong timbre and overtones in the lives of the study participants. This voice clearly exists in the social milieu of the Korean American culture. These young people have learned from an early age to honor and respect their parents. They are also to follow through on their parental expectations as the ultimate sign of obedience. In the process, parental expectations have become the motivating factors for success in their lives. These young men and women realize that their parents, especially being first generation immigrants, live vicariously through their achievements and successes.

Isabella reminisced about how she was obligated to pursue a career in either journalism or media. She talked about internalizing her parents' subtle expectations:

Well, my parents had really high aspirations for me to be one of the few Asians in the field, especially Korean. They wanted me to be like on TV, like Connie Chung and be a Korean broadcaster. And I think that there is a lot of pride for them that I was going to Northwestern in the journalism program and it was a pretty prestigious program at the time. So they were really excited about my being there, liked to brag about me to people. So I felt like my parents were real unusual, they would never tell me what to do, but they would subtly kind of let me know—you know, "Oh, it would be nice, wouldn't you like to be like her?" And they would point to TV

---

[26]J. Hendricks and C. A. Leedham, "Making Sense: Interpreting Historical and Cross-Cultural Literature on Aging" In P.V. D. Bagnell and P. S. Soper, eds., *Perceptions of Again in Literature: A Cross-Cultural Study* (Westport: Greenwood, 1989), 7.

[27]Lee and Zane, Handbook of Asian American Psychology, 193.

and such. . . So when I wanted to go to graduate school in psychology, I felt like I would let them down.

Rose talked about how her mother and father were trying to live out their dream through her success. She felt very pressured and grew resentful, especially toward her mother. Yet, she cautiously expressed her frustration, seeking to be empathetic to her mother:

> She was trying in some ways to live her life through me. But that doesn't take away the fact that she did all those things out of immense, tremendous love. I mean albeit there was some holding on and some bad boundaries and some enmeshment in our relationships, but certainly she did all those things out of love. .

Rose recounted that her father, who initially held low expectation for her, started having high aspirations for her to become a medical doctor. She contends that it all stemmed from his profound disappointment with his sons, who struggled with academics. Rose continued:

> There were a couple of times that I got angry at him (my father) because he is so disappointed that I wasn't applying to medical school. I was so angry with my mom he thought that I was doing that to spite her. You know, his sister is a doctor and he had all these dreams for me and obviously Dave and Steve (my brothers) were not fulfilling those dreams for him by any stretch of the imagination . . . My dad is very disappointed in them, so he sort of looked to me. It's funny, he had no expectations for me academically or career-wise cause I was the daughter, but then he started to put a lot of his hopes on me.

Many other young adults feel obligated to receive further education to make their parents' joy complete. In particular, the mothers long to live out their dreams vicariously through their children. Sam talks about how his mother continues to push him to get a Ph.D. He sees it as a form of redemption of her difficult life as a single mother:

> My mom continues to encourage me to get my Ph.D. because I think for her it would be sort of a redeeming factor . . . She has told me that after she divorced she did not date other men. And she did not pursue that direction just because she didn't want people talking or she wanted to let it be known that her house was very a respectful house and she is going to bring up some respectful children. And I think she thinks if I get a PhD that would be some kind of redeeming factor that—"See how well I raised my kid even though I was divorced. He still comes from a good family."

— which I think many traditional Asians would not think that divorced families are good families.

For some, saving their own and their parents' face from public embarrassment is seen as the minimum requirement in terms of their obligation to family. As previously shared, Elisa decided to finish her undergraduate degree, among other reasons, to save her parents' face and accrue some legitimacy for her character.

Filial Piety and Academic Achievement

While filial piety can be manifested in numerous ways, the most direct impact on the Korean American family has been in the area of education. As discussed above, many Korean immigrants state that they came to the U.S. for their children's education. As a corollary, the immigrants equate their children's success in education with social prestige and reward for the sacrifices they made. Toward that goal, the immigrants work hard to ensure their children's entrance into prestigious universities in the U.S.

Many of the immigrants believe the critical step toward achieving that goal is to move to suburbs known for good public education.[28] Toward that purpose, they work extremely hard to relocate. In the family, the parents exert constant pressure to motivate their children to excel in school. Parenthetically, in concert with parents' efforts, the Korean newspapers regularly have feature articles on successful Korean Americans. Moreover, the Korean American church has customarily recognized them as the model Christians. In all, Korean American families "teach children the importance of repaying parents for their sacrifices, and one highly valued path is through high educational achievement."[29] Several studies report that:

a strong home environment with strict monitoring of children's free time, investment in educational opportunities, and parental emphasis on respect

---

[28]Hurh, The Korean Americans, 94.

[29]Barbara W. K. Yee, Larke N. Huang, and Angela Lew, "Families: Life-Span Socialization in a Cultural Context" in Lee C. Lee and Nolan W. S. Zane, eds., *Handbook of Asian American Psychology* (Thousand Oaks: Sage, 1998), 91.

for education and expectation of achievement were correlated with high academic achievement.[30]

According to Laura Uba, Korean parents exert greater pressure on their children to get good grades than the parents of Caucasian American children. She maintains that, while parents' demand is extremely high, encouragement is inadequate.[31]   Koreans parents provide much less academic help and support than Caucasian and other Asian American parents.

Many Korean American children are then left without parental support for academic achievement.   Instead, children are merely pestered verbally to excel by their own effort.   Yet even if children excel in school, parents are not known to acknowledge their children's success.[32]   Studies also show that teachers and peers often assume and expect Korean American children to excel in academics.[33]   Uba asserts that pressure exerted by parents and perceived expectations from teachers and peers are some of the major causes of stress among Korean American children.[34]

Another study shows that undergraduate grade point averages (UGPA) for Korean American freshmen at eight University of California campuses in the fall of 1984 were lower than that of White, Chinese, Japanese, Indian, and other Asian Americans.[35]   The low

[30]Yee, et. al., "Families: Life-Span Socialization in a Cultural Context," 91; D. Mordkowitz and H. Ginsburg, "Early Academic Socialization of Asian-American College Students," *Quarterly Newsletter of the Laboratory of Comparative Human Cognition*, 9 (1987), 85-91; E. Yao, "A Comparison of Family Characteristics of Asian-American and Anglo-American High Achievers" *International Journal of Comparative Sociology*, 26 (1985), 198-208.

[31]Laura Uba, Asian Americans: Personality Patterns, Identity, and Mental Health, 44-45.

[32]Yee, et. al., "Families: Life-Span Socialization in a Cultural Context," 83-135.

[33]Y. Lee, Academic Success of East Asian Americans: An Ethnographic Comparative Study of East Asian American and Anglo American Academic Achievement (Seoul, Korea: American Studies Institute, National University Press, 1987).

[34]Uba, Asian Americans, 133.

[35]Stanley Sue and J. Abe, "Predictors of Academic Achievement among Asian American and White Students," *College Board Report No. 88-11* (New York: College Entrance Examination Board, 1988).

UGPA for Korean American students may be another source of stress and low self-esteem. Low GPA can be construed as a failure to live up to the expectations of parents and others. The story of a 17-year-old Korean American named Jack depicts an identity problem closely related to his parents' expectation.

> He (Jack) was anxious about living up to the occupational aspirations that his parents had for him, feeling torn between wanting to please his parents but simultaneously feeling unmotivated to do his schoolwork and feeling his parents cared only about his academic success and not about him personally. Jack's symptoms included being withdrawn, depressed, having a poor appetite, and having difficulty sleeping.[36]

The gap between the two generations is not due to lack of respect on the part of the second generation for the first-generation. The second generation appreciates the social and psychological sacrifices that first generation parents have made for their children. Most of them share their parents' dream of success in the U.S.[37] The following excerpt from a speech made by a Korean American student at Yale University exemplifies how many second-generation children understand their parents' predicament:

> Listen, [our parents] left their country, the only country they ever knew, with three thousand years of family history and tradition left behind. And for what, the land of opportunity? Do you think their situation here is that great? Mom and Dad were some of the lucky ones. A doctor, at least, can still work as a doctor in this country. Some parents came, giving up Ph.D.s and very respected positions, knowing that all their life work would be rendered absolutely useless in this new "land of opportunity." They had to open grocery stores, laundromats, and restaurants, working sixteen-hour days, always being treated as inferior because of their color and their accents, suffering the "humiliation of the immigrant." But they had their reasons. No amount of sacrifice was too much for their children. Nothing in their lives meant more to them than their legacy—us.[38]

---

[36]Uba, Asian Americans: Personality Patterns, Identity, and mental Health, 113.

[37]Bok-Lim C. Kim, "Korean Families," in Lee C. Lee and Nolan W. S. Zane, eds., *Handbook of Asian American Psychology* (Thousand Oaks: Sage, 1998), 281-294.

[38]Quoted in Hurh, *The Korean Americans*, 67. Paul Hahn, "Narrowing the Generation and Culture Gaps: A Letter to a Younger Brother," *Korean and Korean American Studies* 3 (1989), 23-24.

For most of the interviewees, obligation toward their parents is not necessarily a negative factor in their lives. Many of them genuinely want to express love for their parents in a pleasing manner. The term often used in Asian cultures to express love for parents is that of filial piety. Albert shared his genuine gratitude toward his parents:

I thank God for my parents. They made great sacrifice for us, coming from a very poor country, giving up everything to send me to a Ivy League school . . . They thank God for all the opportunities I had . . . A part of me feels the same way, I'm a product of my parents. I thank God for all the blessings I was given, and I want to follow him. And devote my life to pay back all the sacrifices they made for me.

Even when parents give their children freedom to change their career, some of the study participants agonize about making the change. For example, Kelly so desires to please her parents, who have been so proud of her becoming successful as a newspaper reporter. Even with her parents' full permission after difficult exchanges, Kelly struggles with her choice to change career. She shared the internal struggle to show her filial piety:

This sense of obedience to my parents, even at 26 going on 27, wanting to honor my parents and not wanting to disappoint them and knowing that I could probably just plug on with this journalism thing. And I don't know—get a promotion, do all the things that they can talk about to their friends and glow with pride. And yet knowing deep down inside I would come home feeling just as empty as I did before. To make my parents happy and how upset after a lot of talking and prayer, my parents did come and say to me, "No matter what you do, we are very proud of what you are doing in your life. And we trust you. You are an adult and you know better than we do what God desires for you."

In short, many of the interviewees want their parents to live a comfortable life. They do appreciate their parents' wish for their children not to repeat what they had to go through. In response, these young adults take the voice of filial piety very seriously and allow it to partially dictate the affairs of their lives. Thinking about their aging parents, especially after experiencing significant changes in life situations, has caused them   to re-evaluate and re-direct their life trajectories.

Respect for elders

One aspect of Korean culture that all these young adults appreciate is giving respect to the elders, closely related to filial piety. The study participants spoke of the honor and worth they desire to express to the older generation. Luke values the way in which "Korean people are really respectful to each other. They might not know each other, but they bow to other parents and all. . . I love the honor and respect for the parents."

Dylan concurred with Luke when he said:

I love the (Korean) tradition and the fact that there is a lot of respect for the older generation. It's by culture, not by "well he needs to give me respect first," but you just have respect for the elders and culture.

Dylan vividly remembers how his father took care of his grandmother when she was in the hospital. He shared about witnessing his father's filial piety lived out in a very tangible manner. Dylan told the story:

One thing about my father I remember that I can really point out. I was very happily surprised as, when my grandmother was sick, he went the hospital every day and just to be there with her because he thought that she might be uncomfortable and also to translate for her and stuff like that. He spent significant hours just sitting at the hospital and I thought that was a good son.

Kris spoke about how she and her family honored her deceased father. She recalled a very important action she took out of her respect for her father. She and her fiancée decided to postpone their wedding:

A month before we were scheduled to get married my dad passed away. So we postponed it for a year because we didn't want to get married and then be disrespectful--kind of like a Korean tradition type of thing.

She continued telling the story about how she and her family followed her father's wish about how and where he wanted to be buried. She shared:

> We did the whole Korean tradition where you have to wrap up the dead body in a certain cloth and we watched all of that and that was all very sad . . . He wanted to be buried where his mom and dad were buried in Tae Jeon (a city in Korea) and so he was buried there, and then after that I came back.

Desire to please parents

Many of the young adults expressed their desire to please their parents as much as they are able. They often see it as their duty and desire to pay back all the sacrifices their parents made for them and their future. Albert spoke about how he "just wants to please them and be a good son." He then talked about how he has been growing in his appreciation for his parents in recent years and his commitment to honor them through his life. He shared:

> Getting to know her (my wife) kind of opened my eyes to how much I owe and how much I really love my parents, how to show that not only by words and actions. I'd like to support them, I'd like kind of live out their dreams, to fulfill part of their dreams, why they came to the States.

Some young adults, especially first-born males, talked about their desire to take care of their parents as they grow older. Being the only son in the family, Brian wants to take more care of his parents, even though his parents are still active and do not require any assistance. Brian shared:

> I'm the only son . . . I definitely accept that role and when I was looking for a house it was definitely a key decision of where, how far is it from my parents. I think that was a little bit more important than how far is it from my work. Luckily, my work and my parents are only 5-10 minutes apart. I feel the urge to go home at least once or twice a week just to check up on them. . . They are right up the road. It's very convenient to stop there. I definitely talk to my parents about their future and all.

Exogamy as a Manifestation of the Familial Conflict?

While no one variable or model can fully explain the phenomenon of exogamy, it has been generally construed as the result of acculturation and assimilation of ethnic Americans. For example, the acculturation/ assimilation model has explained the rate of exogamy among Japanese Americans who have had a long immigrant history in America adequately. However, for Korean Americans, who have had a relatively shorter history in America, other models are needed to explain the high rate of outmarriages in recent years.[39] Because outmarriage is perceived negatively and considered as dishonor to the family by first-generation Korean Americans[40], the high rate of outmarriages among Americanized Korean Americans needs to be considered carefully in order to understand the second-generation experience.

According to Lee and Yamanaka, the exogamy rate of Korean Americans is 31.8%, and the majority of outmarriages involved white spouses.[41] The exogamy rate for Korean American females is significantly higher than that of males.[42] Kitano reports that 62.5% and 100% of second and third-generation Korean American females living in Los Angeles County in 1989, respectively, have outmarried.[43] One of the push factors for the female to outmarry has been the persistence of male superiority in the Korean culture which often continues even in the Korean American family. Moreover, the white male has also been

---

[39]Harry Kitano, Diane Fujino, and Jane Takahashi Sato, "Interracial Marriages: Where Are the Asian Americans and Where Are They Going?" in Lee C. Lee and Nolan W.S. Zane, eds., *Handbook of Asian American Psychology* (Thousand Oaks: Sage, 1998), 233-260.

[40]Hurh, The Korean Americans, 73-75.

[41]S. M. Lee and K. Yamanaka, "Patterns of Asian American Intermarriage and marital Assimilation" in *Journal of Comparative Family Studies* 21, 287-305. 79.3% of outmarriages of Korean Americans involved white spouses. The outmarriage rate of Korean Americans was only 2% lower than that of Japanese Americans who have much longer history in America.

[42] Kitano, Fujino, and Sato, "Interracial Marriages," 241-242, 249.

[43]Harry Kitano, "Korean Intermarriage: A Tale of Two Cities" in Ho-Youn Kwon, ed., *Korean Americans: Conflict and Harmony* (Chicago: Covenant Publications, 1994), 85.

traditionally attracted to Asian American women, who they perceive to be more submissive than white females.[44]

There are several other models concerning out-group marriage that may be requisite in explaining the phenomenon among Korean Americans. One model is based on the concept of hypergamy, marriage unions on the basis of differential status.[45] Fujino reports that interracially married Asian Americans have a propensity to barter/bargain to "exchange their higher educational attainment for the higher racial status of their White spouses."[46] This model supports the notion that Korean Americans tend to have a negative view of their own physical appearance and are ashamed of the people they associate with ethnically.[47] As a result, they wish to be associates with Caucasian Americans in order to fit into mainstream American society.[48]

Another useful model under consideration draws from psychological and psychoanalytical perspectives. Freeman and others contend that individuals marry away from their ethnic group as "an acting out of a psychological problem" because they "feel rejected by their own group and become hostile and rebellious."[49] Others suggest that individuals of a lower-status group intermarry in order to compensate and move up to a higher status that they cannot obtain themselves. Grier and Cobbs assert that intermarriage can be construed as a means of managing Oedipal fantasies.[50] They argue that the inadequate repression of attraction to the opposite-sex parent may cause an adult-child to seek a relationship with an individual who is different from the parent. Some of the differences may be in the forms of different race, ethnicity, and culture.

A rigorous indoctrination of old world values was, as a whole, attempted through the Korean American church. In the process, both

---

[44]Lee, Orientals.

[45]Ibid., 251-252.

[46]Ibid., 251; D. C. Fujino, "Asian American Interracial Relationships: Moving from Description Information to a Theoretical Framework." Paper presented at the convention of the American Psychological Association, San Francisco. August, 1991.

[47]Uba, Asian Americans, 83.

[48]Lee and Zane, Handbook of Asian American Psychology, 139.

[49]Ibid., 252.

[50]W. H. Grier and P. M. Cobbs, *Black Rage* (New York: Basic Books, 1968).

generations have experienced much stress, anxiety, self-depreciation, and identity ambivalence. This reality, at least for the first generation, is described as an existential limbo.[51] It is in this cultural tug-of-war that many of the second generation have been raised and are now grown up.

Voices of Absence and Enmeshment

Insignificant or Partial Voices of Parents

One of the characteristics of voice is that the physical presence of the person is not required for a voice to function in the self. Instead, voice has to do with the embodiment of the speaking personality that is internalized in the self. Moreover, the voice often functions in the physical absence of the person whose voice is a part of the self. In order for the voice to function as a speaking personality, an ample amount of either physical presence or other forms of significant encounters are required prior to its internalization in the self.

For some of the study participants, the significant encounter for internalizing their parents as speaking personalities took the form of physical absence of the parents. In other words, the absence of parents in the lives of the study participants during much of their formative years generated insignificant parental voices in the functioning of the self as young adults.

The insignificant parental voices in the self of the interviewees often create a vacuum in which other internalized voices compete to fill the void. This phenomenon often results in dis-equilibrium among the internalized voices in the self. As Molly reminisced on her childhood, an interplay between her parents and her schoolteachers suggests a manifestation of such dis-equilibrium. Molly shared:

> I had a really nice teacher in fifth grade. Her name was Mrs. Yamuchi. She was Japanese. And I really liked her, she was really nice, laid-back, very motherly figure, very grandmotherly figure rather, so I had a good time that year. Let me think, Mrs. Marlin was really nice in third grade, I really liked her, she was another very kind and motherly woman . . . I remember all my teachers' names from kindergarten on up . . . Possibly, maybe I needed some attention that I wasn't getting at home from my

---

[51]Hurh, The Korean Americans, 145.

mom. She was never home and they (the teachers) took an interest in me. I mean all these teachers that I mentioned I liked probably because they took an interest in me. Maybe teachers have their favorites and maybe I was one of them and they paid particular attention to me. . . . I was very quiet, I never said anything in school, when I got home it was a different story. My parents thought why don't you talk in school, you talk at home so much. See, my teachers always say "Oh, your daughter never talks, she's very good." "This is not my kid," (my mother would say) because at home I'm like "ah, ah, ah" and I was very quiet at school. I didn't see much of her, so maybe I wanted her (my mother's) attention. Maybe that's why I used to talk too much at home.

For many of the young adults, the voice of the father is particularly insignificant. They reported having minimal interactions with their fathers. Kris shared the nature of her interactions with her father. She said, "When I was growing up my dad was kind of like one of those quiet, I mean he wasn't quiet, but he really didn't like to talk to us, only to tell us to do stuff basically."

They also perceive that their fathers were emotionally detached from the family much of the time, with an exception of occasional angry outbursts. Isabella was sympathetic towards her father when she spoke about his uneasiness sharing emotional issues:

Yes, there have been times when I have attempted to share what's going on in my life. But he gets so uncomfortable. I'll be trying to talk to him and he will watch TV. And I know he is listening but it's like he is not comfortable with it, so he can't make eye contact with me and talk. And he tries to at times, but it's just he has a hard time with it . . . I don't think he has ever experienced it (having deep conversations with his parents) himself. He doesn't really know what that's like to talk with his father deeply about those kinds of things, since there was a cut-off (referring to his father's childhood as an orphan in South Korea, after coming down from the North) in his own life. And I think my dad, the way he dealt with what happened was to just to become kind of cold, like kind of a hard person. And he had to sort of play this really weird role of being a dad to his younger siblings and yet also just being a kid himself. So he was more of a disciplinarian, I think, growing up and definitely dad was a disciplinarian in our home, so that automatically puts a little bit of a wedge between feeling free to communicate everything with us.

Some of the interviewees deem their fathers to be task-oriented, as well. Dylan talked about his father's expectations of him, "Growing up my father was always like school, or work, or something. ... . Oriented to something like tasks, education, like a task master to us." Thus, the study participants often referred to their fathers as disciplinarians who were simply not there for their children in many ways the children needed them.

Voice of Enmeshment

Some of the interviewees, especially the male young adults, spoke of their enmeshed relationships with their mothers. Sometimes, the enmeshment relationship extends to their sisters, as well. These young adults maintained that their fathers were not only distant from them, but were distant from their mothers, as well.

In many cases, these young adults remember their mothers' over-involvement in their lives, often blurring the emotional boundary between mother and son. Rose shared:

> I would have liked it more if she took care of herself more and let us become a little more independent and let us fall on our face a little more, learn things the hard way.

Luke's account of his life with his mother and three older sisters typifies such enmeshment relationships and how such relationships function as a voice of enmeshment. Luke recounted his relationships with his mother and sisters:

> I think before it used to be very, very controlling. I remember my mother very, very strict. I went out—gosh, she wouldn't let me cross the street sometimes and all my friends were doing all these things and I couldn't do them. Having three older sisters as well was like having four mothers. So they are always telling me what to do. And I didn't really realize what kind of person I was until college . . . I felt like I was this robot in high school, I just did what they told me to do. All I did was follow them and I was quiet, never said what I thought. And I think that was so bad . . . I'm not able to share, I'm not very relational because I just stand there and stay quiet . . . My mom and my three sisters, brought me up like this and so I didn't know what the heck I wanted to do.

Luke continued to tell about the strains of such relationships in his life:

I used to be so quiet and they used to say, "Why don't you say something—kind of in a Korean angry way—why don't you say something?" Sometimes she would say " Are you some kind of dummy?" That really hurt a lot. Verbally, I felt like I was abused. She was to me like a time bomb, she would just go off . . . She has only few friends. She is very disciplined . . . Basically, I was her life. I can't fault for her for caring for me too much . . . My sisters used to give me their credit cards for me to spend money . . . It was good for a while, but I got out of control.

The enmeshed relationship between mother and child could take many forms as new situations arose. One of the more common incidents among these young adults that often develop into a family crisis is the marriage of a son. Some of the Korean American mothers have a difficult time letting go of their sons in marriage. Young adults reported various crises in the family surrounding their marriage. Some of the manifestations of the crises ranged from the experience of an inordinate stress level in the family to the indefinite severance of family relationships. Kris remembered the experience with her mother-in-law:

It was pretty bad from his side of the family. Because he is the only son, and they just had in the back of their mind—they had their own perception about me. Because he has always been kind of a mommy's boy and he always listened to his mom. And his mom has always kind of raised him like—basically he was extremely close with his mom. And his mom was making all the decisions for him, even when he was older. So it was really hard for her to kind of see somebody else like making decisions with him. And I can't really speak for her, but she didn't want to let go of her son. And I wasn't what she had perceived in her mind.

Another form of the enmeshment relationship that often manifests in the relationship between the parents and their adult-child is the parents planting doubts about the adult-child's decisions. Some of the young adults spoke of their parents questioning the decisions they have made, especially when problems arise based on the decisions they made. While appreciating their parents' concern for them, especially in regard to career and marriage, these young adults complained about their parents being inquisitive and planting doubts in their lives.

While Betsy realizes her parents' deep concern for her safety and comfort, she feels like they are discontent with what she is doing and question her judgments. She shared:

. . . They bother you a lot.   Even now sometimes they really bother me, they are like, "You should have taken a CPA test", even though it would be a waste of time because I am not going to go into accounting.   Or they are like, "You should have found a job in a northern suburb." . . .   "Just let me be," I want to say to them.

Television: Voice in the Absence

The power of Media
A filler in the absence.   Many of the interviewees spoke about the addictive nature of TV watching in their growing-up years.   They also talked about its enduring power over their lives as a powerful voice. For them, TV watching started as a time filler when they were home alone.   Daniel spoke of the TV watching habits he acquired from his growing-up years that continue to this day:

> Once we got in the house, there was really nothing else to do except watch TV, we didn't have any family time.   So just by nothing else to do, we watched a lot of TV and that just became a habit, I think.   So high school was the same—high school was pretty easy for me.   And once I got in college it was just a habit—you'd go home and even in college you have work to do, but you watch TV first.   It was a big part of my life and it still is.   If I have nothing to do then TV automatically goes on and I know there are a lot of things I could read.   I know that there are other things I should be doing but my first choice would be watch TV.   It helps me relax.

Its Addictive Power.   These young adults spoke of walking into an empty house, turning on the TV, and having it on constantly.   While Abigail shared about her addiction to TV watching, she referred to TV as a companion for the latchkey generation:

> Since my mom was never home, I came home from school, I turned the TV on, and I just watched it until ten o'clock at night, started my homework at ten or eleven o'clock and it was always like that.   I know every show on the television.   I have kind of an addictive personality and so, yeah, one thing about TV, once it's on I cannot turn it off.   It was just so difficult.

Abigail then reflected further on her TV watching habits.   She shared that she was able to uncover some of the issues associated with her TV addiction:

During my college years, that was one thing that really—I just did not want to go home because I knew that once I went home somehow I could not avoid the TV set and once it was turned on, I could not move. Something about like being in other environments-I was totally okay, we have TV in the dorm rooms, in the lobbies, but I never stopped to watch it, it was always like when I went home I could not turn it off. (Interviewer: Any reason? I mean TV is TV. If you are addicted to TV, you would watch it wherever you go. No?) Right, but I think it had a lot to do with my home environment, too. Even now, even at home, I still — I have to try — whenever I'm in a home environment, it is very difficult.

At this point, Abigail discussed how she has tried to break the addictive pattern. She also shared the struggles she had to deal with through the process. She said:

I just really have to ask the Lord to help me in this in order to break it. After a certain point, God really did that because I would go home and I'd watch the TV for two or three hours. Then I would get these massive headaches, I could not—I had to turn it off. And I would fight clouds of depression and that type of thing. God literally had to give me a physical reaction to watching too much TV, to really kind of help break me of that.

The Media as a Socialization Tool
The "moral giver". Many of these young adults believe that TV has been a powerful socialization tool in their lives. Molly talked about the profound influence TV had in her life. She also referred to TV as her "moral giver":

We were always watching TV . . . TV was just a constant thing in my life. Interestingly enough, I think of TV as my, scary as it sounds, my moral giver in a lot of ways. I had church but I did . . . My parents, they kind of told us on the spot if we were doing it, but they wouldn't tell us as general guidelines. And TV I felt that was more like that for me, like stuff like the Brady Bunch or something like family shows that you really thought "Huh, that's true." And I kind of listened a lot — it was kind of strange when I think back . . . It played a big role.

TV and social construction of ethnicity. Albert talked about his visit to Korea sparking a critical realization about TV as a socialization tool. He was surprised to witness that Korean Americans like himself were seen as prestigious and esteemed on TV. This incident caused him to reflect on the childhood socialization he received from TV in the U.S. Albert shared:

> Yeah, I still remember when I first realized that (the power of media) because I was in Korea and to see on TV who looked just like myself and were valued because they are on TV. People consider Korean American guy to be good looking, and I remember thinking "Wow, this is a foreign concept!" To think someone of my gender and my race to be considered valuable, or prestigious in a lot of people's eyes, I remember thinking "this is really me? This isn't? Really my type?" (laughter) Because when I was growing up in the States, the blond on TV was supposed to be good looking and macho, and being white was valued. Like those people you want to be like were those I could never relate to. Or I would not try to imagine myself as that person or it was very easy to snap out of it once you look in the mirror.

For many of these young adults, TV constantly reminded them they were different from mainstream society. The media portrays mainstream Caucasian culture as normative and communicates dissonance with their heritage as something inferior. Albert reflected:

> I realized what a huge effect TV had on me, not only what you think, but how you view yourself. If you watch all the popular TV shows like Friends, ER, or whatever, you're watching pretty much white Americans live their lives and what's important to them. And I didn't realize — I thought it's just a show but they had an impact on how I view myself and what I value and what I'm really wanting in life.

The detrimental effects of TV

Some of these young adults freely shared their opinions about the power of media as a socialization tool of the masses. While they pointed out the positive role it could play in the socialization process, they were more concerned about the negative impact of the media. They also cited the media as one of the major socialization tools that has corrupted the society.

Sam was adamant about the negative impact the media has. He asserts that it is morally corrupting people. He linked TV violence's desensitizing effect with societal violence:

> I think the media is just plain doing it for the money, just for the ratings, to see how many people can watch, how bad it can be, how high it can fly, how deep it can go. It's just they do try to do it bigger, better or I think in their case who is worse, who's more corrupt, who's more disgusting, try to

play off that. And I think the more sensationalistic things we see the less surprised we are by that. And the more deviant things that we can do it's OK to slash somebody's head off just because we have seen it so many times on TV. And so many people do it and it's just becomes the norm and people just don't care about ten people dying anymore. It's not even front-page news anymore. It's just the way, the violence and the things that are being perpetuated, just by mere fact of being on TV and in the media a lot, it's just becomes desensitizing.

Positive socialization

Many of these young adults, however, also appreciate the positive contribution the media made to their lives. They speak of the good family values they internalized from shows such as the Brady Bunch, the Partridge Family, and Leave It to Beaver. Some talk about how these shows spoke to their longing for a healthy family. These shows also kept them from resorting to violence and helped them dream about a positive future. Dylan shared how he was motivated by a TV series to stay out of trouble during his growing-up years:

When we were growing up, we were called Chink or whatever . . . I'd be upset, but I didn't fight . . . I think just trying—watching all those Brady Bunch shows where they try to tell you to be bigger and walk away. Maybe roughed up a little bit, but I try to not get into a situation.

Some of these female young adults mentioned how they were empowered by certain TV shows to forge what it means to be a woman. These shows infused them with courage and hope to explore their rich heritages and to become women of their own making. Elisa talked about a TV show that encouraged her to become more independent:

I remember Laverne and Shirley — I thought it was really funny, and I know my dad really didn't like them. But looking back, they were like what a lot of us want to be today, you know just independent, and just living on our own, and just experiencing the world . . . They had their antics but if you thought about it, they were these 20 year olds out on their own, and they were making it. Of course, that was a different time, but you know. I guess in some ways I kind of got lost in the fantasy of being like that or just being independent.

Rose had a ritual of watching a TV show that inspired her about womanhood. She appreciated the female characters of the TV show who, as single parents, valiantly lived out their lives as a close-knit community.

> I would watch it every night, like I would wait until 11:00 and turn on the TV to watch it, turn if off at 11:30, it was a show called Kate and Ally . . . It was about these two women, one had a daughter and a son and the other one had a daughter, and they were both divorced and they are friends and they end up living in a house together, these two women and their kids. The girls are teenage girls in high school, and at the time I was in high school, but the show was centered around the two women, these divorced women living together. It was just funny. I liked the female relationship, the support they were for each other as well as some of the funny things these teenage girls did that I can relate to—like high school. I was really drawn to these two women, Kate and Ally, and their sort of independent lives, caring for their family without a husband. I really like that, being there for each other through that because people have visions of single moms, hard, alone, isolated and at the time I don't think I thought of it that way. I just liked it a whole lot, I really loved all the characters, the four women that were in it.

Chapter 7

The Present Lives of
Second-Generation Korean Americans

The interviews conducted for this study have culminated in a rich set of data that informs the research questions of the study. The data reveals several aspects and themes of the socioculturally constructed nature of the self among second-generation Korean American young adults. The interviewees, by and large, welcomed the opportunity to reflexively articulate narratives pertaining to their self-construction and self-integration. A description of the themes and functions of the internalized multiplicity existent in the lives of second-generation Korean American young adults follows.

Five salient aspects emerged from the interviews. First, second-generation Korean Americans strive to find and develop a career of their choice. Second, they search for independence from their families, in terms of their residence, finance, and identity. Third, they strive to negotiate the challenges involved in forging a life style of their preference. Fourth, they are engaged in building and growing in significant relationships. Lastly, they desire to cultivate a spiritual life.

Career: Adjustment, Employment, and Calling

The study participants talked about a few significant adjustments they have made or are in the process of making, in terms of their career paths. First, some spoke of a change in major during their college years, usually during their sophomore or junior years. As they contemplated their career path in light of their lack of interest and/or poor academic performance in their intended major, they decisively made decisions to change their major. Molly reflected on her struggle to continue pursuing the major she began with. "I just wasn't motivated, or maybe because I didn't know what I wanted to do, I didn't care." However, once she changed her major and transferred to a college that specializes in training teachers, she said that her approach to her education changed drastically. Whenever she encountered difficulties, she said to herself, "Well, this is what I need to do because it's my major. I think I was more career oriented at that time, and I just didn't think about anything else."

Second, some have made career changes after graduating from college. They often made the adjustment based on certain life experiences that confirmed one of their avocational interests to be their actual vocational calling. Daniel shared:

> When I was in college, I wasn't really interested in the electrical engineering that I was doing. Working with Sunday school and then at the college we had the college youth group and a lot of incoming freshman—they never studied. They always had trouble with some math classes, so I volunteered time to help with tutoring and it was a lot of fun. And one day it just clicked like maybe this is what I'm supposed to do. I think I just kind of fell into it.

Daniel went on to receive a master's degree in science education and taught at three different high schools in as many years before settling down at the high school where he currently teaches mathematics.

Third, others spoke of the difficulty they encountered searching for a job that utilized their college major. In the process, they perceived themselves as failures and seriously sought jobs in unrelated fields. Others went on to receive further degrees or acquire expertise, such as computer programming. Dylan shared:

> I was interviewing but I wasn't being hired anywhere. So I had a choice to go to Korea to teach English or this computer career program at DePaul ... but I eventually came to the decision that I'm going to be in the United States, living here, so might as well concentrate on establishing a career here. Because I did that, I was able to receive this job at Allstate, which seems perfect for me, the schedule, the atmosphere, and the culture.

Although a range of employment was found among the interviewees, many of them are in people-helping fields. Some of the employment options include schoolteachers, psycho-therapists, physical therapists, lawyer, dentist, medical doctors, and consultants. They are genuine in their desire to help others lead better lives. For instance, Julia works as a psychotherapist, specializing in family counseling. She wants to be a support and help people through transitions in their lives. Yet, she is realistic about her role when she says, "I realize I can't change people . . . I try to help them know that they have the power to do something about it (their situation)." Betsy talked about one of the reasons she chose to go into teaching:

What I liked about Korea (when she worked there for a few months) is there is a sense of community. It's just like even in my office, they looked out for me. I don't know what it was, but they made sure that things are going well, whereas I don't know if this is possible in American company . . . When I was visiting school, or a village or whatever, they would really look out for you . . . I don't know if it's what I've seen or if it's just a general Korean culture, but I was very impressed with the care and love I experienced there. And I wanted to live like that. A good fit, I thought, for me was teaching a small group of special ed. kids.

Albert reflects on his ambiguous role as a Christian lawyer. He is often perplexed by the unrealistic expectations of clients. He says, "I am involved in a Christian law firm so a lot of times our clients come to us as Christians, expecting us to be like Jesus Christ himself, I think . . . It's tough to meet those expectations." Kelly is in the transition from being a newspaper reporter to a Christian campus group staff worker. She believes she is well prepared for staff work in that "I've been out in the 'real world' so when students I talk to now, who are agonizing over career decisions, I understand that, I've been through it, I'm still going through it."

Whether they are employed or in transition, most of the interviewees continue to struggle with the issue of calling. Even those who are employed in the fields in which they were trained and are secure in their employment continue to search for the sense of call. While Albert, the lawyer, enjoys working with various types of people and confronting problems that arise in the various institutions of society, he feels like he is being:

A hired gun. (They say) "I want this, you do it for me." And at times I don't mind because I see why a certain situation calls for it. Other times I feel like "what am I doing?" In five years from now, I don't want to be a lawyer.

Then, there are those who have not given up their hope of getting into medical school. Although Rose has enjoyed working for a youth resource foundation for some time, she has continued to enhance her chance of getting into medical school, and she finally feels ready to apply to medical schools. In a similar manner, Luke has been convinced that he should be in a medicine-related field, and he has worked as a physical therapist. He expressed his feeling of anxiety about applying to medical school.

Sometimes I feel like "I'm not going to make it," but He (God) is kind of giving me a peace about this decision. And since I had a hard time with my academic aspect in college years, I felt like I can't make it.

Among eleven female interviewees, Kelly is the only woman who has a child from her marriage. She spoke of her double role dilemma as a workingwoman and a mother. She told about a recent decision:

I went part time in February after fighting five months with management at work to get it. And so now I feel a little funny about going to them in a couple of weeks and saying "Well, I'm going to quit." . . . I still felt like I was holding on to that (my job) very tightly.

The concern for the double role that Kelly faces was also shared by many of the female young adults.

Value of self determination

Many of the interviewees, while they want to keep their internalized value of family, appreciate the freedom and self-determination that American culture offers. They value the level playing field, the overt commitment of the American society. They have worked hard to make their dreams come true. Sam, who was primarily raised by his mother and grandmother and had to endure public stigma in the Korean American community, shared his appreciation for the opportunity to achieve the American dream:

I appreciate the opportunity, the freedom, the ability that a person with humble beginnings can make it big, and the American dream. I appreciate that I can raise my family in a way that I would see fit, rather than the way maybe my government would see fit. I appreciate the many ways I can be actively involved in my community and in making it a better place.

In reminiscing about the paths he took to get to where he is now, Sam feels fortunate to live and have been educated in the U.S. He talks about how he was able to decide on his vocation:

> Going to college was another defining moment in the sense that you know like my peers where their parents paid for most of their schooling and I paid for my own. Of course, there were the help of the scholarships and grants and things like that. But I feel my education was earned. I earned my education and worked so much and had so many jobs. From that I realize that I am more of an experiential learner. I decided on the type of profession that I wanted to be in, and how I was going to better myself and how I was going to grow.

For some of these young adults, especially the women, freedom and self-determination are perhaps the features of American culture they most appreciate. They often spoke of the freedom in American culture compared to the lack of it in Korean culture. Rose remembered one of many arguments with her mom about self-determination and boundary issues after coming back from studying abroad in England:

> I spent a year with little contact with any of my family and I really liked the independence. I liked being my own person, making my own choices, and not having the weight of expectations and pressure. So when I came back all of my fights with my mom were –you know . . . I would eventually say "Because you're Korean and I'm not." . . . I made Korean bad and American good.

Georgia echoed Rose's passion for independence and self-determination when she made a plea toward parents:

> Young adults should have the ability and the right to make their own decisions, their own choices even to make their own mistakes. And I think parents should help with that, but not try to live their own dreams and things like that through them.

Joel also talked about why he was pulled toward going and living in Korea. While there were many attractive features about Korea for him, the main factor was independence from his parents and others:

I guess I had established a lot of friends there (in Korea) when I was there and a good church that I would be attending, a good place to grow as a person, independent from my family, independent from my friends and to really grow mentally and to grow spiritually.

Value of hard work

Most of the interviewees have mixed feelings about the value of hard work that was promoted during their growing- up years. While they appreciate their parents' hard work to support them financially, they regret the absence of their parents at home. Moreover, while the young adults value their parents' emphasis on education, they felt their parents pressured them and often overwhelmed them with unrealistic expectations. Dylan spoke about the transmission of the first generation's work ethics to the 1.5 and second generations:

It seems that to me in a sense Korean people work harder in a sense that they are driven by success or driven by a extreme mentality to perform until the body cannot perform any longer. Well, definitely first generation has that drive and I think part of 1.5 and second (generations) might have that as well instilled in them from the first generation.

While some of these young adults did not have to work early in their lives, others had to work hard in their family businesses. Kris talked about when she internalized her work ethics and value of hard work:

Probably about seven or eight years old. (Interviewer: So you would just go out to the store and play?) Not play, I would work, like actually do like ringing up. I mean I would be behind the counter helping my mom, and doing stuff.

During her adolescent years, Kris had to run the business on several occasions entirely by herself:

When I was sixteen or seventeen, they had to go on some business trips and they left the whole store up to me. I was like counting all the money, I was depositing the money, I was making orders, I was ringing up registers, and I was doing everything. So I felt like there was a lot of responsibility . . . I learned to work hard.

Despised values: comparison and competition

Many of the interviewees contend that comparison and competition work confluentially to destroy self-esteem. The confluence of the two factors has been a source of shame and guilt. Many of the young adults said that they still struggle with the issues of inner defectiveness and destructiveness toward themselves.

Elisa talked about the high standards that the Korean American family, church, and community have for the second generation. She shared her frustrations about their unreasonable expectations and arbitrary preferences:

> I don't really like being Korean because Koreans have such high standards for their kids. (They say) "You have to be this. You have to have a certain type of occupation to have status or to be accepted." And I just get tired of that.

Rose's reflection on her competitive tendency illustrates well the confluence of comparison and competition. Rose was consumed to prove herself to others when she was teased by Caucasian schoolmates for being different. Moreover, her reflection serves as a vivid image of how second-generation Korean American young adults have been constructed by both Korean and American cultures and the interaction between the two.

> I remember from a very young age that I was very competitive . . . When I was like in grade school and junior high I got teased a lot because I was different . . . sometimes I wore the same clothes for a few days in a row and Americans don't do that, I would bring funny things to lunch. I became really defensive about people who teased me. I became very tough and learned how to stand up for myself. And in that process I became very competitive academically because that was a place where I can say, "well, in your face" like you're an idiot and I'm an A student so I don't care what you say about me. And so there was a lot of defensiveness there and I became competitive in school and in academics.

At home, Rose internalized the way her mother made judgments about people. Since Rose valued her mother's opinion, she wanted to be accepted by her mother as a daughter of whom she would be proud of. She said:

> Even though my mom didn't always compare me academically with others, all my life she would make comments about people, compare

people. There were good people and there were bad people. And there were ugly people and pretty people. There were smart people and dumb people. A lot of splitting . . . categories, comparing, hierarchy, putting people in order. So yeah, that I would have to say drove my need to be competitive, because I didn't want to be one of those people. I mean I don't want my mom walking down the street and saying, if I were a stranger, thinking of me as the bad as opposed to the good in that splitting.

Search for Independence: Freedom in Terms of Residence, Finance, and Identity

As young adults, second-generation Korean Americans seek to become independent in one to three aspects of their lives. They are securing residence, stabilizing financial situations, and forging their identity in order to maximize their independence. Upon graduating from college, many initially moved back home with parents as they transitioned into a new phase in life. The timing of departure from home to a new residence seems to be negotiated carefully by the interviewees in conjunction with obtaining financial independence. These young adults generally employed two strategies.

One group of study participants decided to move out as soon as they were able to do so, either postponing or taking a slower route to their financial goals. This group of young adults often spoke of the financial burdens while still enjoying independence. Elisa said she could no longer tolerate being treated like a child who needs constant supervision:

If I didn't move out, it was never going to change. I noticed, when I used to be away at school, they would give me more respect. But at home, forget about it. I simply needed to get out.

The other group of young adults decided to live under the same roof with their parents for two reasons. First, they wanted to save up money for the future. They spoke of preparing for a wedding or buying a house. The second reason is that they wanted to develop stronger relationships with their parents. These are generally the young adults who had recently lost one of their parents. A robber murdered Molly's mother in her own store in Chicago a few years ago. After her mother's death, Molly did not wish to leave her father alone in the house. She said:

> I think I've become a lot more paranoid about my father. That's one
> decision that factors in not moving out. I don't want to leave him alone
> and I can't go out too much because I have to go home for my dad. So
> I've become a lot more attached to him.

Melinda lost her father recently to liver cancer and decided to move
back home. She said, "The decision, I guess, was kind of made for me
when my father passed away." With much willingness, she is ready to
set aside her plans indefinitely and be at her mother's side.

Regardless of their search for optimal freedom in residence and
financial situations, these young adults are by and large committed to
re-establishing their relationships with their parents. Many have come
to recognize family dysfunctions from the past that shaped their own
lives and that continue to create unhealthy patterns among the family
members. Some of them have begun working through the issues of
family dysfunctions at a personal level, often through individual
counseling. Many desire to relate to their parents as adults and try to
befriend them. Kris felt positive about the progress she has made in her
relationship with her mother when she said:

> Now that I'm married, it (her relationship with her mother) is better. I call
> her every day and I talk to her about pretty much everything. Well, almost
> everything. In English and Korean, but mostly English.

Others feel they have to be distant from their parents for the time
being because they are not ready to tackle issues in their present stage
of life.

Financial independence as a source of value struggle

Some of the study participants saw financial independence as a value
to maintain in their lives. Kris, having learned early the value of hard
work, is focused on obtaining financial freedom. She has a part-time
job on top of her regular job to secure her family financially. Luke is
contemplating moving to a new company within his field of work for
higher pay. Many of these young adults, however, as previously
discussed, struggle with a preoccupation with financial independence.

The interviewees do not wish to repeat the life style of their parents.
They remembered their parents being too busy and frantic about
making money. They commented that their parents' values of financial

stability and success overshadowed their commitment to provide a quality education for their children. Perhaps the parents were convinced that they were working hard for their children's education, namely for the cost of their college education. While appreciating the hard work on the part of the parents, the young adults said that they needed time with their parents and support and encouragement. Molly still regrets all that transpired during her growing up years. She said:

> We were latchkey children . . . We would cut school a lot . . . My parents found out when the school called and said, "Your children haven't been in school for three days." . . . We got spanked big time . . . Even after that, we had freedom but it was so weird because they (my parents) might call or something and tell us to do certain things, we would never do it . . . We would say okay and we wouldn't do it. We were very unsupervised. . . I want it to be different for my own family. It has to. . .

Voice of Womanhood

Attempts to accept the societal expectations of women
One salient voice that operates in the lives of female second-generation Korean American young adults is the societal expectations of women that they perceived and internalized as necessary for acceptance and success in society.

A few of the women shared that they were once convinced that they needed to be attractive in the male-dominated society. They talked about getting their cues from peers, but mostly from the media. In discussing some of her favorite TV shows, Michelle shared that obsession with appearance caused much grief in her past:

> When I start to watch some of the ones like Friends, where they get a lot into image, body image and stuff like that. (Interviewer: I just learned about Friends today. I was interviewing somebody, until then I didn't know.) Really? Oh, good. That's probably good that you don't. I think those kinds of things have caused me to fall. I remember watching a lot of those in college. And I just remember the only thing important to me in college was having a good physical image. And especially being in California where all the women are very much into their figures and things like that, it was hard for me to get out of that image. And a lot of my time was spent on developing my outer image and not my inner. So I know that once I start watching those shows I think I will be tempted to fall back into that thinking and I don't want that to happen.

Michelle continued to talk about how she was also influenced by magazines on fitness:

> I used to be a magazine person but I think I stopped doing that for the same reasons why I stopped watching TV. I used to read a lot of like Shape and Fitness, and all those women's magazines. I used to read a lot of articles in those magazines like "How to get a better man" or "How to have a shapely body in 10 weeks." So you see those pictures in the magazines and they are all very beautiful women. And they are all talking about how to make your look better. For me I know that that's a weakness for me and so I just decided to throw them all away and stop looking at them because I don't want to have that around.

Some of the women shared that, in order to succeed in society, they needed to act and think like men. Acting like a man, they mean, is keeping their emotions in check and having clear boundaries with co-workers. It also means participating in the stories that interest men, such as sports. Thinking like men, for them, is thinking linearly and abstractly. Melinda was being philosophical about the issue when she shared:

> I mean I know there are this Glasnost, multiculturalism and stuff like that. But I still see it as a Caucasian man's world. They are trying to have some diversity in a lot of ways. But when you scratch the surface, I don't see it in terms of underlying things that are going on. And I think having grown up with an older brother and as a second class person in a sense, I feel like I've learned to operate in a more masculine way of thinking. . . knowing that that's the way I'm going to get anywhere, that's the way I'm going to be heard.

Many of the women also believe that society has shifted from one norm to another in the last forty years regarding women in the work force. They feel that the society expects women to work, especially if they received a college education. While some women are committed to their career, others try to convince themselves that they have other options. Some want to stay home for their future children or work part time or do job sharing. Kelly, who has a daughter, shared about her struggle to be a working mother. She also reflected on the societal pressure on women:

Bethany was born and I was home with her for six months on leave and then I went back full time. We convinced ourselves that we have to have two incomes because blah, blah, blah. So we were telling ourselves and we were telling our families and friends that financially there was just no way we could do it (the two incomes). I went back full time and I was miserable, I hated it and I had a very different outlook on what I was doing. Suddenly it just wasn't worth the time . . . Then Bethany was born and I realized that my career had become much too important. It was taking really much too much of my energy, and we wrestled with the options. The obvious option is to straight out quit work and stay home, but I think Paul also realized my nature that I like to be busy. And I don't think I could watch my Barney all day long, five days a week. And I have a lot of respect for women who can stay home full time because a couple times a week is all I can take. But I just felt there was also something else that I could do, that somehow would work within our family structure. I didn't want to spend too much time away from my family. I wanted the flexibility to take her with me and journalism just wasn't going to be that.

However, Kelly still fights with the internalized voice that says an educated woman should work. She articulated that voice when she said:

Well, this is what you've been wanting to do since high school. And we really do feel that you are gifted in the writing and blah, blah, blah. You spent four years (in college) studying this. What else would you do with your life?"

Forging an Identity as a Korean American Christian Woman

Many of the women have been reflecting upon what it means to be a Korean American Christian woman. They realize that they need to draw from multiple sources, such as their mothers, mainstream culture, women of majority and minority, various Christian views of women, etc. Their search for the kind of womanhood they want to possess has been triggered by positive or negative experiences in the past.

Michelle shared about how the break up with her former boy friend started her search for her identity as a Korean American woman:

I was dating a Caucasian guy very seriously at the time and I was dating him for the entire four years that I was in college. And I think just through my relationship with him, it really showed me also who I was. And I think even, you know, after school he broke up with me. And I think that was one of the things that made me realize how much I needed God. Just because I didn't know but all over the four years I just started to depend on him a lot. I just thought I lost myself in him. He became the center of everything I did. And when he left I realized how empty my life was and how a lot of my decisions was based on thinking that we would be together. I did a lot of things according to him or his life. And so when he was gone that's when I started seeking for something to fill that space and then God opened my eyes to be the kind of woman He wanted me to be.

Melinda shared how her interaction with her mentor, who was a Chinese American woman, challenged her to explore the kind of person she wanted to be:

A Chinese American woman I knew kind of became a mentor-friend. Because our church did not have a lot of female leaders, yet the women were stronger than the guys and the women had more leadership, I think a lot of us were excited to see women doing the ministry, someone older . . . And so since I finally got the opportunity to meet her, we've seen each other several times. I see her at different places and if she's near, I try to go visit her. And we have kept in touch and I know that she is someone I can keep accountable to. All in all, she has served as a wonderful model for me.

Voice of the American Dream

Achieving the American dream is a salient aspect of the lives of the interviewees. They have set their goals to accomplish financial success, develop self, and achieve an autonomous life.

Financial Success

When speaking in terms of attaining financial stability, they usually mean having enough buying power to afford the kind of life style they have in mind. While they readily spend money on what are deemed as necessities of life, such as vacations, they are also mindful of investing for the future. They hope to have a higher standard of living and eventually exceed their parents' assets. Isabella shared that achieving financial stability has been an important concern in her decision-making process. In the process, she also talked about how her parents have influenced her and how she can factor God into her financial decisions:

> I think often some of the cultural things that I think rub off on me — "What are people going to think? — like financial provision. "Am I going to provide financially for this move or my kids?" — that's the big thing, financial security that is something that my parents really emphasized. "How much money are you going to make?" are things I have been struggling with a lot, especially lately, trying to factor in God as well. "How is God going to help me through this, or is this going to please God?" as opposed to "Is it something that I feel I need to have it?"

Development of Self Through Formal Education

The study participants often see attaining as much education as possible as the best way to develop themselves. As previously discussed, many of them have completed or are in the process of completing their graduate degrees. Some are planning on further studies, as well.

In their mind, education is a significant measuring rod in terms of a person's future success and character. Moreover, they tend to see education or obtaining an academic degree as acquiring more social commodity. Thus, education is often seen only in light of formal education, education and development of self stopping when schooling is completed. Elisa said "I guess now that I am done with education, I have set some goals for myself. I guess I want pretty much the American Dream, to get married and have a house and settle."

Brian, in comparing his family and his wife's family, talked about how he felt inferior about himself and his family due to the different levels of education they received:

> There's also a difference in our family background. My mother didn't go to college, my father dropped out of college whereas both of her parents attended college. And then obviously the income level is different between the families .. . . I just felt badly about that.

Brian has been actively preparing to go to medical school to become a medical doctor. He has been working as a physical therapist, after obtaining his master's degree.

Autonomy Valued

Many of the interviewees want to enjoy as much autonomy as possible in their lives. Forced to be self-reliant during their growing-up years, these young adults believe self-reliance or autonomy has become a salient voice in the drive to achieve the American dream. Sam reflected on how his identity has been shaped by the necessity for self-reliance during his growing up years:

> I had to defend for myself a lot as a child, even in my community because my mother was not around much. I had to fend for myself from my (older) brother because when we were kids we used to fight a lot. He used to beat up on me a lot and I used be the kind of kid that cries a lot and I think that taught me a lot about self-reliance. . . I have been on this integrity kick lately. I feel very strongly whatever I say I need to be doing. I know that I should do it and I can do it most of the time. And if I believe that if something is incorrect then I need to change it myself. With God's help, I know I can do it.

For many of these young people, however, obtaining autonomy is a matter of degree and differs from how autonomy is understood in mainstream society. For them, achieving autonomy is not necessarily getting rid of encumbrances from their past, but reassessing, reorganizing, and maintaining the past to their advantage.

Challenges to Forging a Life Style of Their Preference

The study participants are generally busy juggling various spheres of their lives. These spheres include employment, church, friendships, parents, family, and education. They reported that each sphere has its unique challenges. These challenges often work confluentially to add to the stresses of life. One of the on-going stress factors they recounted is the combination of racial prejudice, stereotyping, and ignorance. Isabella spoke of the fact that she has to second-guess her clients in counseling situations:

> Sometimes, I would have a real negative reaction with a client right away in my first meeting. I'd think "Hmm, there's something racial going on" – like that would be a question in my mind. "Are they being prejudiced against me because I'm Korean?" So that's one of the insecurities I have.

At another level, these young adults often spoke of their struggle to keep balance between their career and their Christian life. They lamented the fact that their Christian discipleship has become the most expendable sphere in their lives. Daniel reflected on his life, as well as his peers:

We're so busy with our careers. We are more concerned with careers than church. I think our generation is at a point where we're starting careers, starting families. We're too busy with that stuff. We are not focusing on the church, not focusing on God like we are supposed to. That's what I see among my friends. They are more concerned with their careers and the future. I think we worry about the future too much, especially, financially. We don't have God as a priority right now.

Moreover, the interviewees live their lives moving from one sphere to another, where each sphere seems distinct from others. They work with predominantly Caucasian co-workers or clients in their places of employment. They generally assimilate well into the ethos of their employment place and the society at large. However, while they do have some friends at work, their friendships with co-workers rarely spill over into personal life.

In their churches, these young people worship mostly with fellow English speaking second-generation Korean Americans, including a few other Asian Americans. A considerable portion of their friends comes from the people in their own churches. In family interactions, these young adults attempt to relate to their parents using Korean language, being mindful of Korean culture. Thus, these young people lead lives moving in and out of the above-mentioned spheres, as well as other distinct spheres of their lives. As they endeavor to juggle the various spheres of their lives with their busyness, there is seldom time to reflect on their own lives or to integrate the various spheres of their lives.

The authority of mainstream society

Many study participants recalled their desire to either fit into the mainstream society or be a Caucasian American lasted for many years beyond their childhood and adolescence. Rose reminisced about her desire to be accepted as white by whites during her high school years:

> Once I got to high school I really felt like I had acculturated into the American sort of way of life even though my home life was very Korean. At school I felt very much accepted and just like everyone else. In fact, I even remember asking my friends, "When you look at me do you see a Korean?" And they thought that was the most ridiculous thing, because they said "I look at you like I look at everyone else" which is very American. And I think at that time I was hung up on "I wanted to be American, and not Korean."

She recalled how difficult it was for her to leave a place where she was accepted by the mainstream society and to move on to a new phase in her life where she had to try all over again to be accepted by new people she met:

> I was involved in this thing called Senior Stress Group where seniors came together and talked about stress of leaving high school and everyone else was so ready to leave high school. . . And I was sitting there so sad that I didn't want to leave because I just like I had everything I need, I'm accepted here as American. . . I ended up going to Northwestern and saying goodbye to my friends. That was really sad.

Many of these young adults have thought about why they wanted to assimilate into the mainstream society. As Rose's above narrative indicated, they wanted to be accepted by the mainstream society. They wished to lead a normal life in the U.S. without being labeled as somebody who was different. However, they consider that perhaps most salient socialization tool that was utilized by the mainstream society to shape their lives, as such, was the media.

The interviewees claimed that media, as an authority, dictates to the hearts of people as to what or who should be valued through the combination of explicit, implicit, and null messages. Albert said:

> When I grew up in the U.S., Caucasian guys and gals on TV were supposed to be good looking and macho or beautiful. And those were people I could never relate to or I would try to imagine myself as that person.

Moreover, Sam reflected on the Hollywood portrayal of Asian Americans:

As an Asian American I always feel like I get a bad rap from Hollywood. Asian males, karate and the Bruce Lee and the Jackie Chan things, that's all the positive roles that we play in the media or negative rolls like assassin or nerds.

Many of these young adults spoke of their attempts to break out of the mold that Hollywood and the mainstream society tried to put on them in their growing-up years.

Some study participants talked about the detrimental effects of the media in terms of its overpowering effects in their lives. They deemed media as an outside-in authority, rather than as a inside-out authority with which they would have power to control its impact in their lives. They claimed that the scenes and values they have internalized from TV often mold their lives. Sam continued:

I used to watch TV a lot by myself when I was a kid. I remember when I was thinking about something or looking at situations, I used to go back to old TV shows that I used to watch, and I remember little things I watched from TV. If I am not careful, it can overtake me. I think when I was dating Isabella, most of my decisions as far as dating went were influenced by what I had seen on TV and in the movies. So, I know there are other areas in my life that I am probably not aware of that are being influenced by the media and I just want to be continually aware of those things.

The authority of Korean American culture

As discussed previously in this chapter, most of the interviewees asserted that their parents used their authority to instill Korean culture and values in their lives. In terms of the enculturation processes, their parents heavily utilized the various programs offered by the Korean church. These young people remembered attending Korean language school on Saturday mornings, either at their churches or neighboring Korean churches. For some, Korean language school was conducted on Sundays while they waited for their parents to be done with their activities at the church. These classes were often taught, in their recollection, by first generation Korean Americans who had very little training in teaching and knew little about American culture, often destroying what little motivation the children had to learn about Korean language and culture.

The study participants also talked about their parents sending them to Korea to visit their relatives over summer vacations. They spoke fondly of playing with their cousins and sightseeing in Korea. Most of those interviewed for this study have had multiple visits to Koreas where all expenses were paid by their parents.

Some interviewees contended that Korean culture functions like authority in that it inculcates the Korean Americans with values and preferences, thus providing normative standards for the people. Georgia talked about how Korean culture could dictate the ways people interact, when contrasted with freedom in American culture:

> I like the freedom that I feel here in the States, but if I were in Korea, I'd have to be very private. It's a very inter-related society and I think I would suffocate, if I were there just because my business is everybody's business. And everybody has an opinion and advice. That's how I feel like being with Koreans here (in the States).

For instance, the interviewees spoke of how formal education is deemed as the most important credential for status and respect in both Korean and Korean American society. Elisa talked about why she decided to finish her college education although she was not excited about doing so:

> You know I wanted to be able to say, "Yes, I graduated from college." And I guess how I would be looked upon or noticed in the Korean community was important. It's always like how things appear, you're not credible if you don't. I guess it's all partly appearance. What it (Korean culture) tells you is important

Brian shared the most demoralizing experience he had in his life during his encounter with his then future father-in-law. His girl friend's father required Brian to document all his educational credentials in order for him to consider approving Brian and his daughter for marriage! He talked about the painful experience in tears even after several years have passed since the incident took place and they have been married:

> I think it was very difficult for her (his wife, then girl friend) because basically she was caught between her parents and me. And a couple of times we were thinking of eloping. They wanted certain documents on my background and my education and all of that, so it took me a while to gather all that stuff. I had to like call down to school to get all the legal documents with signatures on them. I had everything except my college

diploma, but instead I brought my check stubs and a list of friends and their phone numbers. I had everything, went there. And her father refused to even talk to me because I didn't have the diploma, so at that point I really just wanted to walk out of there. But then I realized I couldn't. . . because she (his girl friend) would have to make a choice right there to stay in the house or leave with me. And knowing how she was raised it would have been a very difficult choice for her to make. So I went back later and showed them my transcript, and I bowed in front of her parents and formally asked for permission.

The revised authority of parents

As previously discussed, the interviewees have not always appreciated their parents' use of authority in raising them. However, many of these young adults desired to consider the wishes and advice of their parents in their decision-making processes and other affairs of their lives. These young people exhibited a mature and secure sense of their self. They are also committed to growth in their relationship with their parents. Daniel described how his heart toward his father has been changing and how he hopes to continue incorporating his father's wishes into his life:

I am beginning to understand him more. I think I am accepting him more in the last three to five years. When I was in college, though, I would always ask the question, "Why is he like that?" But now I'm like, "He's like that so let's get on with life." So, I would bring up some stuff in my life and we talk. And I try hard to listen to what he says.

Rose's relationship with her mother has been much more volatile that Daniel's relationship with his father. Rose spoke of the progress she has been able to make recently, despite the hurt that she and her mother caused to each other:

The last half a year, we had tons of fights and cries. And you would not believe screaming matches and me accusing her of all these things. She was devastated that I was so hurt and that my self-esteem was so low. And she was just flabbergasted by all this, but recently we came to an understanding that there were many good things she gave me in my life, a lot of support. And pushed me in ways that were good, that did make me who I am, that without that I couldn't have reached my potential. She's right, and she did support me in many ways.

Rose also talked about how her reconciliation process with her mother has positively changed her appreciation for Korean culture:

> There are Korean values that she holds valuable, she sees things in the American culture that are not good, and so that kind of opened my eyes too. But, yeah, there's good in both and I want to glean good from both and keep out the bad from both.

Relationship and Community Valued

Building and Growing in Relationships

In the midst of their busy schedules, the study participants work on building and growing relationships. Many desire to build friendships with people from diverse walks of life. Many are also committed to rebuilding their relationships with their parents and other family members. Those who are single are eager to meet a potential marriage partner, although some break off their potential marriage relationships. Those who are married talked about growing in their relationships.

First, many spoke of their desire and effort to build relationships with non-Korean Americans. In other words, they expressed their desire to "escape" from their ethnic ghetto. The ethnic ghetto is not, in a sense, geographic, but of Korean American Christian culture. Dylan talked about his effort to diversify his friendships, which have been mainly with Korean American Christians, yet he has had trouble breaking out of the circle:

> I mostly hung around Korean Americans who attended my church. In my sophomore and junior years in college, we tried to take classes together, to do projects together. I didn't really hang around with a lot of non-Koreans or non-CFC (my church) people. But during my second semester junior year I joined a business fraternity and one of the main reasons I joined was because I wanted to break out of just knowing Christians or knowing Korean Americans. And I developed some friendships through my business fraternity and I still talk to some people today, but ironically, I think two are Korean and one is Chinese (laughter). So maybe I do have that comfortable level with Asian Americans.

As discussed above, having been a part of Korean American churches most of their lives, the majority of friendships have been with fellow second-generation young adults. Thus, corollary to their desire to have non-Korean American friendships is their desire to see their English speaking Korean American churches or congregations become more multiethnic in make-up.

Second, many interviewees desire to re-establish relationships with family members. They wish to relate to them with respect and in peace. Rose spoke of her on-going struggle with her mother, whom she has a deep love for:

> She (my mother) always wants to give me advice—I don't mind advice, but I feel like if I don't take it she gets mad at me, so now we have this little thing where she has to say before she gives me advice "you don't have to do this, BUT . . ." It's a formula that she must use if she's going to give me advice, because I said, "Just remember that I want your advice, I just don't know if I'm going to take it, so please preface any advice you give me with that statement."

Most of the study participants are genuinely committed to accepting their parents as who they are. They realize that their parents will not change much in terms of character and the perception of their children. Despite finding many faults and dysfunctions in their parents in recent years, these young adults strive to understand and love their parents for who they are. Moreover, they make much effort to maintain their sibling relationships even though they realize that they are taking divergent ways in life from their own.

Third, those who are single and planning to get married have definite criteria for their future spouses that are remarkably similar. They all want to marry a second-generation Korean American Christian, while entertaining the possibility of getting married to a Christian from other Asian American groups. They talked about a similar cultural and religious heritage as crucial in mate selection. They are often mindful of how well their spouse will fit into their extended family. Dylan typified their outlook on marriage well:

> I think there is a level of comfortability once again with Korean American or Asian American, Korean American more than just Asian American. It's hard enough meeting girls as it is, but I don't have much chance to meet girls to get to know in a more intimate way as I do with Korean American girls who are Christian . . . And you know in thinking about my mom and grandmother, I am sure it would be much easier for them to want to treat her well, or being able to express their happiness and love if they were Korean just because of the language.

Fourth, some singles are currently engaged in re-evaluating their significant relationships. Luke said that he has become very cautious about his relationship with his Caucasian girl friend of many years:

> It's kind of funny and we've had some discussions and now I really can't say with much certainty. You know, I think having different peer groups and growing in different ways, we're seeing conflicts in growth patterns and so that's an issue we're trying to address. I feel like we've been growing apart. So we're going to try to be patient a little bit more to see if it (marriage) is the right thing.

Then, there are some singles currently dealing with the aftermath of break ups of either a significant relationship or an engagement. Michelle is still recovering from the end of her four-year-long relationship with her college sweetheart. Upon graduation from college, her Caucasian boyfriend decided to go his own way, which devastated Michelle. Joel, who was engaged to marry a Korean American woman, decided to break up the engagement at the last minute. He said that he finally realized he had much to work on in his personal life and that he was not being fair to his fiancée.

Lastly, the study participants who are married spoke of growth in their marital relationships. They desired to grow deeper in their communication patterns, financial stability, and other common marital issues. The foremost concern in their marriages, however, is their commitment to forge a healthy marriage in the context of their extended families, especially with both sets of parents. Deeming marriage as the rite of passage in becoming adults, the interviewees seek to exert more independence from parents. Yet, they are ever careful in giving respect to their parents and maintaining the relationships. For Kelly and Paul, maintaining the relationship with their parents is crucial so that their children will have a relationship with their grandparents in order for them to learn about their Korean heritage.

The authority of peers

The study participants have held and continue to hold their peers in high regard and allow them influence in a significant manner. As discussed previously, these young adults often consider their cohorts as a group of people who authenticate their own existence as second-generation Korean American young adults. They see one another as giving permission to accept who they are and to lead life at the margin of various spheres of identity. Albert spoke of how he was able to reclaim the Korean side of his identity when he visited Korea with his friends:

> I'm proud to say I'm American. At the same time I'm very proud to say I'm Korean. And my Korean heritage is very important to me. It wasn't so important to me as I was growing up, I thought I was just American. But in college, some of my friends and I went to Korea. So, we were exploring, wanting to know more about Korean and we fell in love with it. We realized that we were quite different from Koreans in Korea, but we (he and his friends) knew we had each other.

The interviewees spoke of the importance of their peers in their decision-making processes. They count on their peers to encourage and support them in times of crises and transitions of life. Their peers usually consist of their cousins and friends from their home church. Molly considers her cousins to be her best friends. She talked about how much she counts on her cousins for advice and whom she chooses to talk to:

> I guess I'm the type of person who depends on different people for my different needs. Fortunately, I have lots of cousins who are my best friends. For example, in terms of vocation, I would probably go to Betsy because she's in the same vocation. With other stuff, I would call a different cousin because she is very. . . Well, I consider her as one of the very few people I consider as a very good head on her shoulders, and so I value her judgment a lot.

Kelly talked about her best friends as authorities she allows in her life. She loves to confer with them on the phone and through e-mail. Even when they are not around, Kelly asserted that her friends are still with her in her decision-making process:

> For me, I have a few best friends that I love to chat with. They are my best friends from my college days. We were inseparable in school. . . Even if we don't get to talk to one another, I think about "What would Cathy say if she knew I was thinking about this or doing this?"

Egalitarian relationships valued

Reactions against how certain Korean cultural values were practiced
 Some of the study participants spoke against Korean Americans' abuse of the hierarchical structure in the family and in the community. Some talked how the fathers have usurped the authorities of their wives and children. They still struggle with the fact that their fathers will not likely change their way of treating members of the family. Abigail shared her struggles with her father, who has been utterly unreasonable in the way he has treated his family members for years. She said:

> When I graduated from school I didn't go back home to live because there's no way I could tolerate how my parents' relationship was structured. It is very, very difficult because in a lot ways my father kind of has usurped his authority in my family . . . He has to be in control and get his way on everything . . . Because he was so caught up in making it (the business) big, like he compromised a lot of his resources and kind of came to a point where he became bankrupt, literally bankrupted . . . He has been struggling in his own manhood, that type of thing.

Many of the interviewees are distressed by the manner in which female members of the family have been treated over the years. Some talked about how they and their siblings were treated differently based on their gender. Especially, they shared male siblings receiving preferential treatment in many ways. Dylan was sympathetic to how his sister was compared to him and his brother, and she almost became an outcast of the family.

 While many of the study participants realize the inequity of the gender situation in the Korean American family, some have internalized the preference for male in subtle manners. Speaking of his experience with his wife's pregnancy, Paul shared one of his fears and how he has embraced a girl for now:

> During the (my wife's) pregnancy I was kind of nervous. I kept thinking if it's a girl I can't play ball with her and "What do I do?" "What will I do with a girl, a daughter?" Once she was born, I had no regrets. But we will make sure that we will have a boy. We are working on that.

Once a kid, always a kid

Many of the study participants felt that they are still being treated as little kids by their parents and their church members. As previously discussed, the young adults struggle to be accepted and treated as adults in their relationships with their parents. The young adults reported similar treatment from the first generation adults in the church.

Part of the reason is that the first generation has seen these young people grow up from their pre-adolescent years. Even if those young adults started attending the church in recent years, they are often lumped together with the young people who grew up in the church because of their association with the other men and women. Melinda is one of those young adults who decided to go back to her home church where she grew up. She talked about her perception by the first generation.

> They (the first generation) have seen us grow up, they've changed our diapers and all that. But it's bad because they still see us as kids and when we see them, like I remember when we started driving, they were all shocked. And some, I remember, asked "You guys have your own checking account?" Because we're single, too, we are not legitimate (adults) yet. . . I'm afraid that we are not going to be taken seriously in the church for a long time.

In reflecting on the hierarchy that exists in virtually every sphere of the Korean American community, a few young adults offered theological critiques about the gap between the two generations. However, their critiques are somewhat simplistic in that the existent problems in a hierarchical culture will be resolved only if the biblical commands supercede the cultural mandates of that culture. Luke's remark is an example of such reflections:

> Yeah, that basically worries me that the Confucianism, the children living for their parents and seeing their parents as the utmost authority and with respect. You could change that around and say "Well, God has given my parents to me to respect and to follow." And the parents can also say that God has given us these children, and they must obey us because they are our children. And going to the Bible talking about honor thy father and mother, and do this because it's right. But also at the same time I think a lot of the time it's the parents' decision to become the ultimate authority. So I would say even higher than the loving aspect of the family is this Confucianistic hierarchy. I think it does more damage than help . . .

That's why before I said being Korean isn't really Christian. Sure, there are a lot of good aspects about Korean, but if Koreans were Christians, you are perfect already. You don't need to have the hierarchy.

In a way, Luke saw that Korean culture, or any culture for that matter, has not much to offer to the life of a Christian. Thus, while critiquing the misuse of the hierarchy, Luke devalued the whole aspect of Confucian culture without making attempts to understand the complexity of the relationships between faith and culture.

Forging more dialogical relationships

Some of the study participants, however, were more intentional in reflecting on the nature of their various relationships. They tended to be more aware of the issues of power dynamics in relationships. Isabella reflected on her marriage relationship with Sam as a complementary relationship. She was grateful that they function more like partners and co-owners of their marriage:

I think also just feeling like God was really completing me in many ways through Sam. Some of my weaknesses, he was really strong in, and I felt some of my strengths he was weak in. So, in a way he was a real completion—I felt more complete when we are together and that we could be co-partners in our lives. So that feeling of knowing that we were going to push each other to grow rather than to stagnate or to go back was a real important part.

Some of the young adults strive to build and maintain relationships that are characterized by respect and mutual support in their work places. They want to avoid competition and self-promotion whenever possible. Moreover, when they are given authority to create a work environment under their control, they work hard to create a cooperative environment. Daniel, who is a high school teacher, said:

I feel more comfortable when I'm working together instead of trying hard to beat the next person. . . I think I like, even when I am teaching kids, sometimes I enjoy being the person in charge, the head guy, but I would much more like to teach on the same level. It's just that I know a little bit more and just trying to let them know.

Care for individuals in community valued

The value of community, for the young adults, did not stop at a nebulous level. Having had experience with those who showed genuine care for them during their growing-up years, the young adults realized that the formation of community happens when individuals in the community live out the life of service. In that light, many young adults shared their dreams to be a catalyst for the enhancement of community somewhere. Elisa reminisced about an American lady who provided a warm and caring place for her and her friends to be enjoy participating in the youth group:

> Mrs. Holmes, Deborah Holmes, she had done a lot with our group at (my church) for quite some time and she was really a great lady. I think she might have gotten a bit frustrated though because I guess all her hard work, I think eventually in the later years, culminated, but in the early years I think we were still struggling but she planted a seed, she definitely planted a seed there . . . She was very warm, a very good listener. She genuinely cared for each of us and we felt like we were a big family together.

For Elisa, caring for individuals in the community became a motif in envisioning a community. Elisa talked about her experience with an elderly community and her desire to provide some kind of care for the individuals in that community:

> I think the elderly are important to society. They have a lot to share, a lot of valuable information because I had done a internship when I was at (my college) as part of my requirements to graduate . . . It (the topic) was just how to better their lives within the community, how the community could better serve. I mean they were all very nice and a lot of them are really lonely. Some of their stories, the people they have met, people they have been with, and just their experiences is just really incredible. I hope to go back and work with them.

The enhancement of community in the church is perhaps the most prominent theme the interviewees expressed about the future of the Korean American church. They grieved over the lack of the sense of community in the first generation church, but they were not very optimistic about creating a sense of authentic community among the second generation, either. However, they still expressed desire to see the realization of an authentic community. Julia, sharing her longing to have spiritual mentors in her life, talked about how her church community could benefit by having spiritual mentors:

> I've been praying about having spiritual mentors in my life and that's something right now that I don't have, someone that's older than me, someone that who has spiritual maturity . . . Someone who I can interact more daily, consistent contact with somebody. So that's something I have been praying about. Having spiritual mentors in my life and for my friends will be great for the church.

For some, a sense of community in the work place is a very important factor in deciding where they should work. Betsy talked about her job where she works with a small group of people, nurturing each individual to function as a learning community:

> I got hired (at a public school in the north side of Chicago). I got hired to work in the special ed. group, so that was where half of my day was in special ed. group. I really liked that, as opposed to the regular elementary classroom, because special ed. involves working more with a group of individuals. You have a small group of kids, and everything is individualized whereas I feel like when you are an elementary teacher you have to learn how to control a whole group of people. You can give a lot more individual attention like working with the kids one-on-one. Of course, you should do group work, too. Some people don't but I would prefer to do group work.

Authenticity valued

Socialization of secrecy
Many of the study participants expressed serious concerns about how the members of the Korean American community interact with one another. Their main concern stems from the persistence of gossiping that destroys relationships and hinders people from sharing their personal lives with others. Moreover, Korean Americans are especially afraid of how they might be perceived by others, if others know the problems or struggles of their lives or families.

Some of the young adults still remember the specific instruction about their family life that they received from their mothers in their growing-up years. The instruction was for the children to keep the family issues in strict confidence. Georgia talks about how her mother was anxious about others finding out about her family life:

> My mother, for example, does not really like it when I share about my family life—I think that's a Korean culture. We don't talk about things that are not as healthy. You always talk about all great things. You never talk about the undercurrents because I think people use it against you, even your friends. And it's very unfortunate that she feels that way even though she's a Christian. I see a lot of unhealthiness in our lives.

Sam shared about his mother deliberately keeping him from finding out about her divorce. Among other reasons, she was particularly concerned about how Sam and the family would be perceived and judged by Korean American people. Sam talked about the cover up and the impact it had on his life:

> I think my environment in which I grew up as a child was very influential. When we first came to the States—my mother and father got divorced, and that is something most Asian parents are not. I think there is a lot of shame in Asian culture for divorce. She didn't want people to know. So my mom never told me that our parents were divorced. She just mentioned, "Oh your father is away, military or business or something." I never found it peculiar at that age when you're young you just trust whatever your Mom says, so I had never seen my father until I was 6 or 7, at least as I recall. That probably was a defining characteristic in my life.

Some of the young adults also lamented how Korean Americans judge others by their outward appearance. They thought that judgment based on appearance encumbers people from being more open with one another. Rose shared her perplexity with the way in which people make superficial judgments:

> What I find bad is this image, this saving face, this name brand, this outer appearance, and this judgment on a lot of things. I am just like –"Why are you judging me on that? I'm a person and I have a lot inside. If you've got to know you would really appreciate, but instead I see a lot of judgment based on appearances and names and prestige and things that really are useless to me. I despise them, but that's not just the Korean culture, that's American culture, too . . . It drives me nuts.

Reflections on the interaction patterns of Korean Americans

For the above reasons, the study participants learned quickly that they are not to share the intimate aspects of their lives with others. They are often hesitant to share their lives with people around them. Isabella, a psychotherapist, shared her reflection on the inability of Korean Americans to deal with others about real issues.

> Korean Americans don't like to confront people. They are not very assertive in terms of like there's a problem and let's talk about it. So as a counselor you really need to know how to confront people in a loving way but yet very directly and that was something I found to be really difficult. I didn't know I would even have the skills to do that.

In sharing how Korean Americans interact with each other, Kris made a statement about his ethnic identity. He presupposed that Korean Americans do not open themselves up and share what they are feeling.

> I'm not really like Korean American because whatever is on my mind, I'll let you know. As you can tell right now, I feel very free to let you know what's going on and what I'm feeling and what I'm thinking.

Sam made an observation about why maintaining status quo is valued in the Korean American community. He contended that it stems from the unwillingness on the part of its people to deal with real issues that threaten the fabric of its community, relationships. Sam talked about how he tries to go against the norm of the community:

> I think that great pressure for stability, not rock the boat, not be different is just huge factor. And I really think that sometimes it is sinful. I desperately don't want to be like that. And among some good friends of mine I am known—if there is something wrong, then I am going to bring it up and that's what they really appreciate in me. If there is something wrong between our relationship I will come and I will bring it up. That's something that I wish we could change.

A same problem for a different reason in American culture

While the interviewees appreciate the freedom and opportunities to succeed that are available in the mainstream American society, they all agreed that Americans are by and large too individualistic. They contended that individualism in society causes the worth of other persons to rest only on the service they can render toward a person's own success.   In the process, people's relationships often become tenuous and temporary or easily fractured.

Sam poignantly described his reflection on how American individualism destroys the fabric of American society.   He self-reflexively talked about his ability to observe the state of American society from a more communal mindset:

> I think that we have too much freedom, not enough restrictions in America. I think people have a daring individualistic notion, like what are you going to do for me type of mentality. And I think that infiltrates almost everything from society, from politics to economics, social issues even religious issues are too individualistic. Coming from a more group-oriented mindset, I think that's why I see so clearly the negatives (of an individualistic society). And I tend blame a lot of societal problems on our individualistic nature. I sort of feel that's why people are out for themselves and not out for the betterment of the group, so I tend to blame most of America's ills on individualism.

Dylan shared his reflection on the American ideal of freedom that is somewhat similar to Sam's:

> It's kind of funny . . . Everyone respects what you do. It's a very open-minded society, but the same reason is kind of a concern as well because it's so open, there seems to be no absolutes, no right or wrong. And because of that I think that's where part of some −a lot of straying from God, a lot of disrespecting, or some characteristics I think can be drawn out from there . . . I guess it's kind of strange that I like it and not like it. And I guess also the way things are being tolerated, like things on, let's say like on TV and other stuff.

Well-developed stories and biographies valued

While discussing their views of media, some of the female interviewees shared their appreciation for a couple of genres of media. They valued TV dramas or movies that have good character development and are made up of wholesome stories. Melinda talked about the attractive features of her favorite programs on TV:

> I really enjoyed the Cosby show and Northern Exposure, in the beginning, the latter part I didn't like it . . . Cosby show was funny, it was based on good family values, kind of idealistic, it was in good taste and I felt like there was a point where values were brought across nicely . . . For Northern Exposure, when it first came out it was very different from all the other shows and it was interesting, had interesting characters. And the

character development was really good in the beginning, and it was just getting to know some of the characters that I liked.

For others, they expressed their love for reading biographies. They talked about the ways in which biographies open up the stories of real people, their triumphs and failures. Authenticity of people's lives was what attracts the young adults to enjoy reading biographies. Julia shared:

> I love biographies of people. Actually, Oprah Winfrey, J.F. Kennedy and the Kennedy family are some of those I have always enjoyed reading. Also, Billy Graham, Gandhi. I am always interested (in biographies). That fascinates me because I'm always interested in people and their background and what it is that made them who they are.

Critiquing how the Korean language has been used to create further inequality between generations

Some of the Korean American study participants offered an important insight as to how Korean culture shapes the lives of people in terms of the use of Korean language. *Hangul*, the Korean language, possesses two distinctive levels, one that is used among peers, and another that is used in conversations between the young and the old. The honorific form between the young and old is used in every sphere of relationships in the Korean culture, including parents and children.

Some believed that this form of language perpetually distinguishes first and second generations where the first has virtually all the power to dictate every aspect of conversations. Thus, some of these young adults saw the honorific language as a crucial authority or a weapon in times of family confrontations and first and second-generation discussions at the church, among other instances.

Rose shared her observations about the use and choice of language in the arguments between her and her mother:

> I'd start in Korean (in honorific form) because I know that's easier for her until I get really worked up then I'll go off in English. She starts in Korean and then she gets more Korean. She doesn't speak to me in English at all. She tries to overpower me with fancy Korean stuff.

Kelly also pointed out how the Korean language changes the relationship between young and old people. She recalled how her relationship with her future mother-in-law was shaped when she got married her husband:

> I did the dutiful daughter-in-law thing. Call once a week when Paul was still at work, call his parents, call just to see how they were doing. And that's so hard—what do you say—you don't know them. And they know I speak Korean so they speak Korean to me and that automatically changes the relationship. I was her son's little wife, you know.

Voices of Mutual Support and Acceptance

From the Peers

Interactions among fellow second-generation young adults, especially those who are Christians, have provided the study participants with opportunities to explore their identity issues. Moreover, through frequent interactions and encouragement, many of the young adults grew in their self-acceptance and assurance about their identity, way of life, and vocation. Thus, the strength of the voice of acceptance and mutual support is founded in the mutual authentication and legitimatization of their common experience of the past, present existence, and future hope among the young adults.

Peer encouragement has been an invaluable source in terms of the decision-making process among these young adults. They speak of the significance of their friends' words in affecting their ability to rise up to challenges and opportunities. The interviewees also speak of the fact that peer encouragements are, not mere therapeutic devices, but based on the enduring observations made by those who are either long-time friends or understood their life's predicaments. Kelly spoke of the support and assurance from her peers about her future:

> Having the affirmation, friends saying—you know, we heard that you are thinking about doing this—we think it's great. We can totally see you doing that. That has really been an encouragement during times where I felt like "I don't really feel prepared to make this decision or to make this jump."

The interviewees also noted a positive peer pressure for them to get involved in ministry opportunities as a significant theme. They believe that their cohorts have not been encouraged by the Korean American church to get involved in ministries outside of their local churches. Moreover, they shared their frustrations about doing the work of ministry at the church without receiving proper training. However, when their peers encouraged them to get involved with them in ministries outside of their comfort zone, many of the young adults agreed to do so and they reported coming away with significant impacts from those ministry opportunities. Dylan spoke of following his friend's excitement by joining a short-term, inner city ministry opportunity:

> She was very blunt, hard, and goes right to the point and that's what I liked about her. She didn't beat around the bush and felt that if there was something that she needed to say she would say without any hesitation or conscience and I thought that would help me take a look at my life a little bit more . . . So I felt it would be a good experience, and indeed it was a life-changing experience for me . . . I have begun to consider making changes in my life . . . My outlook on life is now different.

The study participants also spoke of how their peer recommendations have facilitated their career and marital decisions. Dylan talked about his friend who encouraged him to enroll in job training that would make him more marketable. Dylan said that he heeded his friend's advice and landed a dream job upon finishing the program:

> (My friend) was thinking about taking the same course as well. I think basically because I felt comfortable with someone else going in there together was one of the main reasons why I decided to go into the program. . . It turned out to be one of the most important decisions I've ever made in my life.

For Daniel, receiving approval of his future wife by his trusted friends was a very important process in terms of marriage. He counted on his friends to share their honest opinion about his future wife, and his friends took the request seriously. Daniel said that he did not have to ask them for the approval. Instead, he thought about what his long trusted friends would say to him about her from their perspectives, and was convinced that they would approve of her wholeheartedly. Daniel said:

> It (My friends' approval) was important to me. Even though I didn't outwardly ask them the question, I knew, just like my mom, that they liked

her and they would approve of her. I didn't just ask "Do you like Caroline? Do you think I should marry her?" But I knew that they approved. And they knew that I knew that they approved of her.

By Mothers

The mothers of the interviewees, in general, have consistently played a key role in supporting and reassuring them over the course of their lives. The mothers have provided almost blind trust and enthusiasm for their children, even to the point of detriment at times. They have thus been the continual source of the voice of acceptance. In other words, for many of the interviewees, mothers have been their biggest supporters. Dylan talked about the unilateral support and assurance that functioned as a reassuring voice in his life:

> My mom just would show support for whatever I wanted to do. She didn't really have much objection to what I wanted to do. But she also knows what I'm thinking even before I talk to her. She would always ask how I was doing and she knows exactly how to respond to me too . . . So she was more supportive on whatever my decision would be than other people around me.

Many of the study participants did not forget the significant role their mothers have had in their lives. When these young adults are faced with making important decisions, they actively seek out their mothers' advice or figure out their wishes. Or, if not directly, they seek the mothers' voices of acceptance and support that have been internalized. The young adults are committed to reciprocating the love and acceptance they received from their mothers. In a sense, they try to respond to their mother's voice with the kind of decisions that would please their mothers. Daniel said that he was glad that his mom liked his girl friend:

> I did talk to my mom, mostly, and I could tell that she approved right away. I could tell just by her actions, and the way she asked about (my girl friend), when we were dating. She was happy, very happy and (my girl friend) also had the personality and kind of a Korean culture thing that my mom liked . . . I could tell that my mom liked her, and that was important.

Brian talked about how he was able to receive approval from his future father-in-law to marry his daughter. He received much help from his future mother-in-law, who accepted her own daughter's decision to date and marry her boy friend. Brian is forever grateful for his (now) mother-in-law, when he says:

> Her mother was more accepting so I got on her good side. She respected her daughter's decision. And then she helped us out by helping me prepare for that meeting with her father, officially asking for his permission.

Many study participants are as dependent now on their mother's voice of support and encouragement than ever. The mother's voice of support and encouragement is deeply rooted and functions as a critical source in the lives of the young adults. Joel recalled the ever-present voice of his mother throughout the years, especially in the last few years:

> My mom was always there behind the scene. There was one time where my dad did come home drunk and I don't remember if I did anything wrong but all I remember is getting physically beaten and my mom tried to intervene, she said "if you don't love him that much, why don't you kill him" and then he stopped. Then I just remember my mom crying and I was crying, my dad just left the room. My mom and I, we always had a good relationship. She was always there when I needed her and she was always the one to comfort me. And even these past few years, without having a job or not knowing what to do, she was always understanding, always trying to encourage me, "You know, why don't you try this or something good will come up." So my mom was very encouraging of me.

From Parents Who Were Authoritatively Present

Some of these study participants attribute their healthy self-image and outlook on life to their loving parents who were actively present during their growing-up years. These parents tended to be less authoritarian and instead were authoritative and trusting, giving their children more freedom and presenting clear choices along with their wishes. Kelly is grateful to her loving parents for helping her become who she is:

> My parents have always been very affectionate people. They hug you, I still hug and kiss my dad and I still call him daddy, never father. And I remember at my college graduation, my parents gave a small dinner for our family. And my father got up to speak and he wept as he talked about how proud he was that his little daughter who couldn't speak English when she started school had graduated and she's going to work and pay

her own bill. And when he stood there and he started weeping I thought "Wow," I just don't know too many kids in general who ever see their parents openly weep like that. And for my dad to do that in front of his family . . . because he was talking about me in a very, very strong manner. I think now I consider my mother one of my best friends. I know the day will come when she's not going to be with us any more. I just don't know who I will talk to on the phone, who I will call when I'm grouchy, who is going to make me meals when I need to nurse my baby and all these things. And I also relate to them now as a brother and sister in Christ, which has been a very meaningful and blessed experience.

Melinda also shared the voice of trust and assurance that she has internalized from her parents:

> My parents—they trust me to do my own decision making. . . I think they have always trusted me and they know that if I really wanted to do something I'll do it. If it sounds good to them, they will be like "OK" or if not, they may share some concern and back off . . . I miss my dad a lot (He recently passed away.), but I know he will be pleased with whatever I decide to do.

From Multicultural Environment

Growing up in the city of Chicago has provided some of the interviewees with a healthy sense of their ethnic identity. Through multicultural interactions, they were able to view themselves as part of the mosaic of the U.S. They recalled that their peers or the people in their neighborhoods were not color blind. Instead, these people lived their lives in light of their own cultural heritages, as legitimate citizens of the U.S. They were also eager to share their own cultural heritages with fellow Americans from different ethnic and cultural backgrounds. It is in this kind of context some of these young adults grew up and were able to accept their Korean American heritage, perhaps more easily than those who grew up in the suburbs of Chicago.

Having grown up in the city of Chicago, Dylan believes that he has a healthy sense of who he is, especially when it comes to his ethnic identity. He reflected on this:

> I think I was one of the first Asians in our neighborhood and one of the first days I met someone right away and there was no problem. We became friends and we used to play with all the kids in the neighborhood. And when we got mad at each other, I don't remember getting down to the point of where he insulted me for being a certain race, instead he insulted

me how dumb I was or something . . . In high school, you think you're older and more mature or more tolerant . . . (Interviewer: Was the makeup of the high school pretty much multi-ethnic?) Oh, yes, absolutely. And that's one thing you have to or the school definitely tried to push. You know, the diverse city because they had to, it was the melting pot.

Voice of Companionship

Most of the interviewees reported growth in several areas of their relationships. In regards to the relationship with their parents, these young adults were encouraged by the development of mutual understanding and respect between the two parties. They also appreciate the freedom and trust their parents give more readily to them.

The married interviewees expressed their appreciation and admiration of their spouses as their life's companions. In discussing her husband's gentle advice, Isabella said her husband acted as the voice of comfort and encouragement as she contemplated changing her career:

> I think he sensed I wasn't completely happy and he has always had much more confidence in me than I have in myself . . . I felt that it was sort of like a holding environment where I felt I could move around a little bit. I knew that he was going to support me whatever I do.

Some attribute their spiritual growth to the companionship they experienced in para-church organizations during their college years. Elisa said "it was with a Christian campus group and friends from the group that I was able to meet God in a fresh way." Melinda stated that the missions mobilizers of a Korean American missions agency provided "a home away from home" for her. She also recounted that they "have been a tremendous influence" for her spiritually.

Voices of Spiritual Longings

The study participants generally described their spiritual life as the most neglected aspect of their lives. They reported their church experience to be monotonous and their personal spiritual experience dry. Elisa expressed the dullness in her spiritual life:

I have been too busy to focus on God and the Bible lately. I know that I
am supposed to fear God, but I guess right now, truthfully, I don't. I guess
because I'm just so caught up with a lot of my daily activities and I really
haven't been spending a lot of time in his Word as I should. Yeah, right
now I do see myself as having slipped away from where I want to be
spiritually.

These adults feel their churches are not nurturing them properly.
They complained about the lack of depth in teaching, preaching, and
fellowship. Some reported having significant spiritual experiences
outside of their churches. Dylan spoke of a corporate worship time at
the Urbana Missions Conference as if he were witnessing a glimpse of
heaven: "I remember that as a kind of 'Wow!' Kind of just in awe—no
words could describe the experience. I guess the experience of maybe
what heaven is going to be like." Isabella, a former journalist, said her
search for a significant spiritual experience in her life culminated in her
visit to Toronto Airport Church:

I think I experienced God there in a way that was so different. The Holy
Spirit really touched me in a really unique way. I experienced some of the
spiritual manifestations that they see up there. But more than that it was
actually feeling for the first time that God loved me, and that was a piece
that was missing in my spiritual life . . . And I saw a dramatic change in
my life after realizing that . . . I was doing it (believing God) was more
fear-driven than love-driven.

Although the interviewees are concerned about the lack of spiritual
nurturing from their churches, they plan to stay where they are, partly
because of their church friends. They also expressed their commitment
to work with the younger generation by passing on their faith and
tradition. In light of this, many of the young adults are involved in
some aspect of ministry at their churches.

Desire to Grow Spiritually
    While most of the study participants expressed a desire to grow
spiritually, they seemed to lack vocabulary to adequately talk about the
spiritual dimensions of their lives. They articulated their longings to
grow spiritually in three ways.

Desire to Grow in Their Knowledge of the Bible. Some of the study
participants emphasized the reading and study of the Bible more
consistently as the basis for spiritual growth. Melinda used

interchangeably the phrases "spiritual growth" and "growing in the knowledge of the Bible," viewing individual Bible reading as the primary way to grow spiritually. She shared somewhat apologetically about her recent struggle in studying the Bible, "I admit that these days it's not been a strong discipline of mine but I have been convicted of it recently." In explaining why Bible reading is so important to her, Melinda referred to her view of the Bible: "I see it as a kind of guide book. It comforts you and challenges you to be a better Christian."

Desire to Understand and Use Their Spiritual Gifts in the Church. Some of the male interviewees view the discovery and utilization of their spiritual gifts as the primary means to grow spiritually. They asserted that spiritual gifts should be the tools through which Christians construct their identity and grow spiritually. Certain spiritual gift inventories put out by Willow Creek Community Church in South Barrington, Illinois were referenced as accurate instruments to discover one's spiritual gifts. Once an individual has discovered his/her area of gifting, they contended that the church should actively seek to put each member in a place where these gifts will develop and grow. Joel shared how he matured and grew focused in his spiritual life through the discovery of his spiritual gifts:

In March I had attended a spiritual gifts analysis at Willow Creek and there God gave me a vision about leading a men's ministry, getting a men's ministry going at my church . . . I realized that men are struggling in their responsibilities in the church, whether it is sexually, or whatever. I really realized that men are struggling and they need accountability, they need each other, and I'm thankful that the vision that God has given me is starting. . . I am organizing it and I just want people to realize the need for accountability and the need for ministry, where men can get together and really share.

Desire to Be Purged of Personal Sins. Many of the interviewees struggle with the issues of guilt, shame, and forgiveness. While they have an adequate theological understanding of sin and forgiveness from the evangelical perspective, they still wrestle with integrating these theological constructs in their own lives. The young adults often fault themselves for not being able to measure up to the holiness of God.

With remorse, Isabella talked about her struggle with the sins of her past:

I want to give my life to God . . . But I have struggled in my Christian life for a real long time, with sin, and just not really being able to feel like a child of God. I have been really ineffectual and not really victorious in my Christian life.

Albert came across as a duty-bound person who desperately needs God's approval in his spiritual life:

I know that I need to follow God with my whole heart and with my life . . . I know in my heart that this is what I need to do, to follow God's plan . . . But I compromise with sins everyday. I just don't know how I can follow God's plan. I don't know how to push myself to grow . . . to be holy like Him (God).

Sources of spiritual authority

From the data, at least six sources of spiritual authority emerged illustrating the authorities that second-generation Korean American young adults have incorporated in their spiritual journey.

Nurturing Caucasian Sunday School teachers

Almost all the interviewees spoke of at least one Caucasian Sunday School teacher who accepted them as they were and had genuine concern for their lives in their growing up years. These Caucasian Christians, however, were at the Korean American churches for only a year or two. Most of these teachers were there to fulfill their field education requirements from schools such as Moody Bible Institute and McCormick Theological Seminary.

Despite the short tenure of the teachers at the churches, the study participants remembered fondly being in classes with these Caucasian teachers. They appreciated the fact that the teachers were well prepared, but also had flexibility to accommodate the needs of students. The teachers were respectful and genuinely concerned about what was going on in the lives of the children. The young adults reminisced that the support and encouragement they received from the Caucasian teachers made the church experience fun and created excitement to learn about Christianity.

Abigail talked about how she managed to go through her tumultuous Junior High years and how a Caucasian Christian planted a seed in her life:

Our youth group leader was a Caucasian woman and she worked with us for maybe about a year and a half. It was during my junior high years. And they were very difficult years for me. You know, you go through those difficult growing times and I was a very insecure person... I lived for youth group days, I really lived for it. We had a Caucasian woman to teach the Sundays and the youth group. And I thank God, as a child, he ministered to me through her. The feeling of acceptance, being myself there. I mean as far as the Word, I don't think I literally took a lot of that in, but Debby was there and like became the foundation in which God was able to, for later truths to be revealed in his book, so well up into this time.

A handful of Korean American youth pastors

The study participants shared that during their adolescent years they sought nurturing and caring authority figures. In their reflection on the past, they think they longed to fill the void left by parents and church leaders who did not seem to be concerned about spiritual issues and adolescent issues facing them. As adolescents, these young adults often looked to youth pastors in the Korean church.

They spoke of attempts to get connected to youth pastors and be known by them. However, they spoke of a "revolving door" experience with the numerous tenures of youth pastors who stayed for a short while and then left the church for various reasons. Yet, the interviewees savored the very limited number of youth pastors who made an indelible mark in their lives. These youth pastors exhibited gentle and caring spirits and demeanors. They were able to relate to youth well and were bridge builders to the parents' generation. They were also eager to model and teach the Christian faith with authority. Sam talked about his former youth pastor as if the pastor were his own father:

My youth pastor was a very significant person. He was my role model, a first male Asian American role model. I don't know if he did this intentionally or proactively but I felt that he kind of took me under his wing among all the other responsibilities that he had. And he helped me nurture some gifts and define myself. He also showed me what kind of person I should be. And I really appreciated that about him, and as far as my ministry and how I think now about vision and planning, I am much influenced by what he taught me.

Isabella also spoke of her youth pastor who related to her life well. She said her youth pastor earned her trust and respect because her father, who was an elder at her church, respected the youth pastor a lot:

(My youth pastor) seemed really knowledgeable about the struggles that kids our age were experiencing. . . And also really seeing how he was able to relate to us and yet also really connect with the parents, so he was sort of being like the mediating kind of person, with the two generations. And also it helped that my father really respected Paul and liked him a lot and so kind of gave me more of a respect for him as well.

Dylan talked about how his former youth pastor helped him to think more clearly about God and people:

My youth pastor really took me under his wing. And he helped me with a lot of processing and being open to different views about the Bible and about people. He had a tremendous impact in my life.

Elisa spoke of the profound influence her former youth pastor had on her, even after she went away to college:

He was a great figure. My church was very fortunate to have him serve with us. He had a really big impact. I know that he had taken time with a lot of us when we all went away to school. . . I remember I had a sit-down talk with him. It was truly life changing.

Encounters with spiritual authorities from the outside of the Korean American church during college and young adult years

Many of the study participants shared they were able to connect with good Christian role models during college years who profoundly impacted them. An important distinction is observed in that, while the interviewees tend to speak of having *individual* role models during their pre-adolescent and adolescent years, they spoke of being part of some sort of spiritual community and having multiple mentors during their college years. Sam reminisced about how the Christians he met during his college years were different than those he was used to. He spoke of his experience with a campus Christian ministry group and its impact:

I went to this Christian fellowship thinking it would be just like a church. But they were different, they were living out their faith, and they were really striving to know God and do His will. It was completely different from what I had seen back at my home church. I wanted to be like them, and be serious about God.

Some study participants spoke of internalizing a non-Korean American pastor as their authority. They said this particular pastor had remarkable empathy and understanding of the experience of the second-generation Korean Americans because of his background. He was born and raised in Korea in a missionary family and finished high school in Korea before coming to the U.S. for college and further training. Besides pastoring an English speaking Korean American congregation, he has had pastoral ministry with English speaking Korean Americans at large in the Chicago area for the past 15 years and has quite a following.

The young adults appreciate his gentle and pastoral spirit. Describing him as a counter cultural pastor, Georgia showered him with high honor. He "is more than a child of God. His life is God. Everything he says is about God, but he doesn't preach it. He talks about it but it's different, it's very different. He is a reliable man."

Isabella spoke of a campus ministry staff worker who nurtured her and her husband (then her boy friend) toward marriage during their college years:

I know that in our relationship, in the growth of our relationship, a key person was (the staff person). We talked with him a lot. But really when it came down to making the decision I knew where he stood in terms of how he felt about us and I knew he would support us getting married.

Georgia talked about a Chinese female therapist who helped her become who she is. This therapist, a Christian, shared her life experiences with Georgia, which had a profound impact on her life. Georgia spoke about finally being able to accept her femininity as a child of God. She said:

(My therapist) is more of—she portrays more of the woman to me in God's sense, but still with a brain, opinions, attitudes, personality, character, and her own creativity. (She) has helped me to explore and accept the side of me as a young adult, as a young woman. My direction that I want to go in my future, of who I am as a person, a child of God but as a female in God—different from a male in God, and she has definitely helped me to appreciate and accept my femininity.

The Bible as a spiritual authority

Although most of the study participants claim to be evangelical Christians, they did not know exactly what they meant by such a label. For instance, when they spoke of the Bible, they speak of abstract notions, i.e., inerrancy, revelation, and inspiration of Scripture. Perhaps Rose was trying to make these abstract ideas into tangibles in saying, "The Bible, to me, is God's way of connecting to us physically and giving us some connections to him."

Other interviewees spoke of the Bible as the authoritative book in their lives and the practices of the church. Molly saw the Bible as life's manual:

Bible is the Word of God. It's like a life manual, whenever you come across certain problems or questions, it's going to answer your questions in certain ways. It's accessibility to God, it's one way to have an access to God.

Dylan appreciated the Bible for illustrating godly life principles in several forms, especially through the narratives of real people:

What I have noticed a lot is the way the Bible teaches things is by—I really feel it's comforting that it teaches by— examples. It is through previous people and people's experiences. But I do believe that it is what God wants us to live by, in a sense of direction as well as encouragement, motivation, finding peace, and really knowing who God is through that, and I believe He has given it to us that way.

An ambivalent spiritual authority of prayer

Many of the young adults regretfully expressed that they go to God in prayer as a last resort when all else fails. While they do believe prayer should be an important part of Christian life, they just do not seem to make prayer part of their spiritual discipline. Molly said:

I try to incorporate him (God) in my life, but I'd be lying if I said he's all in everything that I do. I want to give him glory and stuff, and that's a real source of guilt for me, I think, maybe trying to accomplish it, I don't know--it's just something that's been ingrained in me since I was a kid-- you're bad if you don't do this kind of thing, like prayer and stuff. . . And with God, I guess, it's really bad, but I tend to go to him in prayer at my most critical points where I'm just like, "Okay, there's really nothing left for me to do." I'm the type that I'm very self-sufficient. . . It's just solely me in a lot of ways. . . When I come to a dead end that's when I go to God.

Others spoke of doubts as to whether prayer actually "works" or God actually listens to their prayer. They said they tend to follow their own feeling as God's leading. Although they desire to pray more, they are not sure what kind of signs they should expect to see as response to prayer. Finally, there were a few young adults who earnestly seek to experience the power of prayer in their lives.

Spiritual authority attributed to non-Korean American and successful Christian organizations

Some of the interviewees look to evangelical Christian organizations as a spiritual authority providing direction for their spiritual lives. These young adults assert that they need to un-learn the negative things they learned from growing up in the Korean American church. Moreover, they feel the need to re-learn what it means to be a church, have a Christian family, and be a Christian man or woman. They value organizations or movements such as Willow Creek Community Church, Saddleback Community Church, Promise Keepers, and Focus on the Family, among other organizations. Joel talked about his deep appreciation for Focus on the Family when he said:

The reason why I am really attracted to the Focus On the Family is that I feel like a lot of what they talk about are the issues that I am facing now or issues that I will be facing or that are going on in the world. And in order to better understand myself, better understand this world, I want to listen to the Focus on the Family. I believe that it has a good Christian base and it's a good program that helps me to be reminded of who I am and just what goes on in this world.

Chapter 8

View of the Korean American Church

The Korean American church, specifically through the influence of Christian education, plays a key role in the construction of the self and daily functioning of its young adults. The ways in which the church functions in the construction of self among the second-generation Korean American population are manifold. Thus, the church's function in the lives of the interviewees is a significant aspect of the internalized multiplicity.

The Role of the Church in the Construction of Self

Several salient themes emerged from the interview data of the present study that describe how the church has functioned and continues to function in the self-construction of second-generation Korean American young adults.

The Korean American Church as a Place for the Mutual Validation of the Korean American Identity

A place for the Mutual validation of ethnic identity
Most of the interviewees indicated that the Korean American church provided a safe place for them to embrace themselves as English-speaking Korean Americans in their growing-up years. The church has primarily functioned as a safe haven for the young people to gather together with their cohorts. They considered the church as a place where they did not have to constantly explain their ethnic and cultural backgrounds. These young adults asserted that just being with fellow Korean Americans validated their identity. Ironically, they recalled no

significant conversations about their ethnic or cultural identity among themselves. They simply enjoyed being free to deal with their immediate life issues. In other words, their Korean culture and background were assumed unreflectively, and almost set aside, at least in their minds.

Nick talked about the common experience they had at their homes, which enabled them to share funny stories and joke about their families. Daniel said it was the church that brought his cohorts together and "our commonness kept us together." Albert talked about how his Korean American peers at the church provided a sense of his ethnic identity:

> There was a group of friends here at (my church) that made me feel very comfortable with my Koreanness . . . Although we didn't share much similar kind of view of the world, just being Korean was very important to us.

Paul spoke of his pleasant surprise to meet many Korean American friends in the church. He said, "I met a lot of people, other Korean Americans who, to me, were surprisingly normal, yet American."

Speaking of the importance of the Korean American church in his growing-up years, Daniel asserted that the church has functioned as a separate or peculiar culture for him:

> Well, it was mostly because of church, but I think, overall, Koreans tend to just gravitate toward each other. The church made us feel comfortable with who we were. It was definitely the church that brought us together and then I think our commonness kept us together.

Paul went even further to say that the Korean American church had functioned as a social place where being Korean was more important than being Christian:

> I grew up in the church all my life . . . The basic purpose (of the church) was to meet other Koreans. I think religion was kind of secondary, and even now I think people are like that . . . For me, it was more important to have friends who were Korean than learn about God.

The study participants insisted that neither English-speaking Korean American pastors nor first-generation leaders had direct impact in terms of the validation of their Korean American identity. These leaders did not talk to them about the issues of ethnic identity in a palpable manner, giving only implicit validation of their ethnic identity through provision a place for the young people to come together. What some young adults did recall, however, were the few instances where first-generation leaders attempted to forcibly instill Korean pride and superiority in them, often producing intense negative feelings about Korean culture instead.

Trouble in paradise

The interviewees readily admitted the Korean American church was far from a paradise during their growing-up years. They spoke of the formation of cliques and their detrimental effects in the lives of the second generation. Isabella recollected a painful experience of the persistence of cliques among her peers at the church that she attended all her life. Her story is all too common in the experience of other young adults in the Korean church.

> Growing up at (my church) was a real hurtful time, I think, because there were so many cliques. They were really hard to break into. The guys at (my church) formed this little club, called the Cub Scouts. And they were very aggressive and mean, cruel to people, especially to their little girls (sisters). I just really found them to be a source of a lot of hurt and problems with self-esteem for many . . . also rejection of Christianity at that time . . . I hated coming to church . . . Yes, growing up it was definitely not a good place.

Isabella, like many other young adults, said there was no choice but to go to church with their parents. Since many of the parents held positions of leadership (elders, deacons, etc.) at the church, the young adults were required to be in their best form in front of other first-generation adults. One of the ways to avoid bringing shame to their parents was to attend church without absence. Some young adults complained that their parents still demand that they attend the same church in order to continue showcasing them. Young shared his perception of how cliques were formed in the church and the chilling effect they had on his life:

> I remember growing up in my youth group. It was very segregated, a lot of cliques and I remember I didn't fit in, and wanting to just forget about God, not wanting to get involved at all, and so there were many times where my parents literally had to force me to go to church . . . The cliques

were based on how popular you were, how good-looking you were, how much money you had. And it seemed like the rich kids all stuck together, while the not-so-rich kids, not so wealthy kids were kind of left out. And the wealthy kids were the ones who were involved in the youth group, in the leadership, and I felt like I didn't belong. I felt very excluded, like it was a very cold place . . . I felt a lot happier at school than I did at church.

Other young adults whose parents did not hold positions in the church were given more autonomy to make up their mind about church attendance. Michelle shares the reason why her siblings no longer attend church. She says that it all happened during her high school years:

When I was (at a church) it was the people (her peers) -- that's why my sister and brother don't come to church. . . I would see them in church and they were very nice, very good, but then I saw them outside of church and they were not so nice . . . And we felt criticized, we felt judged when we were there . . . I remember there were some days where my sister and I would go into service for the youth group and then my sister would pretend she was going to the bathroom and she would go out to the car and she sat in the car the entire service because she felt so unwelcome and unwanted in the group. And I remember feeling that way as well. I think we just saw all the bad things. When we had a bad image of people, then we had a bad image of church and of God, so that's why we stopped going . . . And for my sister and brother, that was the end of it.

The problem with cliques within the church extends to yet another level. Each English-speaking second-generation congregation has its own distinctive boundary markers defining its existence. Each church thus has its own normative rules and practices that members are expected to follow and abide by. Molly talked about a problem this kind of arrangement raises, especially if differences of opinion exist:

I feel like in a lot of ways if you don't believe their way then you really don't belong there . . . They are not very open to reflect on why we do what we do kind of stuff . . . So sometimes I don't feel like sharing things because I feel like they are going to be very judgmental towards me so I keep a lot of things in. Sometimes I feel like I can relate to them well but other things I feel like I can't relate with them at all.

Many interviewees had concerns about the Korean American church being too ingrown. They see the church as self- focused and too comfortable maintaining its own culture and heritage. This concern is directed toward English-speaking second-generation Korean American congregations that resemble first-generation congregations in their practices. Molly remarked:

> We simply don't disperse. We just kind of stay in one group, everyone knows everybody, which is nice. But, outside of the church or in the community, no one knows you or we don't know them . . . So not to say— I'm probably guilty of this myself to a degree, because I've haven't kept in touch with a lot of my friends I had who were non-Korean. And I feel like in a lot of ways the Korean church does its own stuff and we are quite content with it.

The Korean American Church as a Place for Keeping Korean American Culture Alive

Instilling conservative Korean values

While some study participants maintained the Korean American church functions almost as an ethnic ghetto and wished it was more outward-looking and encompassing of mainstream society, they generally agreed that the church was good at instilling Korean values in the lives of its English-speaking second-generation Korean Americans. Sam's comment exemplifies the voice of many young adults:

> My church heavily emphasized Korean culture. They (the first-generation) drilled us to respect your parents and keep the Korean heritage. Learn Korean language. Don't rock the boat, be a good kid, study hard, the things that are all related to the Korean culture.

Moreover, the Korean American church has socialized its people to keep conservative values in general, which is consistent with the tradition passed down by American missionaries to Korea at the turn of the twentieth century in Korea. Luke describes such socialization processes during his growing up years in the Korean American church:

> My church was very conservative so it was no drinking and dating was very, very minimal. In the church the guys didn't usually talk to the girls, or shouldn't do it in open. And during youth group there were some times when the men sat in the front two pews and the women sat in the last two pews or whatever. There was always some segregation and separation.

The transmission process that backfired: Boredom in their
church experience

Most of the study participants spoke of the Korean church as a
torture place. All the interviewees remembered the times when they
were required to sit in Korean-speaking worship services during their
adolescent years. They either had to listen to a sophomoric English
translation of the service using headsets or endure a Korean service
they could not understand. Paul's comment typifies this aspect of the
church experience, which had a profoundly negative effect:

> There was a point in time where they decided all of the kids should be
> with their parents during the service, I don't know if it was to promote
> the Korean service or promote togetherness or simply make it look like
> it was more people in the service. But I didn't understand a thing so I'd
> bring a book to read, never pay attention to the Korean service — I
> couldn't understand it anyway. After a while they tried to translate the
> service — they bought a bunch of these old radio transmitters. There
> was someone up in the elders room, with a radio and listening in trying
> to translate, it was more like broken English because it was very hard to
> understand. We had to listen. We were bored to death, plus the
> earpieces were uncomfortable.

Some of the interviewees find it ironic that the first-generation
leaders incorporate the English-speaking second generation at any cost,
but also consistently exclude the second generation from leadership
roles. Rose reflected on such practice:

> I always felt like there were things behind closed doors that we (the
> second-generation) weren't allowed to know about. A lot of what I term
> Korean bureaucracy in the church, a lot of like of hush-hush stuff going on
> among the first-generation. Obviously if they are hiding it from us, then it
> must not be good for us to find out . . . Why do they do that?

Hypocrisy in their church experience

Many of the study participants candidly spoke of hypocrisy in the
Korean American church. They grieved over the lack of integrity in the
lives of its people. This indictment was geared toward both first and
second generations. These young adults pointed out that people in the
church carry a judgmental spirit, especially toward those who deviate
from the norms of the church.

Some of the interviewees used very strong language to express their
reaction to the people in the Korean church. Albert, a mild mannered

man, reminisced about his feelings toward the church during his college years:

> When I went to Korea I was sick of Koreans and Korean Americans. Well, more accurately, I was sick of Christian groups, I was sick of them because there was so much hypocrisy and dishonesty. I was very hurt by them, and very hurt and disillusioned.

Nick shared an observation about Korean American Christians that he has witnessed over the years:

> Christians behave worse than non-Christians in church related activities. Basketball is a great format to reach Korean Americans or volleyball is a wonderful format. But whenever I go to these tournaments, church guys, the Christian guys are worse than the others . . . swearing their head off . . . . Well, we want to reach non-Christians and invite them to come, but then the non-Christians leave the tournament saying like 'These Christians guys are worse than we are.'

Nick and other study participants were perplexed by the discrepancy they witnessed between what the Christians say they believed and how they actually behaved.

Another "stumbling block" that caused these young people to be concerned about the church was gossip. Chris revealed how gossip among the people in the church affected his church attendance:

> I felt like they were saying like all this church stuff out of their mouths, but then they turn around and they talk behind your back. And if you're going to be a Christian, you should act out what it says in the Bible as much as possible. And if you can't, then you should be sorry for the things that you have done, so that was the one thing that turned me off, and then sophomore year, after that, I never went back to church again . . . until recently.

The Korean American Church as a Place for Christian Formation during Growing up Years

The study participants were generally in agreement about their experience of the Korean American Church and its Christian education as a faith community in their growing-up years. By and large, these young adults perceived their spiritual experience in the church to be uneventful or even counter-productive to their Christian formation, with the exception of occasional periods of respite. They spoke of lack of planning and preparation, in terms of programming. They also detailed the lack of intentionality and coherence in execution.

Counter-productive Christian formation

Most of the study participants were eager to share horror stories about the boredom with which they dealt at church. As previously discussed, many had the experience of Korean-speaking worship services, often with bad English translations. They also spoke of staying at church for long durations on Sundays to wait for their parents to get done. Moreover, they spoke of a mediocre Sunday school experience.

Many interviewees shared distasteful endurance of Sunday school and children's worship hour. They claimed knowing, even at an early age, that their teachers were not well trained or well prepared to teach them. The teachers spoke very little English and were too authoritarian in their interaction with the children. These young adults were quick to point out the mediocrity of teaching as well as the lack of consistency in caring for children and youth. Isabella recalled her experience:

It (the church) was not really a place where I felt like I was learning anything. There was no real teaching or haphazardly prepared teaching at best. Besides, the people that came through to teach us stayed only for short periods of time . . . youth pastors and teachers and all.

The interviewees also expressed frustration with the ways in which they were taught. Molly aptly articulated her experience with the children's ministry at her church:

Every time I've gone to a Korean church I have had bad experiences with the teachers. I always thought they were mean, I always thought they were strict, I didn't want to go, I didn't like the way they taught, or I didn't like what I was learning. We were learning Korean, Korean writing, Korean letters and stuff and I thought 'I don't want to do this.' I didn't want to go to school on Sunday, too. I thought of it more like a school, I had to go, kind of dreading it.

Continuing her reflection, Molly, who had also attended Caucasian churches, made comparative remarks of her experiences in both churches:

I looked forward to going [to the Caucasian church]. It was more fun, they made it towards more kids. At Korean churches they teach you like little adults. They expect you to do certain things, and sit down and do this, they don't want you to talk, and they don't want you to do anything.

Molly's experience at Korean American churches and Caucasian American churches can be analyzed as a contrast between teacher- vs. student-centered, content- vs. process-driven, hierarchical vs. egalitarian, or transmissive vs. romantic approaches to education. However, it is remarkable that Molly and other young adults chose to look through the cultural or ethnic lens.

Some of the study participants wondered whether the church should be the primary place for Christian formation. Having grown up in the Korean American Christian home, they struggled to understand the relationship between the church and the family. The young adults believe the family or home should be as much or even more important for Christian formation. When these young adults talked about the family as a primarily locus of Christian formation, they often have in mind the extended family. They lamented the fact that their parents have been and continue to spend too much time attending church programs, further separating both nuclear as well as extended family. Paul raised this concern:

You know, one of the things we gripe about is that there are too many meetings at the church. When I was growing up I didn't like it either but I learned to adapt—used to bring my homework to church. These days, it seems whenever we call, (my parents would say,) 'We can't do it today, got a church meeting tonight, got a prayer meeting tomorrow. Friday night we can't do it, we have to go to church'... What family service? It's like they almost resent us calling to get together because they don't have time for our family . . . We (second-generation) can criticize all we want, but we are doing the same thing. We are too busy with all the meetings and stuff at the church.

Caucasian pastors and interns

Periods of spiritual oases were often marked by the presence of one of two types of persons. As extensively discussed in chapter seven, the young adults spoke glowingly about those people who had significant influence in their lives while growing up in the church. One type of person was the Caucasian American youth pastor or intern who usually spent about one (or two years maximum) year with second-generation Korean Americans in the Korean American church. These predominantly Caucasian Christians came to the Korean American church either as a part of their field education training or as a hired gun. Yet they were faithful, understanding, and caring. These people accepted the second-generation students as they were and believed in them.

Their faithfulness and friendship. Dylan remembered a Caucasian youth pastor named Bill whose faithfulness and friendship made a deep impression in him about God:

> Bill was the one person who we all thought was very wacky . . . We realized that he had kind of a crazy personality but he really had a love for God that drove him to do crazy things . . . Looking back I am really appreciative of that. I don't know what it was, but something clicked. I remember he was part of that . . .

Coupled with Bill's faithfulness and friendship was the refreshing and free spirit that Dylan observed in Bill's life, "I think having Bill as my youth pastor was very significant in growing up. . . He made me realize that I can be "cool" and be a Christian at the same time."

Their love. Others speak of the love that they experienced from Caucasian teachers who were genuinely concerned about their lives. Rose talked about a Caucasian woman who taught her Sunday school class for just one year:

> I just remember that warm feeling in my Sunday school class. There was an (Caucasian) American woman named Diane, I think. And I just remember that warm feeling, that fuzzy stuff from her. I remember saying to myself that this is what church should be, experiencing God's love like this.

For Rose, then, her teacher Diane was able to help her viscerally experience what the church of Christ ought to be. Chris talked about the Christian love she experienced after the death of her father. As Chris was having a difficult time sorting through many issues in her life, she encountered a Caucasian pastor who voluntarily spent a lot of time with her. Chris says:

> I was very depressed after my Dad's death . . . I didn't know . . . what's this life all about. And then I realized there has to be a good God who takes care of you and stuff like that. I really felt like I really needed to

accept Christ into my life. And at the time Robert was really counseling me about my dad's death and stuff. And he would come over a lot and he was like a really good example . . . For the first time, I understood God's love . . . basically through him.

Their sensitivity and sharing of the Gospel. The study participants also appreciated their Caucasian pastors and interns for their cultural sensitivity and desire to work with Korean-speaking parents and church leaders. Interestingly, many of these young people shared they became Christians during the years when these culturally sensitive and "kid-friendly" Caucasian Christians were present at the church. Kelly shared her experience with Luke, a student at Moody Bible Institute. When asked why she remembers Luke, she said:

More than any of the Sunday school teachers I had before or even after, he was very sensitive to the cultural differences. And though he could not relate to them (first-generation teachers and parents) I think he understood that he was coming in as an outsider. And he came when I believe I was in 4th grade and that was how I accepted Christ. I just remember him taking a lot of time to talk to us, one on one, never making fun of the things that we were going through . . . just really taking us very seriously and having fun, goofing around, willing to try to get to know our parents, which was neat because I also remember a lot of (Korean) Sunday school teachers not knowing who your parents were.

Their authenticity. The interviewees also appreciated the authenticity that the Caucasian Christians exhibited to them during their growing-up years. Daniel talked about how his relationship with a former Caucasian youth pastor has and continues to impact his spiritual life:

Don would always invite us over to his house, and we still once in a while go visit him. I remember his wife had cancer and remember just being close to them. He was really suffering with her, I remember that, and he would be very vulnerable with us about his struggles. It was just a very close relationship . . . We (Daniel and his friends) saw Jesus in him. It was just incredible.

English speaking Korean American college students
and young adults in the church
Another type of person who influenced the lives of the study participants was the English-speaking Korean American college student or young adult. Like the Caucasian pastor or intern, the college

students and young adults often had relatively short stays at the church due to their transient life stage. Yet, the interviewees consistently pointed to these people as having significant spiritual impact in their growing up years. These Korean American Christians tended to be more Americanized and treated the second-generation children with respect and dignity. They exhibited deep care for the children and were able to empathize with the children's predicaments in their family, church, and society.

Generally in their early twenties or late teens, these mentors voluntarily chose to minister to the adolescents and children in the church. Dylan talked about Mr. and Mrs. Chung, who sacrificially ministered to him and his peers during his junior high years:

> They spent lots of time with us in teaching and hanging out with us . . . I think that, because of them, some level of seriousness of God came in my life . . . One of the things I think the most about growing up is the relationships, the friendships, that I had with them kept bringing me back to church . . . which eventually let God click in my life.

In their growing up years, the interviewees naturally gravitated toward Korean American college students and young adults who spent time with them. These Christian leaders appeared as attractive, winsome, and energetic persons to the children. Rose talked about some of the models that she had in her growing up years:

> There were a couple of Sunday school teachers who were younger, like Don, Luke, and Steve. I remember them because I felt like they related to us more rather than these Korean mothers who couldn't even speak English . . . I think they built the foundation for why I wanted to teach Sunday school. And that's what I used, I think, that and my spiritual growth in college to really have a vision for what I wanted to duplicate.

Breakthroughs in the Self-Construction Process:
College ministries and non-Korean American churches
as a place of nurture for young adults during their college years

Some interviewees spoke of the impact of having good role models or disciplers for their spiritual growth during their college years. Whereas during their growing-up years, these second-generation young adults were deeply influenced by Caucasian Christian workers, the young adults pointed to a handful of Korean American or other Asian American Christians as having significant spiritual influence during college years.

Asian American collegiate para-church ministries
    Most of interviewees spoke of the profound influence Asian American collegiate para-church ministries had in their lives. The influence they spoke of is not necessarily limited to the spiritual dimension of their lives. These para-church ministries on campus provided them with a sense of belonging, permission to explore their ethnic identity, and emotional support, among other things.
    For some, meeting fellow Korean American and other Asian American Christians provided not only a sense of belonging, but also permission to explore their own cultural heritage. For the first time, these young adults sensed the need to explore issues of ethnicity and culture from a Christian perspective. However, they admitted their inability to formulate, articulate, or even think Christianly about issues such as ethnic identity. Nick recounted the lack of preparation as a college freshman:

> We were nice kids, good kids in the youth group . . . In terms of our walk with God and our faith really weren't there or it was just more of a sort of lip service type of thing and just hung out in church and did things. Then by God's grace we went out to school and many of us received a wake-up call . . . We were all in different places and started exploring life's issues with vigor . . . We knew that something significant had happened . . . meeting God through (a college group).

Many young adults say they stopped attending church due to negative experiences in the Korean American church while growing up. However, Asian American collegiate para-church ministries served as a re-entry point for some young adults to embrace Christianity in their lives again. These young adults spoke of the members of a para-church ministry befriending them and naturally sharing the Gospel through their lives. Brian talked about such a college experience after fifteen years of absence from church:

> I was fortunate enough to hang out with some Christians who belonged to (a para-church ministry). . . After attending a meeting (put on by the ministry), I called this one guy and really asked a lot of questions. And he and his friends really took a keen interest in me. I did go to a few (of

their) meetings and informal Bible studies . . . We started hanging out together and I became a Christian through them . . . I never officially went to a church service, it was strictly involvement with (the people in that para-church ministry).

Some of the study participants spoke of their involvement in more charismatic churches where they felt free to worship God with emotion and exercise more spectacular spiritual gifts. Abigail shares how her involvement with a Christian fellowship led to a profound spiritual experience:

It was a campus fellowship . . . It was a charismatic group but it seems like in that group there was such a good accountability. And the teaching was just right on and people were really moving in the gifts but they were doing it with Biblical principles . . . I had never thought that God could speak and speaking through people and praying over me, words, knowledge, prophetic . . . God just really drew me and even in those moments God created the atmosphere for me to be able to give of those areas of my life step by step and weep with people. It made me really hungry for Him and grow in Him.

Mentors

Some study participants spoke appreciatively about Asian American Christian mentors during their college years. These mentors were fellow college students, generally one or two years older than the interviewees. The interviewees also talked about Korean American or other Asian American ministry leaders, whose age ranges from 25 to 35, as having had significant influences in their lives. Luke shared how his discipling relationships with older male Christians, who are English-speaking Korean Americans, have impacted his life:

My Bible study leader and three older guys had a lot to do with my spiritual growth . . . The guys were one year older than me, but they were sort of similar to me. And they knew what I was going through so we shared a lot of struggles . . . I would tell them about my sins and problems and some of the things I found that they have same as mine . . . Sharing with these guys I felt like I've got a lot of baggage . . . We prayed for one another and made an agreement that we wouldn't be afraid to ask each other personal questions. That really helped a lot. Having all these older brothers helped a lot.

Among the interviewees, there tended to be more talk of the influence of role modeling among the male young adults than the females. The reason for the phenomenon is quite simple. When the male interviewees talked about role models, they emphasized the hierarchical nature of their relationship with the role model. Although the females had plenty of relationships that resembled the role modeling of which their male counterparts speak, they tended to portray their relationships simply as significant friendships. Betsy recounted the relationships that she was able to develop with older Christian women through her para-church small group during her college years. She spoke of the provision of vision to live as a Christian.

> I joined a small group in my freshman year and that's where things started to really happen for me. They looked out for me . . . I just remember the relationships within that Bible study with the other members . . . As people invest in me, I think that's why I was at church. Yeah, it was because of people, older people. I remember someone told me to stay away from guys, 'What you should do in your freshman year is to spend time with older, more mature women.' Actually it wasn't so much me going to them but they would come to me. So that was really good for me. That was my whole freshman year and I continued all the way through senior year.

Non-Korean American churches

According to the study participants, significant spiritual encounters continued to be outside the confines of the Korean American church during college years. Many of them attended Caucasian American churches in the vicinity of their colleges and universities. Generally, they were not concerned about the church's denominational affiliation. Rather, they were attracted to the churches where the members of the para-church ministries they encountered belonged. Rose shared why she started attending a non-Korean American church and how she became very involved:

> My faith grew through (a para-church ministry) that I was really involved in, my spirituality really deepened through the Word because of their focus on it . . . And I started coming to (the church) with my (para-church ministry) friends. I started getting fed. A lot of people from (the para-church ministry) went to (the church). . . I just really began to embrace the Pastor's philosophy on church and how to run a church about letting the people do it. It was no longer 20% of people doing 80% of the work like in the Korean church, I saw 90% of the people doing the work. He

just supported everyone to do that work, so much volunteerism. He preached grace and freedom, not guilt—I hated people who preached guilt. I put enough guilt on myself, so I loved his preaching of grace and freedom, very Biblical and he would only preach on a few verses of week and yet still give us the big picture—I really enjoyed the feeding.

Rose and other interviewees tend to get attracted to churches where pastors encourage and enable lay people to become an integral part of the church's ministry. They also crave good preaching and teaching grounded in the Bible and grace-focused. They rarely talk about the importance of church fellowship during their college years. Perhaps they felt they had a good faith community through the para-church ministries in which they already took part.

Describing their experience with non-Korean American churches during their college years, the study participants often used comparisons with their Korean American church experience of the past. They charged that the Korean American church, including English-speaking second-generation congregations, is too comfortable with the maintenance of what already exists. Young described his experience attending a Hispanic church during his college years, which transformed his view of worship and Christian life style:

I went to my friends' church, Hispanic church, and I got to participate in their worship and it was truly a blessing to know that God is being worshipped and God is being praised, not only in Korean American churches, not only in the American churches, but in Latin American churches, Hispanic churches as well. And I feel like in some sense God is moving more, God is more powerful in those churches than he is in Korean American churches. I think Korean Americans are very comfortable in their lifestyles and with who they are, that they are just putting God second in their life, and I realized that. A lot of Hispanics they need God, each and every day for survival because a lot of them work for minimum wage jobs and so they—some of them really understand what it means to serve God, to worship God because they are placed in a situation where they need God . . . I feel like many Korean Americans now are just too comfortable.

The Functioning of the Korean American Church as
Part of the Internalized Multiplicity

The Present Experience of Second-Generation Young Adults in the Korean American Church

The interviewees were remarkably unanimous in describing their present church experience as bland and wanting. The young adults were quick to lift up several concerns that they have for the church.

Lack of open and honest fellowship
The study participants decried the lack of open and honest fellowship among the members of English-speaking second-generation young adults. Chris talked about her experience:

> It's been four years and we (Chris and her husband) haven't made many friends. You know, it's just like people aren't open. They don't want to talk. You ask them 'How are you?' They would just say, 'Oh, I'm fine, everything is going great.' End of story . . . I just feel like they are not willing to open up . . .

Many of these young adults asserted feeling uncomfortable sharing their deep longings of heart and life struggles. In her reflection on the lack of authentic fellowship in the church, Chris echoed the sentiment expressed by many young adults:

> They (the young adults) are scared to share what's going on (in their lives.) – you can tell, too, when somebody is holding something back. It's like maybe they have had some bad experiences in the past. . . Actually I feel more comfortable with Caucasian people. I feel like I can just say whatever and it would not be held against you or it's not going to be spread through the community.

Some believe their parents and the church, fearing possible dishonor associated with open sharing, have socialized them to be silent about their life issues and pretend that everything is fine.

Lack of cooperation
The interviewees outlined the lack of cooperation among the people in the church. They pointed out the dearth of interaction between first and second generations in the church. These young people feel the first

generation has shied away from participating and working with the second-generation English-speaking congregation under the same church roof. Even those who have resided in the U.S. for a long period of time and have a proficiency in English seldom make overtures to connect with second-generation young adults. Speaking of the senior pastor at his church, who has had some success in working with second-generation young adults in the past, Daniel remarked:

> I think that he is so busy with the first generation. I don't know if he just doesn't have the time or just feels that's his place. He always talks about how he is too old to take care of the second generation and all. It's sad.

However, the lack of understanding and interaction among people in the church cannot only be attributed to the generational gap between the first and second generations in the church. Some interviewees pointed out the existence of such a gap among various groupings within the English-speaking second-generation congregation.

One congregational gap that some study participants pointed to is the separation between singles, those who are married, and those who are married with kids. Talking about a cohort of people in different stages of life, Luke seemed almost resentful those married with children:

> At (my church), the majority of the members are a certain age group, about late 20s to about early 30s. They are married, they have one or two children. They are young couples with very good jobs, very satisfied and because they are very good at getting comfortable and settling down. So they go to church because it has some good aspects but they are not convicted, not passionate. Some of the congregation members are, some people in the age group are as well but it seems like the majority of the people who do most of the work in the church are either the oldest members of the church, or the youngest members of the church—this middle group, the age group I was talking about—seems not as involved.

Lack of pastoral leadership

Many interviewees commented on the lack of pastoral leadership and pastoral care in the church. They also expressed concern for spiritual lethargy in the church. While discontented with their pastors and lay leaders, they tried to give the benefit of the doubt, attempting to understand the difficulties that the leaders might be going through. Differences in philosophy of ministry from that of the first-generation leadership and also limited material and human resources in the

English-speaking congregation were acknowledged. Moreover, some interviewees were quick to point the finger at themselves for not contributing to the church as much as they should. Dylan reflected on his predicament as a Sunday school teacher:

> Sometimes church becomes such a hassle, not a hassle but more of a burden . . . I haven't prepared my Bible study for my kids and it becomes a task instead of just wanting to worship God . . . I know I have to put more into the church before I complain about the church.

However, some study participants feel the pastors ought to be more present and connected with the members of the congregation. They also desire leaders to be more pastoral in their interactions with the members of the congregation. One young woman states, "The reason why I started attending (another church) is because I was originally going to get married at (the original church), but the pastor there couldn't find a date to do our wedding." Reasons for the pastor's inability to perform the wedding aside, he clearly did not communicate to the young woman that this very special event in her life was valued.

Lack of vision and vigor

The study participants raised wide-ranging concerns about the church. For instance, some felt uncomfortable about their English speaking Korean American churches remaining ethically homogeneous. Others spoke of the persistence of the rigid hierarchal church structure of the first-generation church. In all, the young adults sensed a lack of vision among the English-speaking second-generation Korean American congregation for how the church can play a key role in the lives of its people.

Instead, some interviewees think the church has been more of a stumbling block for its people's Christian growth. Daniel aptly described how the church has caused much grief in the lives of its members:

> I know in my heart that we should be growing (as Christians). But these days I think what hinders me, more than anything, is the church. My church specifically hinders me and it's all about the way that it was started, the way that I am obligated to it.

Some interviewees maintained that many young people come to the church to be either cared for or entertained. They are concerned that many of the young adults complain about the church and its leaders for not doing much to bring enthusiasm to the church. Young made a strong statement about the lack of spiritual vitality he has observed among second-generation young adults:

> When I see the first generation Koreans... I really sense them really worshipping God, and just how much they do give—not only financially, but just their time or just their efforts. But, when I see the second generation they are very hedonistic in their own ways, very self-centered.

Again, Young used a comparative strategy in making his observation about the second-generation Christians. His statement is unusual in the sense that he made positive statements about the first generation, commending them for their devotion to God and commitment to the church. Young continued to lament the life style and approach to Christianity of the second generation. While reflexively assessing himself, he generalizes about the second-generation Korean American Christians and their congregations:

> I find myself catching myself falling into that trap and that's something that I don't want to do, just to be complacent and to live a life of mediocrity and to compromise new things, and I feel like a lot of the churches now are compromising in their beliefs, and watering down the gospel message, and that's just something that I feel God hates.

Some believe that the church is too pastor-focused and the success of the church too heavily dependent on the leader's charisma. As a result, the church's goals change every time the church experiences leadership change, which is less than stable. Nick asserted, as do some young adults, that the church has been in a rut:

> I have noticed about Korean American churched people attend churches like (more popular Korean American or Asian American churches in the Chicago area) usually because of the pastor or well run programs . . . We've gotten to this mentality, if they've got a good discipleship program and teaching, people go there . . . I hear, 'I want to be fed' all the time. I hear that 'I go because Pastor so-and-so is there and I know he is a good speaker and I'm going to get good teaching.' And that's good — I really and sincerely believe that's important — but what happens is then they get stuck in a rut. The maturity level of these brothers and sisters stay in the same place because they want to stay in the cocoon environment of reproducing for themselves what they experienced in their Christian life

and their college experience . . . They've heard many messages, they don't need any more teaching. They need to get involved either in the church or do something for the less fortunate.

Nick's lament about the passivity among second-generation Christians is all too common. Ironically, as discussed earlier, this status quo in the church is remarkably similar to the status quo many of the interviewees grieved over in the first-generation congregations that they grew up in. However, Nick goes on to critically analyze this situation. Thus, some interviewees are very concerned with ending the cycle of mediocrity and status quo.

Lack of grace

Many of the interviewees voiced concern about the general tenor of ministries within the Korean American church. For instance, they lambasted the guilt-driven and shame-producing tone of much preaching and teaching. Talking about the desperate need for grace, Rose shared her reason for currently attending her Caucasian American church,

> I used to hate Korean pastors for putting a guilt trip on me at (the Korean American church) . . . I put enough guilt on myself, so I love his (the pastor's) preaching of grace and freedom.

For some, the grace of God has been understood more as a theological concept rather than the ethos of their churches. Luke reflected on his church experience during his college years:

> Like some people, I felt it (the church) was too stringent, too strict. Some people felt it was almost cult-like, that we did everything the same, we had similar tastes, . . . I felt like I wasn't good enough, I felt that there was something in my life that I'm not doing or taking care of . . . I would say I felt guilty because I wasn't doing all my do's, and at the same time I really didn't understand God's grace. I think that (grace) wasn't really accentuated enough in (my church). Definitely there is a standard, . . . in one aspect they knew a lot of standards and they abided by a lot of them, they were very good at it, but people who didn't meet up to it, they looked down upon. . . I think overall the general feeling of the church became sort of judgmental . . .

Luke's experience unfortunately echoes the experience of several other interviewees. They talked about rules and standards that are poorly articulated, seeming arbitrary to all but insiders of that faith community. They also spoke of how insiders approach outsiders with a judgmental spirit. Luke shared an experience he had with a pastor who was candid, yet shared an unsubstantiated impression at a difficult decision-making time in his life:

> I remember times when I was debating over going into physical therapy or going into the medical field, he said 'Well, what do you want to be' and I told him maybe consider going to medical field, being a doctor or being maybe a physical therapist and he said 'Well, be sure you pray' and I remember he told me "cause you tend to have a lot of pride", I'd say "How?" and he said "Well you tend to think everything on your own, so you kind of do it your own way, it's just the way that you do this."

The church as a safe haven and dwelling place for second-generation Korean Americans

Safe haven

Despite many concerns of the English-speaking congregation, most of the interviewees still see the Korean American church as a safe haven for themselves. They view the church as the central place for coming together to affirm one another's faith, experience, identity and culture. These young adults appreciate being with fellow second-generation church members because they understand one another's past history, present life, and future yearnings. Luke shared his appreciation for the Korean American church interacting based on a set of Korean American cultural presuppositions:

> This is something that I have never really experienced elsewhere, a very strong, thriving second-generation congregation—everybody in my church functions pretty much as Korean American so this is something I really appreciate and really enjoy.

Moreover, they feel comfortable being not needing to constantly explain the superficialities of their lives, such as ethnic origin, foods eaten, and such, to others. While many of these young adults have reservations about the church and the level of interaction among themselves, they enjoy being themselves. Luke remarked that the peer-group in the churches is the most important aspect of being in the church:

I enjoy the sermons but it's not the most spiritually uplifting for me all the time — sometimes it is and sometimes it's not. But I like the peers and I like the friends that I have made at the church, so it's probably that more than anything.

Potential place

Again, while the interviewees are quick to express some critical concerns about the Korean American church, many of them consider the church the future hub of English-speaking Korean Americans. Although they yearn for more autonomy for the second generation, they are committed to being part of the Korean American church. Many of the men and women do not plan on leaving the church to either start an English-speaking Korean American church or join an Anglo-American church.

Daniel typified many of the study participants' sentiments about the church and what it has done for him. Despite its shortcomings, the church has functioned as a character-shaping authority in his life:

I think my character was largely developed by church, going to church, studying the Bible, and things like that—that had a bigger impact than TV or school. I want to be a part of continuing that tradition. Yea, we have lots of stuff that depress me but what else do we have?

Daniel pointed out the dearth of adequate alternatives for second-generation Korean Americans. He believes it is critical to maintain the flow and continuity of generations in the church, despite many differences in culture and values.

In that vein, many of the interviewees would like to stay and make meaningful connections with the first generation. Kelly spoke of the need for autonomy for the second generation rather than continuance of dependent or paternalistic relationships with the first generation:

I would love to see elders of the church... say we want this second generation to be autonomous, to make decisions for themselves, to know that the first generation church. And I want them to admit that how [the first-generation congregation] functions is not in many ways realistic for second generation, this is just not how it functions. I think would be exciting to see giving us autonomy instead of 'Why would you want to leave? We'll take care of you. We have the money and we can bring in people (pastors) for you,' and that kind of stuff.

Interviewees who came back to their home churches after having experienced significant spiritual growth during their college years are cautiously optimistic about the future of English-speaking ministries. These young people often try to avoid direct confrontations with first-generation leaders. Instead, they focused on what has been happening in English-speaking second-generation ministries. Speaking about the encouraging signs of ministry in his church, Sam shared:

> Currently in our church, our efforts and dedication in the past few years are starting to bear fruit, in fact, a lot of the fruits. A lot of young adults and kids (adolescents) that we discipled in the past are now getting to a point where they are on fire for God and they want to take leadership positions and that I really appreciate that so I am able to step back now. They want to go deeper with spiritual disciplines and stuff . . . So, whereas church used to be a place where I needed to serve, like a one-way street, and is now becoming a refuge for my spiritual walk—a very encouraging place for me spiritually.

Others commented that the church provides an opportunity to integrate their faith and life further as they pass on their faith to younger people. For instance, Albert appreciates this opportunity: "I'm thankful for the experience God gave me where I could integrate what I am learning about God and my faith with teaching kids."

Envisioning the Church for Future Second-Generation Korean Americans

Grace-filled church

Many of the interviewees have been reactive to the first generation ways of being the church. Thus, they try to carve out their identity as a congregation in contrast to the first generation. Their views of church have been largely shaped by American evangelicalism that shares similar tenets of faith with the first generation, but is more democratic and modern in its outlook than the first-generation Korean American church. Many of these young people are quick to follow more successful church models of Caucasian evangelical churches, such as Willow Creek Community Church, in South Barrington, Illinois, or the Vineyard church in Evanston, Illinois. The churches the young adults attend all have sophisticated sound systems and semi-professional worship bands. Many of the interviewees have attended evangelical conferences, such as Willow Creek Association's leadership conferences and Promise Keepers.

However, most of them have no intention of leaving the Korean American church. They are, by and large, looking for less legalistic and shame-producing churches that accept people as they are. Grace-filled churches that are more Americanized and mature stand out as well. Envisioning what the Korean church ought be, Melinda spoke of a pan-Asian American church that models such values:

> I love (the church I have been attending). I recognize that it's not a perfect church, but not by far. I feel like it's a few steps closer than a lot of churches that I've seen. There is just a sense of community, working together that we're in this together, we respect one another. . . I'm just thinking I'm this little girl and yet they respected me and wanted to hear what I thought and they saw me as an adult and respected what I thought and said.

For Melinda and other interviewees, acceptance and respect for who they are is extremely important. They also long for a sense of community with a genuine partnership and mutual care. Melinda talked about the care she received from her church when her father passed away:

> And so in that time I felt it would be really good to build a sense of ownership over it too . . . I feel so much care for them and from them and so much appreciation and respect from them and for them. And with my father's passing, I had never been cared for in that way, in such a godly community-like way . . . I know that I idealize (my church), but I have been a recipient of so much love and caring grace from the community, and I have been so blessed and touched by the ministry. I will always speak the praises of (my church) and I have tremendous respect for the leaders. It was such a privilege to sit under their teaching and to be a part of something like that.

When other interviewees envisioned a grace-filled church, they talked about openness and honesty among the members of the church. As previously discussed, the interviewees long to see themselves opening up with their life's struggles. Kelly reflected on a wedding she recently attended:

> We (she and her husband) were recently at a wedding, I was sitting there and looking around other (young adult) families, who also have children.

And none of them seemed to have very strong marriages. And I was very surprised when one woman said that she was having struggles with her in-laws, very similar to my situation in that she and her husband had several conversations that were very much like one's that Paul and I had had. And she and I both shared our frustrations. . . And I was really struck by her openness at that moment and I thought—I had no idea and she said, 'I had no idea that you were going through that.' Just imagine the kind of prior support we could have shared, the comfort that we could have given each other during that time . . . Why does church have to be this way? Why so hush and hush and everyone pretend to be doing fine? I get sick of just thinking about it.

Kelly and others are looking for more openness among the members of a church as the catalyst for the church to grow as community.

Counter-cultural church

Generating ideas for the future, many of the interviewees expressed their preference for a church holding values counter-cultural to mainstream society. Moreover, they long to see leaders who exhibit counter-cultural values in their lives. They look for people who are not too concerned about worldly standards of success, such as numerical growth, large budgets and making a name for the pastor or the church. Georgia talked about such a pastor:

(My pastor) definitely had something that I had not seen before. No fight, no nothing, he talked about church, he talked about being drunk in spirit, he talked about whatever, and people thought he was nuts. But I thought he was an amazing pastor . . . He had a junky car that someone had given him. It was a winter and the lock was frozen and he couldn't get the door to open. It was like a hatchback, he had to undo the back, climb in the back. Here's my pastor crawling through the back, not feeling ashamed, not feeling anything, just doing what he needs to do — going in, the handle comes right off — you know, it's broken, goes in, starts the car and he goes 'Bye' and drives away. He is a pastor who is like how old, as a husband and as a father. Here's a man who had a heart for God that just touched me in a special way. Then, there's me. He showed me something that I didn't know about following Christ.

Some of the study participants are attracted to the pastors who wish to see the church develop to its full potential. They speak of the important lesson learned from pastors who sensed their church would be better served by pastors with a different vision. Her own pastor, who voluntarily stepped down for the sake of the church, touched Kelly:

> I get excited when people step down from positions or pass on opportunities because they know that that is not where God is calling them—where they know that that is not where God has gifted them and we have had a number of situations right now at (my church). We've had some people leave and not all of them have left because of those reasons, but I know of one couple that left a position of leadership knowing that their gifts just do not match the needs of the church. And what a incredible decision they have made—completely trusting in God and I think that is teaching a lot of people that you don't just say 'yes' to every opportunity that comes by. And this whole idea of passing on this church to the next generation, I think, that's valid because our children will to some degree grow up in this church.

Reforming the educational ministry of the church

As previously discussed, many of the interviewees see the Korean American church as a safe haven and community of their future. They also see the church as the main avenue for their generativity. Many of them, after experiencing spiritual growth during their college years, have decided to come back to their home churches in order to pass their faith on to the next generation. However, they envision the church and its educational ministry to be more innovative and transformational than in past experiences. Sam explicates:

> Well, I think the way we are doing it now is inadequate—Bible studies once a week or teaching kids in a classroom setting is inadequate. The Bible is inherently practical and God is inherently in everything, so trying to teach them in an academic style is just not the only way to be done. I think people grow in faith experientially. As a discipler or a person, a Bible study reader or whatever that would teach me what it means to be humble and teach what is means to serve and show me God's creation and show me God's power—things like that. Alternative things like maybe going to work in soup kitchens or going to serve by building houses or going on nature walks and looking at the creation and how it was born and built and things like that rather than just the theology or this is what God did. . . I think that would be far more valuable and far enriching experience.

Generativity valued

Looking back on their church life, many interviewees realize they did not have mentors who were there to walk with them and nurture them in faith. While they are appreciative of some of their Sunday school teachers, they noted the lack of modeling by people in the church. When the interviewees talked about life goals, many of them expressed a desire to spend time discipling younger Christians so that they themselves can perpetuate the tradition of producing people of faith in the Korean American church.

Sharing her appreciation of a rich spiritual heritage in her family, a somewhat rare occurrence in the Korean American family, Julia remarked on her desire to share her faith with young people in the Korean American church:

> We do have a pretty strong family background, as far as spiritually, God has really blessed my family in the sense of as far as spiritually because my great, great grandfather that would be my dad's side, he died for the church in Korea.... God's really close to my family.

Julia continued by sharing what she would like to see happen in the Korean American church and how she wants to be part of it:

> I would like them to be more open and provide more services. And it be a growing ministry where they would have strong core leaders and I would like to see people discipling others because I think from my own personal experience I don't think I would have grown had I not been discipled. I wouldn't have been to this point if I wasn't discipled. And I feel that God is calling me to disciple others, to leave the legacy of faith in their lives.

Chapter 9

Implications for the Self and Christian Education in the Korean American Church

This concluding chapter summarizes the salient themes found in this study. The chapter then proceeds to draw implications from the findings by analyzing the functioning of the self in second-generation Korean American young adults in the midst of internalized multiplicity. The analysis brings together the salient themes of the internal functioning of the self and the strands of the literature discussed in chapters 2, 4, 5 and 6. In conclusion, implications are drawn for the church and its Christian education programs from the interactive analysis of the young interviewees' church experience and recommendations for the church.

Summary of the Present Study

Summary of the General Framework of the Study

This study has focused on two research problems. First, it sought to understand the internalized multiplicity of authorities, values, and voices in the narratives of second-generation Korean American young adults. It also sought to understand how internalized multiplicity functions in the lives of these interviewees. Second, the study examines the role of the Korean American church, specifically the influence of its Christian education on the construction of the self and daily functioning of these young people.

The present lives of second-generation Korean Americans resemble the lives of their Caucasian American counterparts at a cursory reflection.   As Erikson argued[1], Korean American young adults are engaged in the two most salient issues during young adulthood, namely, ego-identity and intimacy. First, these young people attempt to forge who they are and want to be as they reflect on their past, with the intention of declaring themselves as unique and autonomous individuals.   Second, young adults seek to build significant relationships with others. During this time, many of the young adults look for a life spouse.

Indeed, Korean American young adults have the typical issues the mainstream society expects its young adults to contend with. They strive to find and develop a career of their choice, and search for independence from their families in terms of their residence, finance, and identity. They also strive to negotiate challenges that are involved in forging a lifestyle of their preference. Moreover, they strive to build and grow in their significant relationships. One obvious difference between these Korean American interviewees and the general population of young adults Erikson envisioned is that the interviewees are committed to incorporating their spiritual lives in their projects of ego-identity and intimacy. Considering the great percentage of church attendance and involvement among second-generation Korean American young adults, the role of the Korean American church must be one of the central themes of the study of these young people, as was the strategy for this study.

While most of the life projects of Korean American young adults might be consonant with that of mainstream young adults, the sociocultural context in which these projects are carried out has been qualitatively different, occurring in a more multifaceted atmosphere. As previously discussed, Uba maintains that, despite some differences, both male and female Asian American young adults tend to exhibit a similar pattern as that of Caucasian female young adults, whose projects of self-identity and intimacy are often conceptualized as one integrated project. Moreover, Uba argues that race, ethnicity, gender, and age work confluentially as variables that shape the lives of ethnic and cultural minorities in the U.S.

For instance, these Korean American young adults have constantly negotiated the effects of both centripetal (pluralism) and centrifugal (assimilation) forces and their interactions throughout their lives.

---

[1]Unless stated otherwise, all the names cited hereafter in this chapter have been discussed and fully cited in chapters 2, 3, 4, 5, and 6.

These effects are not merely an abstract reality to them, but a concrete reality where various sociocultural institutions have claimed their authorities and values on their lives. Family, church, educational institutions, and professions, among other sociocultural institutions, have exerted their power as the young people attempt to forge their lives. These sociocultural institutions and relationships have had confluential effects in shaping the lives of these young adults, generating internal multiplicity.

Summary of the Themes and Functioning of Internalized Multiplicity Among Second-Generation Korean American Young Adults

By analyzing the inter-relationships among the salient themes that emerged from the lives of these interviewees, some generalizations about the nature and functions of the self are formulated for second-generation Korean Americans. The salient themes of internalized multiplicity and inner functions are as follow.

The theme of internalized authority resulted in two categories. Outside-in authorities include parents, church, and mainstream society. Inside-out authorities include peers, adult figures, and spiritual authorities. The internalized values comprise family as mixed blessing, autonomy, relationships, community, high ethnicity and high assimilation. A variety of the internalized voices surfaced. They are voices of mutual support and encouragement, absence and enmeshment, media, comparison, mediocrity and inadequacy, assimilation, womanhood, American dream, obligation and filial piety, companionship, and longing.

Investigation into the internal functioning of the self resulted in three major categories of themes. First, the relationship patterns with selves in inner life exhibit themes such as incorporation of others, comparison and measuring up to others, projection, obedience to God, and generativity. Second, reflexive action on the self includes themes of self-consciousness, reflection on the constructed self/self-reflexion, coming to terms with past, self-acceptance, and self-avoidance. Third, the future of the reflexive self comprised themes of self- determination, self-improvement, and planning for further self-reflexion.

Summary of the Themes of Church
Experience and Recommendations

Interviewees' reflections on their church experience suggest a few important themes. They believe the church has had a constructive role in their lives. The themes include their gratitude toward loving Caucasian teachers and a few exemplary Korean American youth pastors, mediocre or unimpressive Christian education in the church, the first-generation oriented atmosphere of the church, negative patterns in modeling and socialization on the part of the first generation, their college years as a period of spiritual break-through, and their consideration of the Korean American church as a safe haven for future Korean American Christians.

Several themes emerged from the interviewees' recommendations for the Korean American church and its Christian education. The themes include the church as an authentic community, a grace-filled community, a healing place, a reflexive community, a place of intentional and integrative Christian education, and a proactive and engaging community in the world. Some of the specific recommendations include more understanding and reconciliation with first-generation Christians within the church, addressing the issues of power and position in the church, empowering women in the church and family, equipping the laity, and reaching out to broader communities.

Implications for the self: Socioculturally Constructed
Distributed Self: A Promising Methodology in Understanding
the Self of Second-Generation Korean American Young Adults

The notion of the self in second-generation

Korean American young adults should be conceived as the socioculturally distributed and constructed self. While sharing many similar life projects with Caucasian American young adults, Korean American young adults have a set of peculiar life experiences that permeates the make-up and functioning of the self.

The construal processes of the self of the young adults, however, are neither static nor unambiguous. These processes are fluid and precarious in nature and must take into account the historical and cultural bases of various forms of world construction. As Geertz argued, the make-up and functioning of the self of the young adults can only be understood in a socioculturally relative manner where the ordinary interactions in life intermingle to construct a particular concept of self among second-generation Korean American young adults.

In this study, the researcher sought to understand how multiple games of life are played out according to commonly accepted rules, and to search out significant symbols and underlying regularities in the lives of the young adults. Thus, the notion of self for these young people must be considered as a product of the situations in which it operates, namely Bruner's notion of the "swarms of its participation." The construction of the distributed self should be considered as the dynamic interactions that proceed from the outside-in as well as from the inside-out, from society-culture to the self and vice versa.

Indeed, the study participants have been interacting with various visible and invisible guests in their lives. Therefore, a careful study of the nature and functioning of the swarms of the person's participations among these guests constitutes a plausible study of the self of second-generation Korean American young adults.

The Telos of the Functioning of the Self

Despite the complexity of their life experiences, the interviewees are in general committed to on-going reflection on their lives. They seek to understand how their past experiences have shaped who they are and how the experiences continue to influence their present lives. They understand that their past experiences are not merely a set of events without effects, thus to be discarded. Instead, they believe that their past experiences have had and continue to have profound impact on their lives in the form of internalized multiplicity.

Internalized multiplicity does not reduce to form what Mead calls the generalized other, symbolizing an absent-actual-others. Instead, multiplicity of the self should be conceptualized as Watkins's notion of imaginal others who function as the actors of the person's internalized social reality, namely the self. Each actor or invisible guest matures as a character through four stages as argued by Watkins: animation, articulation of psychological properties, clarification of the perspective, specification of identity of the character. The *telos* of the self of the young adults, the internalized social reality, is then to create, maintain, and grow in mutual respect and peaceful coexistence among the invisible guests.

For instance, the findings of this study suggest that the interviewees strive for self-determination, economic success, and pursuit of happiness. These values and other aspects of the American dream are, however, the very attributes these young people criticize their parent generation for being obsessed with.   In fact, this study's findings indicate that the majority of the interviewees share their parents' occupational aspirations for their children.   As Uba suggests, the aspirations involve prestigious professional occupations that bring financial success and high social status.

This researcher submits that the study participants have indeed internalized their parents' dreams of success, outlook on life, occupational aspirations and other expectations.   Instead of remaining as a set of ideas to be pursued, these attributes were internalized and developed as invisible guests within the self of these young people. As an example, the internalized attributes of the father developed through the stages (the animation, articulation of psychological properties, clarification of the perspective, specification of identity of the character) to become a powerful invisible guest within the self or the internalized social reality of the young person. This imaginal father continues to exert his wishes on the young adult to succeed. In a similar manner, the imaginal father continues to take on additional characteristics of the father, approximating fuller character of the father over time.

When the study participants criticize their parents for their obsessive pursuit of the American dream, they often base their criticism on its manifested negative consequences in their own lives. They deeply regret the absence of their parents during their growing-up years. They despise their parents comparisons of them with their siblings and others in the church, which often resulted in competitions and low self-esteem.

Thus, while the interviewees are committed to pursuing the same American dream as their parents, they seek to achieve it in a different manner. Again, the different manner is not merely a different strategy, but it is the manifestations of other invisible guests possessing a different set of values that reside in the self of the young people, influencing them to approach life differently. One such invisible guest might be a Caucasian American Christian teacher from the past who exhibited genuine love and care for the young adult, as discussed in chapters 7 and 8.

Moreover, there exist other invisible guests who personify different manners through which the American dream can be achieved. These characters may be the person's close relatives or people in the church who are successful. They could also be celebrities such as Tiger Wood or Michael Chang, who are Asian Americans. They may also be Bill Gates or even a TV character, as Caughey suggested.

Social Relations as the Key: An Implication for the Self and the Church

As discussed above, the *telos* of the self of the young adults grows in harmonious relationships among the invisible guests.   However, Hermans and Kempen argue that not all the invisible guests necessarily promote peaceful coexistence and mutual respect. Instead, each of the invisible guests, according to Hermans and Kempen, functions as an individual *"I"* position with his or her own personality and goals. They, thus, conceptualize the self, not as a coherent whole self, but as the sum and interactions of multiple *"I"* positions, i.e., decentralized multiple selves.

Within the self, then, exist suppressed voices and other issues of dominance within dialogical relations among the multiple selves. Following the lead of Hermans and Kempen, the present researcher argues that asymmetrical relationships exist among the multiple selves in the forms of interactional dominance, topical dominance, amount of talk, or strategic moves.

The issues of asymmetrical relationships must be addressed in order to promote a growing harmonious relationship within the self. The self often suffers from the enduring effects of asymmetrical relationships from the past that hinder the full realization of who s/he was meant to be.   This researcher contends that the issues of the asymmetrical relationships can be effectively addressed through authentic interactions of people who share lives in the context of a safe and hospitable community. This researcher submits that, if the self is an aggregate of internalized social relations as Watkins, Hermans and Kempen, Vygotsky and others argue, the movement toward wholeness of the self can and should begin at the sociocultural context that gave birth to and has engendered the self.

An appropriate sociocultural context for second-generation Korean American young adults, the present researcher maintains, is the Korean American church. The Korean American church possesses many necessary constructive components where the young adults can reflexively work on their selves together. In order to accomplish this task, the church needs to, not only simulate, but embody the harmonious and holistic social reality. Detailed descriptions of such a community will be discussed later in the chapter.

Relationships in the Functioning of the Self

As discussed above, the self as the internalized social reality, presupposes social relationships among the invisible guests. As Geertz conceptualized, these social relationships usually operate under both constitutive and constraining forces of culture/society so that persons are not often conscious of them. The relationships among the invisible guests within the self of the young adults seem to operate under the following forces.

Incorporation of others
One such force on the relationships that are operative in the lives of the interviewees is the sense of obligation to incorporate others, including invisible others, as the evaluative measurement of the core self. While these young people detest how their parents and other first generation adults have constantly compared them with others, they have internalized the practice of comparison, measuring up to others becoming a key criterion for their self-assessment.

Interviewees often seem to be too conscious of those around them and too self-conscious of the invisible guests within their self. While both Cooley and Mead theorized that the other as a social mirror would eventually become a singular generalized other with maturation, these young people seem to maintain multiple sets of both external and internal mirrors through which they see themselves and engage in self-assessment.

The incorporation of the multiplicity of others, however, is not necessarily disadvantageous to the proper functioning of the self. Instead, when the multiplicity of others, including the invisible guests, interacts in harmonious relationship and is streamlined to have one unified *telos* or a set of agreed life goals, it may be more advantageous to the proper functioning of the self. The multiplicity of others is more authentic in comparison to Mead's notion of generalized other, particularly in that it seeks to incorporate the sociocultural influences on the person in a more specific and comprehensive manner. Thus, the theory of distributed self in combination with the theory of multiple selves may be a valuable framework for understanding the experience of second-generation Korean American young adults and for promoting wholeness among them. However, as discussed above, the framework can only be effective when the cohorts commit themselves to engage in the project of the self together in a safe and hospitable community.

The transference in relationships

Related to the force of obligation to incorporate others is the force of transference. Here, I am referring to borderline transference in the sense of "transference acting out," as opposed to classical psychoanalysis notion of transference.[2] In the clinical setting, a client or patient who "acts out" transference projects:

> onto the therapist feelings towards parental figures from his past without any awareness of their true origins and also without any perception of the independent existence of the therapist in reality. Instead the patient sees the therapist as literally being that projection. This allows the patient to replay earlier scenarios in the present without feeling or remembering their links with the past. He alternately activates and projects upon the therapist each of the split representations of the self and the mother or other significant figure from his childhood.[3]

Having internalized the multiplicity of others, the young adults may be engaged in transference acting out in various spheres. However, the transference acting out is toward the therapist. Perhaps the most significant kind of transference acting out in the young people involves God and other significant persons in their lives.

Many of the interviewees articulate the feeling of abandonment in their perception of God and other significant persons in their lives. The absence of parents and other church leaders during the growing-up years has been well documented in this study. Moreover, the excessiveness of parental demands and expectations can have a

---

[2] James Masterson, *The Search for the Real Self* (New York: The Free Press, 1988), 129-132.

[3] Ibid., 130.

profound impact on the young adults' perception of God and others. Correspondingly, their perceptions of God and others as the self-assessment criteria may have had downward spiraling effects on their self-esteem.

For example, they may struggle to accept the grace of God as a result of their transference acting out onto God and the consequent bad self-image based on that transference. These interviewees may also be bound up in duties to please God and others, in order to be accepted by them. This kind of self-compliance and submissiveness may bring a state of "feeling good" but is only a pathologic false self, concerned with immediate pleasure rather than long-term recovery, reverting to regressive behavior."[4]

In both projections, the study participants engage in a kind of instant replay of the abandonment and necessary coping scenarios imprinted in childhood. In the process, they carry the past into the present and project it upon God or others around them. These kinds of transference acting out need to be converted into a real transference and skillfully confronted.

For the Korean American church, two cursory implications can be drawn. One is to invest in the lives of some of its people to be trained as group psychotherapists who can effectively help these young adults work through the issues of transference together as a group. Another is that the church needs to preoccupy itself with creating a grace-filled community where these young people can grow in healthy relationships with God and significant persons in their lives.

Enmeshment in relationships

Another related force operative in the relationships of the interviewees is that of enmeshment. They share their concerns about unhealthy enmeshed or codependent relationships with their mothers, resulting in a variety of serious problems, as previously discussed. Lee concurs with the finding of this study when she says that, in many Korean families, the strongest emotional attachment for a woman is often not her husband, but her children, especially her sons. Thus, it will be instructive for these young adults to address boundary issues within the collectivistic Korean American culture. In particular, the characteristics and consequences of enmeshment, such as care-taking, low self-worth, repression, obsession, controlling, denial, dependency,

---

[4]Ibid.

poor communication, weak boundaries, lack of trust, anger, and others,[5] need to be contextually evaluated as a community.

Keeping relationships alive

The interviewees are committed to pass on a more contextualized Korean culture and a more holistic Christian faith to the next generation. Their commitment to generativity rises as a corrective for the absence of intentional parenting and mentoring they experienced in their growing-up years. They envision the Korean American church as the community through which they want to work out their generativity. The Korean American church has an important task ahead in equipping and mobilizing these young adults to engage in transmitting its ideals and values to the next generation and beyond.

Themes of the reflexive project of the self

As previously discussed, the interviewees are often unconscious of the constitutive and constraining forces of culture/society on their lives. These young adults are busily involved in working out their projects of identity formation and intimacy building. While they might not have had many opportunities to reflexively evaluate their own lives, their initial attempts at such evaluation emerged from the analysis of the findings in the present study.

Self-consciousness

As Vygotsky argued, consciousness is the fiction of interaction where interactive experience, whether real or imaginal, transforms into the realm of the delayed internal social reaction structure. In other words, self-consciousness refers to the heightened ascendancy of the self in that fiction of interaction or in the realm of the delayed internal social reaction structure. The study participants seem to be especially concerned about evaluating themselves in the drama of life, especially in their fiction of interactions. Some of the debilitating results may be that they become too conscious about themselves, overly cautious in the decision-making process, and less apt at taking appropriate risks in

---

[5]Melody Beattie, *Codependent No More* (New York: Harper & Row, 1987), 35-47.

their lives.   Moreover, the two principal vehicles of socialization, obligation and shame, reinforce them to maintain sociocultural norms and expectations.   These young people are often too conscious of the norms and expectations, and they often feel stifled by the expectations.

Reflexion on the constructed self
Some of the interviewees have begun to reflect on the sociocultural influences that shaped their lives.   While they often see themselves as a mere product or victim of outside-in influences, they are gaining appreciation for the agenticity that they possess.   Indeed, the person can be construed as the product of all the sociocultural factors around her where her life is not just her own, but represents and reflects surrounding factors.   However, these young people ought to realize that, as Vygotsky contended, internalization involves more than a mere transmission of sociocultural influence by outside-in force.   It involves the willful shaping of that influence into a personally constructed subjective experience of the young adults.

Self-acceptance
The interviewees show some hopeful signs of coming to terms with their past and who they are.   They seek peace with themselves rather than accusing or destroying themselves.   For some, the need to address some internal issues is recognized, self-avoidance strategies are employed instead.   They do not feel ready to tackle the issues they have to deal with.   However, by and large, the young adults are eager to embrace themselves more and grow in the self.

The future of the reflexive self
The study participants discuss at least three goals toward improving their lives. These goals are self-determination, self-improvement, and self-reflexion.   These goals are inter-dependent but not necessarily sequential.

Self-determination.   The interviewees indeed envision their future in terms of the possible selves that Markus and Nurius proposed. These young adults utilize their possible selves as psychological tools to motivate and defend themselves and their present life styles. Possible selves also function as possible future trajectories of their lives.

These young adults realize, as Vygotsky contended, that they are not merely passive agents, but active agents who transform nature and culture. They seek to create and utilize tools in order to strengthen their active self. While some of them dream about building their own unique community of the second generation, many others desire to work within the socio-historical context of the first generation, whether it be the family or the church.

The interviewees are also realistic in realizing that many of the opportunities available to their Caucasian American counterparts may not be available for them. Although it may be convenient for them to blame the lack of access to opportunities on racism, they recognize their lack of social capital, i.e., finance, connections, and heritage, for taking advantage of the opportunities. In Bourdieu's terms, neither first nor second-generation Korean Americans possess appropriate habitus in the mainstream society to produce capital. As a result, the field for Korean Americans is limited. The Korean American church, as the only viable sociocultural institution for both first and second generations, should investigate ways in which it can construct generative schemes resulting in the production of capital and expansion of the field of its people.

Self-improvement. Despite their limitations in mainstream society, these young adults seek to engage in their life callings within their situatedness. They also seek to integrate various strands of their lives and grow in integrity. They express that their desire for self-improvement stems very much from respect for their predecessors and successors in the various sociocultural institutions in their community, namely, their parents, their own families, the church, and fellow Korean Americans.

Planning for further self-reflexion. The interviewees recognize the need for further reflexion on their lives. They also recognize the need for inter-dependent relationships through which they can reflect on their lives. They prefer working on themselves in the context of a safe and hospitable community where they can mutually benefit and grow together.

Implications for the self in action

In this section, three overarching themes about internalized multiplicity are discussed. These themes illustrate how the self negotiates multiplicity in real life. From these themes, implications are drawn toward the enhancement of the functioning of the self.

Peculiar effects of assimilation and pluralism in the U.S.

The interviewee's dream?: High assimilation &
high ethnic identity

These young adults' efforts to assimilate into mainstream society have had significant, as well as peculiar effects, on their construction of the self. In the orthogonal model of Kitano and Daniels, these young people generally fit into Cell B (high assimilation & high ethnic identity). Those who fit into Cell A (high assimilation & low ethnic identity) express their commitment to work on their ethnic identity as a Korean American. However, while the orthogonal model may serve as a useful tool in categorizing second-generation Korean American young adults, one of the variables, namely assimilation, does not capture the complexity of the second-generation experience.

When Gordon proposed the seven step processes of assimilation in the early 1960's, he was rather optimistic that all Americans of any ethnic descent would eventually assimilate into mainstream society. He postulated that they would all want to assimilate into mainstream America. In the second stage of his model, ethnic Americans will enter into cliques, clubs, and institutions of the host society on a primary group level; and in the third stage, large-scale intermarriage occurs.

According to this study, the interviewees have indeed been well acculturated to mainstream society. Being born in the U.S., English is their primary language. They received all of their education in the U.S. and are currently employed in mainstream society. Their cultural patterns and behaviors can pass as Caucasian American. However, they currently do not belong to any cliques or clubs of the host society. Gordon does not include membership in professional organizations related to one's occupation, of which many of these young adults are members, as part of his model. Moreover, all the interviewees, except one, who is uncertain, clearly state their commitment to marry fellow Korean Americans. Some have already done so.

Thus, according to Gordon's model, the study participants are still in the first stage, acculturation, in the seven-step assimilation process. Perhaps these young people, observing that Gordon's fifth (absence of prejudice), sixth (absence of discrimination), and seventh (absence of value and power conflict) stages will never become reality for them, have already foreclosed the possibility of becoming fully assimilated into mainstream society. In the process, they may have already chosen to remain at stage one. Or more likely, the presence of racial and ethnic prejudice, discrimination, and value and power conflict in mainstream society are preventing the young adults from moving into the second and third stages of the assimilation process.

The interviewees' experiences with racism have caused them to realize they will never feel quite at home in mainstream society. They are beginning to be aware of issues ranging from the negative media portrayal of Asian Americans to the glass-ceiling effect in the marketplace. They have begun to explore the various effects of being labeled as model minorities. For instance, many of these young adults would have appreciated having one of their parents home, instead of earning the dubious distinction of having the highest income per family as Asian Americans. They started realizing the lack of appropriate social networks and other capitals needed to succeed in mainstream society. These young people should continue to reflexively evaluate how they have been shaped by the practices of racism and formulate ways to proactively respond to such construction in their lives.

On the home front, the interviewees' parents, while desiring their adult children to be successful in mainstream society, have actively dissuaded their children from intermarriage. As an extension of the Korean American family, the Korean American church has been a safe haven where the young adults were welcomed to interact with their peers. In spending much time at the church, these young people have maintained lifelong friendships with many of their peers, and many have returned to their home churches, reuniting with their childhood friends. By and large, these young adults are content being part of Korean American culture in their private life and working in mainstream society in their public life.

The models of adaptation for second-generation
Korean American young adults reconsidered

For these young men and women, neither Anglo-conformity nor the melting pot has proven realistic as a model for legitimate life trajectory. Based on the findings of this study, the researcher contends that the trajectory these young adults and subsequent generations will follow will likely be the classical cultural pluralism model or ethnogenesis model, depending on their experiences.

In fact, many of the interviewees are well on their way to the lifestyle that the cultural pluralism model predicts for ethnic minorities. There is a definite sense of the persistence of ethnic, social and cultural ties to their parents' heritage. At the same time, these young people do embrace many of the social conditions of the host culture, while maintaining their own. They are all U.S. citizens, mostly by birth. They are committed to American political values and enjoy the common mass media. Yet, they seek to maintain their own community while revising their former heritage. The Korean American church continues to be the center of that community for them. The trends of the cultural pluralism model, at least for the Korean Americans in the Chicago metropolitan area, will likely continue in the future.

Furthermore, as Americans of various Asian ethnic descent join in alliance, whether voluntarily or imposed by the social institutions of mainstream society, the ethnogenesis model will provide an invaluable model in understanding the formation of Asian Americans as a new ethnicity. Efforts of various Asian American groups to obtain more political solidarity and influence are indicative of this ethnogenesis. This kind of construal has been well documented, especially after the civil unrest in L.A. and in the U.S. Census. However, for the young adults in this study, ethnogenesis has mainly been the result of the mutual support of young adults and their Asian American cohorts during their college years. Some of the Korean American young people continue to maintains ties with fellow Asian American cohorts, and it remains to be seen how the ethnogenesis will continue to evolve within the Asian American community in the future.

The young adults and theories of ethnic identity development

According to theories of ethnic identity development, the person of ethnic descent in mainstream society generally experiences four stages in achievement of a healthy sense of ethnic identity. As previously discussed, the four stages are based on Marcia's four stages of identity formation—namely identity foreclosure, identity crisis, moratorium, and identity achievement—where the development of ethnicity in the person is the isolated variable.

Indeed, the findings of this study clearly indicate that many of the interviewees have gone through these processes. In general, they possess a healthy sense of their Korean American identity. Those who grew up in the suburbs wanted to be accepted by their Caucasian American peers at school and in the neighborhood. In the process, they attempted to distance their Korean culture from their public life. At home, in the absence of their parents, they were heavily exposed to TV, through which their desire to fit into the mainstream society deepened. However, they lived as the children of first-generation Korean American parents, acquiring much of Korean culture.

In the Korean American church, they were able to be and act as who they were with their Korean American peers. These young people, however, did not receive much beneficial instruction about Korean culture in the church. Instead, they speak negatively about their Korean language school experience, which took place in the church. Interestingly, it was the Caucasian Christians workers (who came to serve in the Korean American church) who graciously encouraged them to appreciate and grow in Korean culture.

During the college years, the interviewees' involvement in Pan Asian American ministries or Korean American ministries encouraged them to examine their ethnicity as Korean Americans. Through healthy reflections as a group, they were able to explore the issues of ethnicity, achieving their ethnic identity. Included in their reflections on ethnicity were theological reflections on ethnicity, culture, and multiculturalism proving extremely helpful in their ethnic identity achievement.

For those study participants who grew up in the city of Chicago, there was no compulsion to be like or fit in with Caucasian Americans. Living in a more pluralistic setting, they enjoyed interacting with people from many ethnic backgrounds, including Caucasian Americans. They also had more interactions with neighborhood kids from diverse ethnic backgrounds. Interestingly, these young people had more interactions with their grandparents, uncles, and cousins, as well. When they talk about the influence of TV in their lives, they speak of it as entertainment, rather than as a socializing tool of mainstream society, which was the suburban young adults' experience. In all, they seem to have led less complicated lives than those who grew up in the suburbs, at least in terms of their ethnic identity development.

One of the implications that can be readily drawn from the patterns of ethnic identity formation of these young adults and subsequent generations is promotion of the positive values of city life. These values include frequent interactions and exposure to Americans of various ethnic decent, extended family members, and fellow Korean

American peers.   At a more practical level, the Korean American community ought to re-evaluate one of its preferred values, the rapid flight to more desirous housing and education. If the fact that residence in the city of Chicago has had many positive influences on the ethnic identity development of its children, the community as a whole needs to consider its people's lifestyles. For instance, Korean Americans, both first and second generations, could perhaps delay moving to the suburbs. This delay could translate into shorter work hours for the parents, less pressure to come up with a larger mortgage payment every month, and more time with their children.   Although these recommendations are highly speculative, the community will benefit much by reflecting together on the effects of lifestyle on the formation of its families and children.

Implications for the Korean American Church

Due to the complexity and confusion characterizing the Korean American social context and the many factors contributing to the development of the self, the Korean American church is in a position to play a vital role in the growth and future of what may appear to many as a "lost generation." Three implications for the Korean American church are apparent.

A Safe and Hospitable Faith Community as the Method and Place for Christian Education in the Korean American Church

The telos of the community

Christian education practice in the Korean American church must be the primary method for young adults to come together to work on their reflexive selves. As a safe and hospitable faith community, the church needs to facilitate such projects for its people. Since this project is intensely social, as the person interacts with both the actual and imaginal selves, it must take place both in the individual sphere and within committed relationships in the church. By working on the reflexive projects of the self collectively, young people can dialogically engage in the project in both of these spheres.   Through the interactions, they will understand more fully their vocations and experience wholeness in their experience of the self, as well as of the world.

Revisioning Korean American culture: the Korean American
church as the home base

Interviewees do not claim to have mastered Korean culture when
they state that they are Korean Americans. Realizing their deficiency
in Korean language and other aspects of the culture, they express their
desire to acquire more of the Korean American culture. They also
desire to pass on their heritage to subsequent generations of Korean
Americans. However, they are very keen on rectifying certain aspects
of the culture, while preserving some of its treasured aspects. The
Korean American church has been and should continue to be the re-
traditioning cultural center for second-generation young adults.

According to Abramson's four possible sociocultural conditions of
ethnicity, these young adults may be categorized as converts. The
converted ethnicity is essentially relational in nature in that young
people's sense of belonging comes mainly through social interactions
with those in mainstream society. In terms of symbolic ethnicity, they
may be considered as those who belong to the third category where
memories and symbols of the ethnic culture exist, but there are no
primary networks and structural attachments, especially for second-
generation Korean American young adults who have no attachments
with fellow Korean Americans.

However, the majority of second-generation Korean American young
adults do belong to the Korean American church which functions as the
primary sociocultural institution for the community. In this sense, they
do possess some semblance of symbolic ethnicity. Unlike Abramson's
description of religioethnic movement characterizing one dimension of
symbolic ethnicity, the Christian church for Korean Americans is not
rooted in its ethnic heritage. The history of Christianity in Korea is
only about 130 years old at best. What is remarkable, however, is the
high level of church participation of Korean American immigrants and
their descendents, as previously discussed.

For second-generation young adults, the Korean American church
has inadvertently functioned as the center of their religioethnic
movement. As previously discussed, the interviewees express their
preference for and commitment to the Korean American church despite
many readily observable deficiencies. The Korean American church
has been their "home" church and they are committed to rectifying that
church. For instance, although they have yet to come up with
appropriate strategies, they   desire to work together with the first

generation in the church in this process. It is certain that the young people seek to maintain the church as their primary sociocultural institution through the interplay of Korean American culture and Christianity.   In this sense, the Korean American church and its Christian education become a critical center for the future of the young adults and beyond.

Growing in healthy relationship with parents' generation
     The interviewees realize that, regardless of their shortcomings, their parents have sacrificed much for them. The church must consider bridging the cultural gap in its efforts towards strengthening the relationships between generations. Young adults should continue to seek understanding of some of the possible reasons for the cultural gap between them and their parents. Having grown up in a monolingual and mono-cultural culture, the parents' generation has had an extremely difficult time acquiring English as their second language. One of the few viable options for these parents was to be self-employed in small business. They often found themselves fulfilling the role of middleman minority, as a buffer between the rich and the poor of society. For the first generation, it was a significant occupational shift from life in Korea, as previously discussed. Such shifts have caused stress and led to disappointment.   They were often segregated from mainstream society, unable to learn English and constrained to work long hours.

     These adults maintained their authoritarian parenting style and had high hopes for their children. In the meantime, their children grew up speaking English, being influenced by the media, and being acculturated into mainstream culture. They wanted their parents to ease up on their expectations in terms of academics and other demands. As a result, the gap between parents and children widened.

     This author maintains that contextual theologies from Womanist, Hispanic, and Asian American traditions contain much that illuminates the predicaments of the two generations. Moreover, these theologies provide rich narratives and metaphors through which both generations in the Korean American church can come together to reflect and mourn about their past and give birth to new ways of relating to each other.

The relationship with the next generation
     Another issue the interviewees want to address is the way in which they relate to their future children and subsequent generations. They realize that their fathers were socialized to keep a distance from

children in order to maintain proper order in the family. They also realize that Korean culture does not promote verbal or physical expressions of love for children.

Reflecting on their childhood relationships with their parents, these young people are eager to express their love for others through more verbal and physical expressions. They also believe that more intimate relationships with their future children will generate more respect on the part of the children. They desire to give more freedom to their children to experience life for themselves, rather than superimposing dreams onto them.

The church, as an extension of the family, will do well to see itself as the family of God whose members function as family. Young adults can function as surrogate uncles and aunts to their peers' children. They can invite first-generation members to be their older brothers and sisters. However, age should not dictate the direction of influence. The church must educate its people in the concept of mutual mentoring and sharing lives together as co-equals before God.

Soundings of Socioculturally Appropriate Practices of Christian Education in the Korean American Church

The church as a reflexively renewing community

Christian education in the Korean American church ought to seriously consider the sociocultural context of second-generation Korean Americans. The church must engage in analysis of how young adults have been constructed by the environment socially and culturally. Included in this must be an examination of the impact of racism, classism, sexism, and ageism on the Korean American self.

Some of the negative impact of Korean American culture on young adults must also be explored. In exploring these issues, young adults will come to a better understanding of how they have been socioculturally constructed and how the internalized multiplicity functions in their daily lives. Together they can decide how to make their lives more reflexive, becoming praxis-generating persons.

Moreover, the Korean American church should consider how its Christian education practices can help young people (re)interpret and live out Christian traditions. The Korean American church, like all churches, lives within its tradition—constantly passing on its past, living in its present, and moving toward its future. The church should communicate that continuity and change are always connected through relation to a God who has acted in the past, acts in the present, and will act in the future through God's people. Through this process, the participants' Christian traditions can be (re)considered in light of their involvement in the reflexive projects of the self, resulting in a more reflexive and praxis-generating life.

The revisioning of the hierarchy in the Korean American culture through the Korean American church

Most of the concerns the interviewees express about Korean American culture seem to originate from the hierarchy that exists in Korean culture. This hierarchy permeates every aspect of the Korean culture and has had a profound impact. The hierarchy stems from the Confucian moral system where

> the basic metaphor of the Confucian moral system is the proper family: correctly ordered by differences of function and authority, with filial piety the central virtue, the family is the model for society as a whole . . . Relations throughout society were described by a rigorous application of hierarchical distinctions . . . In the Confucian approach to education, correctly ordered conduct was emphasized as it expressed and embodied the correct relations and attitudes at the foundation of a harmonious society . . . Learning was the process of submitting to and mastering the wisdom of the sages . . . Respect was a key symbol of Confucian virtue . . . Independence of thought was not regularly rewarded or encouraged.[6]

Even a cursory look at hierarchical relationships prescribed by the Confucian moral system shows the conflict between the first generation, who were acculturated in the system, and the second generation, who grew up in the U.S. However, this study's findings indicate that second-generation Korean American young adults show their eagerness to address in a reflexive and respectful manner the issues of asymmetrical power relationships that have been operative in Korean American culture, especially in the church.

---

[6]Thomas P. Rohlen, *Japan's High Schools* (Berkeley: University of California Press, 1983), 48-50.

The relationship between man and woman

One of the critical issues these young people want to address is the relationship between man and woman. Both male and female have witnessed the double roles that their mothers had to fulfill as working women and housewives. These young adults are concerned and sympathetic toward their mothers' sacrifice for the family. Although the young adults may not be quite articulate in their commitment to more equitable relationships between men and women in the family and church, they seem to be open to revision of the Confucianistic complementarian relationship between women and men toward a more egalitarian spirit and dynamic nature.

While Chan reports that first-generation parents say they treat their daughters and sons equally in their parenting style, the findings of this study show otherwise. Both female and male young adults share that male children consistently receive preferential treatment. In comparison to the way they were raised in Korea, this researcher contends that the parents have been more equitable in their parenting, but from the vantage point of these interviewees their parents have been partial toward male children. The young adults resolve to raise their children equally, regardless of gender.

When the study participants talk about how they envision their marital relationships in the future both male and female tend toward a complementarian outlook on the relationship. In other words, female young adults prefer to be homemakers, and male young adults feel that they should be the primary breadwinners for the family. These young people are perhaps more concerned to ensure that one parent be home with the children, having experienced the absence of parents during their own growing up years.

The church stands as a place where gender issues must be addressed and modeled with intentionality. Young adults look to the church to openly tackle this thorny issue with care and respect. They are not generally interested in some of the standard issues in mainline denominations, such as the ordination of woman, inclusive language, or the gender debate for God. Rather, they are concerned about basic home issues, such as sharing housework and parenting responsibilities between husbands and wives. While these practical issues must be addressed in the church, the church must realize its constitutive role in shaping relationships between male and female on both practical and ecclesial levels.

Filial piety

The issue of filial piety is another issue with which the interviewees grapple. They are very much committed to honoring their parents and taking care of them in their elderly years. The desire to pay back their parents sacrifice for them is never out of their mind. Yet, they desire to maintain a proper distance with their parents, especially once they are married and have a family. A good balance between paying respect and asserting independence is sought.

This researcher submits that young adults also need to learn that filial piety should be practiced out of love for their parents. Young people must be careful in discerning possible enmeshment or codependent motifs in their practice of filial piety. In other words, the adults should not deem such practice as a way to gain the acceptance and love from their parents that they did not receive in their earlier years.

The church has an enormous task ahead of it in the area of promoting the psychological well being of its young adults. These young men and women need to embrace the lifestyle of forgiveness. This lifestyle calls them to accept themselves for who they are, extend forgiveness to those who wrong them, and receive others' forgiveness for the wrongs they have committed.[7] The church, as the community of Christians, must embody this lifestyle of forgiveness, dispensing grace and promoting genuine peace.

The study participants are to be commended for their keen observations about other issues that arise from the unreflective use of the Confucianistic hierarchy. For instance, while they plan to acquire proficiency in the Korean language, they are quick to point out how the language itself has created and maintained hierarchy in Korean and Korean American cultures. They still hope to learn the honorific language form that is used with elders in the community. Yet, they hope that the elders will reciprocate with respect for the younger ones in the community.

---

[7]Leanne Payne, *Restoring the Christian Soul* (Grand Rapids: Baker, 1991), 19-159.

Holistic practices of Christian Education
for Second-Generation Young Adults in the
Korean American Church

The Christian education processes in the Korean American church should be imaginative in utilizing all aspects of the church in order to connect with the experiences of young adults in the church. The church needs to take seriously the importance of mutual, intergenerational discipleship.

Healthy view of self
Young adults ought to grow in a healthy view of themselves. This study's findings indicate that many of the interviewees struggle with issues of shame and guilt. They report feeling that they are never good enough to measure up to their parents' expectations. This study's findings also concur with literature showing that first-generation parents demand much from their children without providing much support for them to succeed. These young adults also report feeling defective as an ethnic minority. As a result, many of them readily admit the struggles they have with low self-esteem.

Many of the interviewees report their struggle with academics during college years. This is consonant with the College Board Report, as previously discussed. These young people believe they were not adequately prepared to succeed in college. The inadequacies they point out are usually non-academic issues, such as lack of emotional maturity, undisciplined study, and social habits. Their self-disappointment and shame for apparent failure is compounded by their parents' pressure to excel. For these young people, issues of inner healing and self-acceptance must be addressed at an individual level, as well as in the community of cohorts.

The healthy view of self, however, will not be attained overnight. Some of the symptoms and root causes may linger for a long period of time. There may be multiple causes and manifestations of psychosocial dysfunction in the lives of these young adults. Multiple symptoms and root causes require multiple sets of interventions. If the church adopts the integrative approach to Christian education, as previously discussed, the church as the community of Christians can minister to its people in a holistic manner.

Linking up with first-generation leaders

These young people will be helped to learn there are some first-generation adults who can serve as models for their future lives as parents, spouses, and church leaders. Some of the interviewees report having had supportive parents and healthy families. These families often resemble bicultural families. The parents tend to be more Americanized and have more egalitarian relationships with their children. In these families, mothers usually stayed home during their children's formative years. These parents also tend to have commended respect as leaders in the Korean American church. While some of these young adults feel they need to create a new set of traditions for the Korean American community, this researcher observes a fair number of first-generation adults who could provide much needed leadership and serve as mentors for second-generation young adults and their congregations.

Once friends, forever friends

These young people have wonderful building blocks for their future lives right in their midst. They have been deeply shaped by mutual friendships with their peers. These peers have walked through the peak and nadir experiences of their lives together. They have been companions of unwavering support and encouragement in one another's lives. When they were struggling with their ethnic identity, cultural conflicts at home, and disappointments in school and relationships, these young adults were there for one another. Now that many of them are back in their home churches or are committed to a local Korean American church, they should be construed as a critical mass which can take further steps together toward growing in sense of self and building a safe and hospitable community for fellow second generation and subsequent generations of Korean Americans.

APPENDIX 1: PROTOCOL FOR THE INDIVIDUAL INTERVIEW

Interview questions with consultants (human subjects) in the individual interview setting (first interview).

1a. Can you share some of the recent decisions you have made or are in the process of making?

1b. How do your parents make decisions? How are you similar/ dissimilar?

1c. What are the issues that you are concerned about lately? What are you going to do about them? Parents, societal pressure, age, etc. . .

2. Can you describe some important experiences in you life?

3a. What do you appreciate about your cultural heritage, whether you call it Korean or Korean American, Asian American or American? Values?

3b. What troubles you about your cultural heritage. . .?

3c. What do you appreciate about American society?

3d. What don't you appreciate about American society. . .?

3e. What does each culture say about your?

4a. Can you talk about the media, especially in relation to your life?

4b. How much time do you spend watching TV, listening to the radio, reading newspapers and popular magazines? What do you like about them?

5a. What are some memorable experiences in the Korean American church?

-    In your Christian education experience?

-    What is the role of the church in your life?

5b. How does religion (Christianity) function in your life?

-    Can you share any stories from the Bible that are important to you?

-    What does the Bible mean to you?

6a. Can you describe your relationship with your parents?

-    Do you have any legacies/traditions in your family you want to pass on? If yes, what are they?

6b. What kind of relationship do/have you had with your grandparents, aunts, and uncles?

6c. Who are the persons who have influenced you in significant ways?
-    What do/did those persons say about you?

7. Can we go back to those important decisions you made recently?
-    Who was influenced your decision-making?
-    What roles did these people, and the other themes that we talked about today, play in your decision-making process?
-    Do they suggest any conflicting messages to you?

8. How would you describe yourself?
-    Is the way you see yourself now different from the way you saw yourself in the past?
-    What do these people and the themes that we talked about today say about you?
-    Are there conflicting messages regarding who you are? If so, what did/do you do about it?

9. How do these people and the themes function in your life?
-    If you were to provide an image of the relationship among them, what would it be?
-    Through this interview, have you learned anything about your life? These people and the themes?
-    Has the interview been helpful to you?
-    Do you have any suggestions for the Korean American church and its religious education process as they minister to people like you?

10. Do you have any comments you would like to make regarding your feelings/experiences during this interview process today?

Bibliography

Abelmann, Nancy, and John Lie. Blue Dreams: Korean Americans and the Los Angeles Riots. Cambridge: Harvard University Press, 1995.

Alba, Richard D. "Social assimilation among American Catholic National-Origin Groups." American Sociological Review. 41 (December 1976): 1030-1046.

Anderson, Walter Truett. The Future of the Self: Exploring the Post-Identity Society. New York: Penguin Putnam, Inc., 1997.

Ashmore, Richard D. and Lee Jussim, editors. Self and Identity. New York: Oxford University Press, Inc., 1997.

Atkinson, Harley. Handbook of Young Adult Religious Education. Birmingham: Religious Education Press, 1995.

Bakhtin, Mikhail. The Dialogic Imagination: Four Essays by M. M. Bakhtin. Austin: University of Texas Press, 1981.

Bakhurst, David and Christine Sypnowich, editors. The Social Self. London: Sage Publications Ltd, 1995.

Balmer, Randall. Mine Eyes Have Seen the Glory: A Journey into the Evangelical Subculture in American. New York: Oxford University Press, 1993.

Bamberg, Michael, ed. Narrative Development: Six Approaches. Mahwah, NJ: Lawrence Erlbaum Associates, Publishers, 1997.

Banton, Michael. Race Relations. London: Tavistock Publications, 1967.

Blackwood, Vernon, "Historical and theological foundations of Paulo Freire's Educational Praxis." Trinity Journal. Vol. 8, No. 2,(Fall 1987): 201-232.

Baldwin, James. Mental Development in the Child and Race. New York: Macmillan, 1897.

Belenky, M., B. Clinchy, N. Goldberger, and J. Tarule. Women's Ways
Of Knowing: The Development Of Self, Voice, and Mind. New
York: Basic Books, 1986.

Bourdieu, Pierre and Loic Wacquant. An Invitation to Reflexive
Sociology. Chicago: The University of Chicago Press, 1992.

Brinthaupt, Thomas M. and Richard P. Lipka, eds. The Self
Definitional and Methodological Issues. Albany, NY: State
University of New York Press, 1992.

Bruner, Jerome. Acts of Meaning. Cambridge: Harvard University
Press, 1990.

Budde, Michael L. and Robert W. Brimlow, eds. The Church as
Counterculture. Albany, NY: State University of New York Press,
2000.

Chan, Sucheng. Asian Americans: An Interpretive History. Boston:
Twayne Publishers, 1991.

Christensen, C. Roland, David A. Gravin, and Ann Sweet. Educating
for Judgment. Cambridge: Harvard Business School Press, 1991.

Clapp, Rodney. A Peculiar People: The Church As Culture in a Post-
Christian Society. Downers Grove, IL: Intervarsity Press, 1996.

Cobb, John. Becoming a Thinking Christian. Nashville: Abingdon,
1993.

Cooley, Charles. Human Nature and the Social Order. New York:
Scribners, 1902.

Cross, Susan, and Hazel Markus. "Possible selves across the life span."
In Human Development 34 (1991): 230-253.

Collins, Denis. Paulo Freire: His Life, Works & Thought. New York:
Paulist Press, 1977.

Cumings, Bruce. Korea's Place in the Sun: A Modern History. New
York, W. W. Norton & Company, 1997.

Dissanayake, Wimal, ed. Narratives of Agency: Self-Making in China,
India, and Japan. Minneapolis, MN: University of Minnesota Press,
1996.

Doi, Takeo. The Anatomy of Self. Tokyo: Kodansha International,
1985.

Dryden, Gordon and Jeanette Vos. The Learning Revolution: To
Change the Way the World Learns. Torrance, CA: The Learning
Web, 1999.

Elias, John. "Paulo Freire: Religious Educator." Religious Education.
Vol. 71, No. 1, (Jan-Feb. 1976): 40-56.

Elizondo, Virgil. Christianity and Culture: An Introduction   to
Pastoral Theology and Ministry for the Bicultural Community. San
Antonio: Mexican American Cultural Center, 1975.
_____. Galilean Journey: The Mexican-American Promise.
Maryknoll, N.Y.: Orbis,1983.
_____. The Future is Mestizo: Life Where Cultures Meet.
Bloomington, I.N.: Meyer-Stone Books, 1988.
_____. "*Mestizaje* as a Locus of Theological Reflection." In Mestizo
Christianity: Theology from the Latino perspective, ed. A. Banuelas,
5-27. Maryknoll, N.Y.: Orbis. 1995.
Espiritu, Yen Le. Asian American Panethnicity: Bridging Institutions
and Identities. Philadelphia: Temple University Press, 1992.
Feagin, Joe and Nancy Fujitaki. "On the assimilation of Japanese-
Americans." Amerasia Journal 1 (1972): 13-30.
Fong, Ken Uyeda. Pursuing the Pearl: A Comprehensive Resource for
Multi-Asian Ministry. Valley Forge, PA: Judson Press, 1999.
Fong, Timothy. The Contemporary Asian American Experience:
Beyond the Model Minority. New Jersey: Prentice Hall, Inc., 1998.
Ford, David F. The Shape of Living: Spiritual Directions for Everyday
Life. Grand Rapids, MI: Baker Books, 1997.
Foster, Charles R. Educating Congregations: The Future of Christian
Education. Nashville: Abingdon, 1994.
Freire, Paulo. Education for Critical Consciousness. New York:
Continuum, 1973.
_____. Pedagogy of the Oppressed. New York: Continuum, 1970.
_____. "Conscientization," Cross Currents 24 (Spring 1974): 23-30.
_____. Pedagogy of the Oppressed. New York: Continuum, 1992.
_____. Education for Critical Consciousness. New York: Continuum,
1992.
_____. Pedagogy of the Oppressed. New York: Continuum, 1992.
Fugita, Stephen S. and David J. O'Brien. Japanese American Ethnicity.
Seattle: University of Washington Press, 1991.
Furuto, Sharlene, Renuka Diswas, Douglas K. Chung, Kenji Murase,
and Fariyal Ross-Sheriff. Social Work Practice With Asian
Americans. Newbury Park, CA: Sage Publications,1992.
Geertz, Clifford. The Interpretation of Cultures. New York: Basic
Books, 1973.
Gergen, Kenneth. The Saturated Self. San Francisco: Basic Books,
1991.
_____. Realities and Relationships. Cambridge: Harvard University

Press, 1994.

_____. An Invitation to Social Construction. Thousand Oaks: Sage
Publications, 1999.

Giddens, Anthony. Modernity and Self-Identity: Self and Society in the
Late Modern Age. Stanford: Stanford University Press, 1991.

Gilbert, Paul and Bernice Andrews, editors. Shame: Interpersonal
Behavior, Psychopathology, and Culture. New York: Oxford
University Press, 1998.

Gonzalez, Justo L. Out of Every Tribe and Nation: Christian Theology
at the Ethnic Roundtable. Nashville: Abingdon, 1992.

Gribbon, Robert. Developing Faith in Young Adults. New York: The
Alban Institute, 1990.

Grodin, Debra and Thomas R. Lindlof, editors. Constructing the Self in
a Mediated World. Thousand Oaks, CA: Sage Publications, 1996.

Groome, Thomas H. Christian Religious Education. San Francisco:
Harper and Row Publishers, 1980.

_____. "Conversion, Nurture and Educators." Religious Education
76:5: 482-497.

_____. "The Critical Principle in Christian Education and the Task of
Prophecy." Religious Education 72:3 (May-June 1977): 262-272.

_____. "Religious Education for Justice by Educating Justly." In
Education for Peace and Justice, ed. by Padraic O'Hare. San
Francisco: Harper & Row, 1983.

_____. Sharing Faith. San Francisco: HarperCollins Publishers, 1991.

_____. "Theology on Our Feet: A Revisionist Pedagogy for Healing
the Gap between Academia and Ecclesia." In Formation and
Reflection: The Promise of Practical Theology, ed. Lewis Mudge and
James N. Poling. Philadelphia: Fortress Press, 1987.

_____. "Walking Humbly With Our God." In To Act Justly, Love
Tenderly, Walk Humbly. Walter Brueggemann, et al. New York:
Paulist Press, 1986.

Groome, Thomas H. and Mary C. Boys. "Principles and Pedagogy in
Biblical Study." Religious Education 77:5 (September-October
1982): 486-507.

Gubrium, Jaber F., James A. Holstein and David R. Buckholdt.
Constructing the Life Course. Dix Hills, NY: General Hall, Inc.,
1994.

Gutierrez, Gustavo. A Theology of Liberation. New Jersey: Maryknoll,
1973

Harre, Rom. The Singular Self: An Introduction to the Psychology of

Personhood. London: Sage Publications Ltd, 1998.

Harris, Maria. Fashion Me A People: Curriculum in the Church. Louisville: Westminster/John Knox Press, 1989.

Harris, Maria. Women and Teaching. New York: Paulist Press, 1988.

Harris, Marvin. Theories of Culture in Postmodern Times. Walnut Creek, CA: AltaMira Press, 1999.

Hendricks, J. and C. A. Leedham, "Making Sense: Interpreting Historical and Cross-Cultural Literature on Aging" In P.V. D. Bagnell and P. S. Soper, eds., Perceptions of Again in Literature: A Cross-Cultural Study. Westport: Greenwood, 1989.

Hermans, Hubert, Harry Kempen, and Rens Van Loon. "The Dialogical Self: Beyond Individualism and Rationalism" In American Psychologist, 47, 1 (1992), 23-33.

Hermans, Hubert and Harry Kempen, The Dialogical Self: Meaning as Movement. San Diego: Academic Press, 1993.

Hiebert, Paul G., Anthropological Reflections on Missiological Issues. Grand Rapids, MI: Baker Books, 1994.

_____. Missiological Implications of Epistemological Shifts: Affirming Truth in a Modern/Postmodern World. Harrisburg, PA: Trinity Press, 1999.

Hogan, R. Personality Theory: The Personological Tradition. Englewood Cliffs, NJ: Prentice-Hall, 1976.

Holli, Melvin G. and Peter d'A. Jones. Ethnic Chicago: A Multicultural Portrait. Grand Rapids, MI: William B. Eerdmans Publishing Company, 1997.

Hooks, bell. Teaching to Transgress. New York: Routledge, 1994.

_____. Yearning: Race, Gender, and Cultural Politics. Boston: South End Press, 1990.

Huang, Larke Hahme and Yu-Wen Ying. "Chinese American Cchildren and Adolescents." In Children of Color: Psychological Interventions with Minority Youth. ed. J. T. Gibbs and L. N. Huang and Associates, 30-66. 1989.

Hurh, Won Moo. "The 1.5 generation: A Cornerstone of the Korean-American Ethnic Community." In The Emerging Generation of Korean-Americans, eds. Ho-Youn Kwon and Shin Kim, 47-79. Seoul, Korea: Kyoung Hee University Press. 1993.

Hurh, Won Moo, and Kwang Chung Kim. "Religious Participation of Korean Immigrants in the United States." In Journal for the Scientific Study of Religion 29, 1 (1990), 19-34.

_____. "The 'success' image of Asian Americans: Its Validity,

Practical and Theoretical Implications." Ethnic and Racial Studies 12. (1989): 512-537.

James, William. Psychology. Greenwich, CT: Fawcett, 1963.

Jarvis, Peter. "Paulo Freire: Educationalist of a Revolutionary Christian Movement." Convergence. Vol. 44, No. 2, (1987): 30-40.

Jones, James W. Contemporary Psychoanalysis. New Haven, CT: Yale University Press, 1991.

Jum, Joyce L. "Family Violence" In Lee C. Lee and Nolan W. S. Zane, eds., Handbook of Asian American Psychology, 505-525. Thousand Oaks: Sage, 1998.

Karnow, Stanley and Nancy Yoshihara. Asian Americans in Transition. New York: The Asia Society, 1992.

Kasindorf, Martin, Paula Chin, Diane Weathers, Kim Foltz, Daniel Shapiro and Darby Junkin. "Asian-Americans: A 'Model Minority'". Newsweek 6 (December 1982): 39, 41-42 and 51.

Kennedy, Ruby Jo Reeves. "Single or triple melting-pot? Intermarriage trends in New Haven, 1870-1940." American Journal of Sociology 49:4 (January 1944): 331-339.

_____. "Single or triple melting-pot? Intermarriage trends in New Haven 1870-1950." American Journal of Sociology 58:1 (July, 1952): 56-59.

Kennedy, William. "Conversation with Paulo Freire." Religious Education. Vol. 79, No. 4, (1984): 511-522.

Kim, Elaine H. and Eui-Young Yu. East to America. New York: The New Press, 1996.

Kim, Eunjoo Mary. Preaching the Presence of God: A Homiletic from an Asian American Perspective. Valley Forge, PA: Judson Press, 1999.

Kim, John T. Protestant Church Growth in Korea. Belleville, Ontario: Essence Publishing, 1996.

Kwon, Ho Yoon. Korean Americans: Conflict and Harmony. Chicago: Covenant Publications, 1994.

Kitano, Harry and Stanley Sue. "The model minorities." Journal of Social Issues 29 (1973): 1-9.

Koh, Ton-He. "Ethnic identity: The Impact of the Two Cultures on the Psychological Development of Korean-American Adolescents." In The Emerging Generation of Korean-Americans, eds. Ho-Youn Kwon and Shin Kim, 29-46. Seoul, Korea: Kyoung Hee University Press, 1993.

Kuo, Wen H. "On the Study of Asian-Americans: Its Current State and Agenda." The Sociological Quarterly 20 (Spring 1979): 279-290.

Lawrence, J. and J. Valsiner. "Conceptual Roots of Internalization: From Transmission to Transformation" in Human Development 36: 150-167.

Lee, James. The Content of Religious Instruction. Birmingham: Religious Education Press, 1985.

Lee, Jung Young. Marginality: The Key to Multicultural Theology. Minneapolis: Fortress Press, 1995.

Lee, Lee and Nolan Zane. Handbook of Asian American Psychology, Newbury Park: Sage, 1998.

Lee, Robert G. Orientals: Asian Americans in Popular Culture. Philadelphia: Temple University Press, 1999.

Lee, Sang Hyun Lee, and John V. Moore. Korean American Ministry. Louisville: PC(USA), 1994.

Levine, Gene N. and Darrell Montero. "Socioeconomic Mobility among Three Generations of Japanese Americans." The Journal of Social Issues 29 (1973): 33-48.

Low, Ron. "A brief biographical sketch of a newly found Asian male." In Roots: An Asian American Reader. eds. Amy Tachiki and Eddie Wong and Franklin Odo and Buck Wong, 105-108. Los Angeles: UCLA Asian American Studies Center. 1971.

Ma, Sheng-mei. Immigrant Subjectivities in Asian American and Asian Diaspora Literatures. Albany, NY: State University of New York Press, 1998.

Magolda, Marcia B. Knowing and Reasoning in College. San Francisco: Jossey-Bass, 1992.

Markus, Hazel and Nurius, Paula. "Possible selves" In American Psychologist, 41, 9 (1986): 954-969.

Masterson, James F. The Real Self: A Developmental, Self, and Object Relations Approach. New York: Brunner/Mazel Publishers, 1985.

Margolis, Diane Rothbard. The Fabric of Self: A Theory of Ethics and Emotions. New Haven, CT: Yale University Press.

Matsuoka, Fumitaka. Out of Silence: Emerging Themes in Asian American Churches. Cleveland, OH: United Church Press, 1995.

McAdams, Dan. The Stories We Live By. New York: W. Morrow, 1993.

McAdams, Dan. The Person: An Introduction to Personality Psychology. Fort Worth: Harcourt Brace, 1994.

McDargh, John. Psychoanalytic Object Relations Theory and The

Study of Religion: On Faith and the Imaging of God. Lanham, MD: University Press of American, 1983.

Mead, George Herbert. Mind, Self, and Society. Chicago: University of Chicago Press, 1934.

Metzger, L. Paul. "American Sociology and Black Assimilation: Conflicting Perspectives." American Journal of Sociology 76 (January 1971): 627-647.

Mezirow, Jack. Transformative Dimensions of Adult Learning. San Francisco: Jossey-Bass, 1991.

Min, Pyong Gap. Asian Americans: Contemporary Trends and Issues. Thousand Oaks: Sage Publications, Inc. 1995.

Moore, Mary Elizabeth. Education for Continuity and Change. Nashville: Abingdon, 1983.

Moran, Gabriel. Religious Education as a Second Language. Birmingham: Religious Education Press, 1989.

Nagata, Donna K. "Japanese American Children and Adolescents." In Children of Color: Psychological Interventions with Minority Youth. eds. J. T. Gibbs and L. N. Huang and Associates, (1989): 67-113.

Nakanishi, Don T. "A quota on Excellence?" Change (November/December 1989): 39-48.

Nunez, Emilio. Liberation Theology. Chicago: Moody Press, 1985.

Nelson, C. Ellis. Where Faith Begins. Richmond, VA: John Knox Press, 1971.

Okihiro, Gary. Margins and Mainstreams: Asians in American History and Culture. Seattle: University of Washington, 1994.

Pai, Young. Cultural Foundations of Education. New Jersey: Merrill Prentice Hall, 2001.

Paik, Irvin. "That Oriental Feeling." In Roots: An Asian American Reader. eds. Amy Tachiki, Eddie Wong, Franklin Odo and Buck Wong. Los Angeles: UCLA Asian American Studies Center. (1971): 30-36.

Pang, Valerie Ooka and Li-Rong Lilly Cheng. Struggling to Be Heard: The Unmet Needs of Asian Pacific American Children. Albany, NY: State University of New York Press, 1998.

Parks, Sharon. The Critical Years: The Young Adult Search for a Faith to Live by. San Francisco: Harper & Row, 1986.

Palmer, Parker. To Know as We Are Known: A Spirituality of Education. Cambridge: Harper & Row, 1983.

_____. The Courage to Teach. San Francisco: Jossey-Bass, 1998.

Perry, William. Forms of Intellectual and Ethical Development in the College Years. New York: Holt, Rinehart and Winston, 1970.

Phinney, Jean. "Ethnic Identity in Adolescents and Adults: Review of Research" In Psychological Bulletin 108 (1990): 499-514.

_____. "Ethnic Identity in Adolescents and Adults: Review of Research" Psychological Bulletin, 108:3 (1990): 499-514.

Rigdon, Joan E. 1991. "Exploding Myth: Asian-American Youth Suffer a Rising Toll From Heavy Pressures." The Wall Street Journal, 10 (July, 1 and 4, 1991).

Rizzuto, Ana-Maria. The Birth of the Living God: A Psychoanalytic Study. Chicago: The University of Chicago Press, 1979.

Roland, Alan. Cultural Pluralism and Psychoanalysis: The Asian and North American Experience. New York: Routledge, 1996.

Russell, Letty. Church in the Round. Louisville: Westminster/John Knox Press, 1993.

_____. Household of Freedom. Philadelphia: Westminister Press, 1987.

Seidman, Irving. Interviewing as Qualitative Research. New York: Teachers College Press, 1998.

Seymour, Jack L., Margaret Ann Crain, and Joseph V. Crockett. Educating Christians. Nashville: Abingdon, 1993.

Seymour, Jack L., and Donald Miller. Contemporary Approaches to Christian Education. Nashville: Abingdon, 1982.

_____. Theological Approaches to Christian Education. Nashville: Abingdon, 1990.

Shane, Morton, and Estelle Shane and Mary Gales. Intimate Attachments: Toward a New Self Psychology. New York: The Guilford Press, 1997.

Sowell, Thomas. Marxism: Philosophy and Economics. New York: Morrow, 1985.

Spradley, James P. Participant Observation. Fort Worth, TX: Holt, Rinehart and Winston, 1980.

St. Clair, Michael. Object Relations and Self Psychology: An Introduction. Stanford, CT: Brooks/Cole, 2000.

Steinberg, Laurence "Ethnicity and Adolescent Achievement" American Educator (Summer, 1996): 28-35, 44-48.

Strom, Robert S. H. Park, and S. Daniels, "Child Rearing Dilemmas of Korean Immigrants to the United States" International Journal of Experimental Research in Education 24 (1987): 91-102.

Stevens, Richard. Understanding the Self. Newbury Park: Sage, 1996.

Sue, Derald W., and Sue, Stanley. "Ethnic Minorities: Resistance to Being Researched" in Professional Psychology 3 (1972), 11-17.

Sue, Stanley and Derald Sue. "Chinese American Personality and Mental Health." Amerasia Journal 1 1971: 36-49.

Takagi, Dana. The Retreat from Race. New Brunswick: Rutgers University Press, 1992.

Tuan, Mia. Forever Foreigners or Honorary Whites? New Burnswick: Rutgers University Press, 1998.

Valsiner, Jean. Human Development and Culture. Lexington, MA: D.C. Heath,1989.

Vogel, Linda J. Vogel. Teaching and Learning in Communities of Faith: Empowering Adults through Religious Education. San Francisco: Jossey-Bass, 1991.

Vygotsky, Lev. Mind in Society (eds. Michael Cole, Vera John-Steiner, Silvia Scribner, and E. Souberman). Cambridge: Harvard University Press, 1978.

Walzer, Michael "What does it mean to be an 'American'?," Social Research. 57:3, 591-614.

Warner, R. Stephen and Judith G. Wittner. Eds. Gatherings in Diaspora: Religious Communities and the New Immigration. Philadelphia: Temple University Press, 1998.

Watkins, Mary. Invisible Guests: The Development of Imaginal Dialogues. Hillsdale, NJ: Erlbaum Associates, 1986.

Weir, Allison. Sacrificial Logics: Feminist Theory and the Critique of Identity. New York: Routledge, 1996.

Wertsch, James V. Voices of the Mind: A Sociocultural Approach to Mediated Action. Cambridge: Harvard University Press, 1991.

Westerhoff, III John H. Will Our Children Have Faith? Toronto: Morehouse Publishing, 1976/2000.

Wimberly, Anne Streaty. Soul Stories: African American Christian Education. Nashville: Abingdon, 1994.

Wuthnow, Robert, and James D. Hunter, and Albert Bergesen, and Edith Kurzweil. Cultural Analyis. New York: Routledge, 1984.

Wynter, Leon E. and Jolie Solomon. "A New Push to Break the 'Glass Ceiling'." Wall Street Journal, B1. 15 November 1989.

Yang, Fenggang. Chinese Christians in America : Conversion, Assimilation, and Adhesive Identities. University Park : The Penn State University Press, 1999.

Yep, Jeanette, ed. Following Jesus without Dishonoring Your Parents. Downers Grove, IL: InterVarsity Press, 1998.

Yoo, David K., ed. <u>New Spiritual Homes: Religion and Asian Americans</u>. Honolulu: University of Hawaii Press, 1999.

Index

Steve Kang is a 1.5-generation Korean American, having immigrated to the States with his family in 1977. He is assistant professor of Christian Formation and Ministry at Wheaton College in Wheaton, Illinois. Some of the courses he teaches include culture and ministry, educational research, educational processes, and psychological and sociological foundations of education. During his undergraduate years at Cornell University, he published an article on the discovery of a new organic compound in Journal of Organic Chemistry. His graduate training is in the areas of Theology and Religious Education from Trinity Evangelical Divinity School and his Ph.D is in Religion in Society and Personality from Northwestern University. He has pastoral ministry experiences with youth, young adults, family, and in church planting. He has contributed to journals such as *Religious Education*. Steve is married to Chris, and they have two children, Ashley and Andrew. They reside in Wheaton, Illinois.